GEORGIA GENEALOGICAL

RESEARCH

by

George K. Schweitzer, PhD, ScD
407 Ascot Court
Knoxville, TN 37923-5807

Word Processing by
Anne M. Smalley

ISBN 0-913857-10-6

1

TABLE OF CONTENTS

4

Chapter 1

GEORGIA BACKGROUND

1. Georgia geography

The state of Georgia (hereafter abbreviated GA), the last settled of the original thirteen colonies, is located in the southern region of the eastern seaboard of the US. It is the largest state east of the MS River, its area being almost 59000 square miles, its length about 320 miles, and its largest width about 260 miles. In shape, it resembles a rectangle with a large portion of the upper right corner cut off (see Figure 1). It is bounded on the east by SC and the Atlantic Ocean, on the south by FL, on the west by AL, and on the north by TN and NC. GA has about 100 miles of direct coastline, but the meanderings of the many inlets give it a much greater length of actual coastline. The capital of the state is located at Atlanta in the northwest region, and the state is divided into 159 counties, more than any other state except TX. The major cities of GA (with their approximate populations in thousands) are Atlanta (425K) in the northwest, Columbus (169K) in the west center, Savannah (141K) in the southeast, and Macon (117K) in the central region. Other cities of GA with populations of 37K or over include Albany (74K) in the southwest, Augusta (48K) in the east center, Athens (43K) in the northeast, Warner-Robins (40K) in the center, Valdosta (38K) in the central south, and East Point (37K) in the northwest.

An understanding of the progressive settlement of the state and the genealogies of its early families is greatly enhanced by an examination of its three major geographic regions and their features. These are pictured in Figure 1. The first region consists of the Coastal Plain, which makes up the southern half of GA. The rivers of the eastern portion of this plain drain into the Atlantic Ocean, while the rivers in the western portion make their way to the Gulf of Mexico. The plain is very low and flat along the coast and gradually rises into gently rolling hills inland. There are marshes in many places along the coast, with the large Okefenokee Swamp in the extreme southeast. Off the coast is a chain of sandy islands (the Sea Islands) extending from SC to FL. From north to south, the chief ones are Tybee(TI), Ossabow(OI), St. Catherines(SCI), Blackbeard(BI), Sapelo(SI), Sea(SeI), St. Simons(SSR), Jekyl(JI), and Cumberland(CI). The coastal areas were

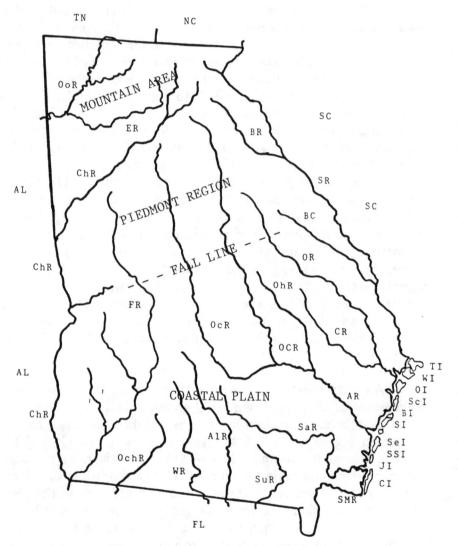

Figure 1. GA Geography

the earliest to be settled (1733-4), Savannah being the first. The second region, which is called the Piedmont Region, occupies about a third of GA, the central and part of the northern areas. The border between the Coastal Plain and the Piedmont Region is known as the Fall Line because the land undergoes a sharp drop from north to south. The line runs across the center of the state roughly from Augusta to just south of Milledgeville and Macon to just north of Columbus. The land in the Piedmont is rolling upland country with some moderately deep river valleys. The altitude gradually rises from about 400 feet along the Fall Line to approximately 1500 feet in the north. The third section of GA occupies the remaining one-sixth of the state in the north. It is known as the Mountain Area and is made up of a small plateau region in the west (the Appalachian Plateau), a ridge and valley section (the Appalachian Valley) in the west central area, and the Appalachian Mountains (the Cohuttas and the Blue Ridge) in the eastern portion.

Figure 1 also depicts the major rivers of GA. It is important to have a good understanding of their locations because they provided the main early transportation and communication routes of GA. The patterns of settlement therefore centered around them and the valleys which run along them. The rivers also served as natural boundaries for early subdivisions of the colony (parishes) and for describing the locations of land. The rivers which flow into the Atlantic Ocean were especially important in the colonial period (1733-76). Using Figure 1, first take note of the Savannah River (SR) which constitutes almost all the border between GA and her eastern neighbor SC. Take special notice of two of its tributaries, Briar Creek (BC) in the south, and farther north the Broad River (BR). Now direct your attention to the Ogeechee River (OR) and the Canoochee River (CR) which runs into it. Then pay attention to the Altamaha River (AR) which is made up of the confluence of the Ohoopee (OhR), Oconee (OcR), and the Ocmulgee (OcmR) Rivers. Cast your glance down a bit and you will see the Satilla River (SaR) and beneath it the St. Marys River (SMR) which constitutes the coastal borderline with FL. All of these rivers, as you have seen, flow into the Atlantic Ocean, most of them entering the ocean through large inlets and/or island networks. Let us now take a look at the streams which empty into the Gulf. The longest of these is the Chattahoochee River (ChR) which rises in the northeast, moves southwestwardly, then becomes the border between GA and AL. In the southwestern corner of the state it joins the Flint River (FR) at Lake Seminole which is drained through FL into the Gulf. Now notice the four rivers which empty south central GA into FL, then flow into the

Gulf of Mexico: the Ochlockonee (OchR), Withlacoochee (WR), Alapaha (AlR), and Suwanee (SuR) Rivers. In the northwestern corner of GA you will see the Oostanaula (OoR) and the Etowah (ER) Rivers which flow together then move into AL as the Coosa River.

2. The trustee period (1733–54)

When the first permanent white settlers came into GA in 1733, they were entering a land which had been inhabited by Indian tribes for many centuries and which had been explored by numerous representatives of several European nations for about two centuries. The Cherokee Indians had towns in northwestern GA and ranged widely over the surrounding territory, and the Lower Creek Indians lived in central and southern GA and also ranged widely. In 1497 Cabot explored the North American coast claiming the lands for England; in 1513 the Spaniard de Leon went ashore in FL; and in 1524 da Verrazano explored the Atlantic Coast in the name of France. These three early explorers set afoot the long-term controversy among Spain, England, and France for control of North America. In about 1540, the first Europeans entered GA, these being members of an inland expedition led by the Spaniard de Soto from his FL base. Spaniards went on to settle St. Augustine, FL in 1565 and proceeded to establish missions and military posts along the GA coasts to stave off French claims to the area. Then, after about 100 years of Spanish control of GA, but no settlement, Charles II of England granted all of what is now NC, SC, and GA to eight English noblemen in 1663. These proprietors of Carolina (NC, SC, GA), however, made no attempts to settle the GA country. The permanent English settlement of Charleston (1670) secured England's claim to Carolina and the permanent Spanish settlement at St. Augustine (1565) secured Spain's claim to FL. Both countries asserted that they owned the lands which now are GA.

In 1732, King George II of England granted to 20 trustees the land between the Savannah and Altamaha Rivers and its extension to the Pacific Ocean. The trustees planned to make the area a haven for British unfortunates and dissenting Protestant sects, a military buffer between the Carolinas and Spanish FL, a claim against the French in the back country, and a silk producing society to supply England with this commodity. The trustees offered land to settlers, but the land could neither be sold nor mortgaged; it could only be held for life and passed on to male heirs. The land was to be developed, mulberry trees (for silk worms) planted, no slaves could be brought in, no rum or brandy sold, and no land holder could leave GA without permission. On 12 February 1733 the first group of 120 settlers led by Oglethorpe established the town of Savannah about 18 miles up the Savannah River. A treaty was made with eight tribes of Indians in the nearby regions, the Indians permitting the settlement of the land. Oglethorpe supervised everything, administering oaths, giving out land, issuing permits to leave, convening court, and overseeing the Common Council which had named three bailiffs, two constables, two tithingmen, eight conservators of the peace, and a recorder. He then began constructing several small forts at various strategic places, staffed them with small contingents of soldiers, and sent families to cultivate the land around some of them. Ships began arriving with supplies and further emigrants, one ship with about 40 Jews, then one with over 250 settlers, then a sizable group of Salzburgers who had been expelled from Germany, then others. The Salzburgers established a settlement called Ebenezer on the Savannah River about 25 miles north of Savannah. In the first 15 months of the colony's existence, Savannah and Ebenezer had been founded, Fort Argyle and other smaller forts had been set up, small villages (Abercorn, Highgate, Hampstead) were settled, some people from the Piedmont in Italy, from Switzerland, from France, and from Wales came, a lighthouse was erected on Tybee Island, farms were started, and silk growing was begun.

In 1735, a colony of Swiss and Moravians (left for PA after 5 years) settled on the Ogeechee River near Fort Argyle, a military outpost called Augusta was established far up the Savannah River, and early in 1736, a group of Scottish Highlanders established New Inverness (now Darien) on the Altamaha River. Later in 1736, Oglethorpe returned from a visit to England with 225 people and supplies, 125 of the people being Germans who were sent to Ebenezer (shortly moved to New Ebenezer) and 25 Moravians who went to Fort Argyle. Another settlement which was called Frederica was set up on St. Simons Island at the mouth of the Altamaha River. By 1737, over 1000 people had come to GA, over 50000 acres had been granted, five main towns had been set up (Savannah, New Ebenezer, New Inverness, Frederica, Augusta), and forts had been built on the coastal islands and the Altamaha River. See Figure 2 for these early settlements. Fearing they were about to lose all of GA, the Spanish threatened to destroy the colony in 1739, and England and Spain declared war on each other. Oglethorpe, after driving a Spanish raiding party back into St. Augustine, organized in December 1739 a successful invasion of FL which

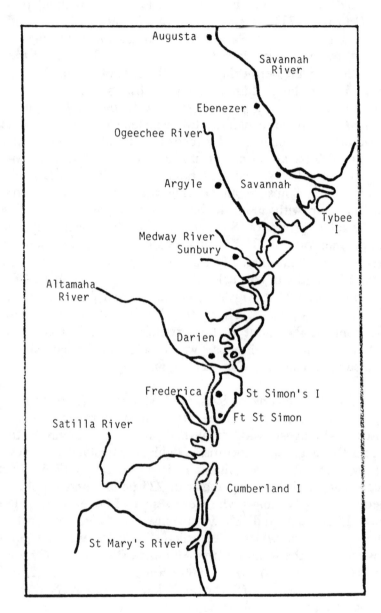

Figure 2. Early GA settlement.

took several Spanish forts. In May 1740, a second invasion in an attempt to capture St. Augustine ended in failure. In July 1742 a very large Spanish force landed on St. Simon Island, Oglethorpe abandoned Fort St. Simon, withdrew to Frederica which he had fortified, sallied out in a surprise attack, and roundly defeated the Spanish in what came to be called the Battle of Bloody Marsh. The Spanish retired to their ships, the war was effectively ended (even though GA tried again to take St. Augustine in 1743), and GA's southern boundary became the St. Marys River.

In 1741, the colony was divided into two counties, one centered at Savannah, another centered at Frederica, but the arrangement never really functioned. In 1743 Oglethorpe left GA in the hands of a president, but the settlement began to falter. The number of new settlers dropped precipitously, the colonists were dissatisfied with the land regulations and the prohibitions on slavery and rum, many left for SC, the silk growing enterprise failed, many indentured servants became ill or refused to work or ran away, and several threatening incidents with Indians occurred. In response to this dismal turn of events, the rum, slave, and land regulations were first relaxed then abolished, a provincial assembly was created, new groups of settlers began to be added to the 1500 who were in residence in the middle 1740s, and other trade and agricultural enterprises began to be successfully developed. Among them were lumber, tar, pitch, furs, deer skins, and rice. In 1752, a group of 280 Congregationalists from SC settled with over 350 slaves on the Medway River, halfway between the Ogeechee and the Altamaha Rivers. Their town was called Midway. In June of this same year, the trustees of GA turned control of the province back to the British monarch. The King ordered that the trustee government should continue until a royal government could be set up, this taking a little over two years. The population at this time was approximately 3000, about 800 of them being black slaves.

3. The royal colony (1754-76)

On 29 October 1754, the first royal governor arrived in Savannah with the structure of a new government in hand. The major changes were that GA was given a legislature and a well-ordered court system. The governor set up a General Assembly consisting of two houses: an Upper House was made up of a 12-membered Governor's Council, and a Lower or Commons House which was made up of 19 members elected by GA landowners from designated towns and districts. All matters involving money had to be initiated in the Lower House. The Governor and his Council granted lands, acted as a Supreme Court, and regulated the militia. The Governor was chancellor of the province, acted as ordinary (handling wills and estates), and called and dissolved the Assembly. Lower courts presided over by justices of the peace were established and above them was a General Court with a chief and two assistant judges.

The new governor got the system operating, visited the towns, improved the defenses, and made a treaty with the Indians, but was unable to get along with the General Assembly. His replacement arrived on 16 February 1757. The work of the first governor was continued in all areas, and the prosperity of the colony continued in response. Notable in the successful exploitation of their lands, the prosperous Congregationalists around the Medway River asked for and got the setting up of a port city called Sunbury. This town was rapidly populated quickly becoming second in size only to Savannah. To regulate and govern the increasing peoples of the colony better, GA was divided in 1758 into eight parishes: Christ Church including Savannah, St. Matthews including Ebenezer, St. Pauls including Augusta, St. Georges including Halifax, St. Philips including Argyle and Hardwicke, St. Johns including Midway and Sunbury, St. Andrews including Darien, and St. James including Frederica (see Figure 3). Even with the parishes, however, most record keeping remained in Savannah. The districts, towns, and regions which were coalesced to form these parishes were: Christ Church (Towns of Savannah and Hardwick, District of Savannah, Sea Island north of the Ogeechee River), St Matthews (Districts of Abercorn, Goshen, and Ebenezer), St. Pauls (District of Augusta), St. Georges (District of Halifax), St. Philips (District of Ogeechee), St. Johns (Town of Sunbury, Districts of Midway and Newport, Islands of St. Catherine and Bermuda), St. Andrews (Town and District of Darien, Sapelo and Eastwood Islands, and Sea Island south of the Ogeechee River), St. James (Town and District of Frederica, both Great and Little St. Simons Islands).

A third governor came 11 October 1760, arriving just in time to strengthen the colony's fortifications against a possible spread of a massive Cherokee uprising all along the SC frontier. However, in 1761 the SC militia supported by British regulars attacked and crushed the Cherokees who sued for peace. This uprising was part of the French and Indian War against the British, which Spain entered in 1762. In this same year, England defeated the Spanish Navy, and shortly received FL from Spain, as well as the territory east of the MS River from France. On 10 October 1763 the British Crown declared St. Marys River to be the southern boundary of GA. The territory below the line became the provinces of East FL and West FL. The King forbid whites to settle west of the headwaters of the rivers flowing into the Atlantic Ocean, and he ordered VA, NC, SC, and GA to make a peace treaty with the Indians, which they did. Out of this treaty, GA received permission to settle a coastal strip down to the St. Marys River and a broad strip between the Savannah and Ogeechee Rivers extending above Augusta. In 1765, four new parishes were added in the newly acquired territory, since settlers poured in because of the removal of the Spanish threat from FL. The new parishes were St. Davids, St. Patricks, St. Thomas, and St. Marys. And then, in 1773, another Indian council and trade settlement brought the Creeks and Cherokees to cede two very large parcels of land: a section far up the Savannah River and a tract west of Savannah and Darien between the Ogeechee and Altamaha Rivers (see Figure 3).

The population, agricultural productivity, territorial spread, and commerce of GA, all of which had started to rise in the late 1740s, accelerated their growth rates throughout the period 1754-76. The repeal of the land and slavery restrictions, the beginnings of representative government, the presence of a stable administration, the removal of the French and Spanish threats, and the cessions of Indian lands brought about these remarkable trends. Both white immigrants and black slaves poured in, as these population figures show: 1753 (2400 whites, 1100 blacks), 1760 (6000 whites, 3600 blacks), 1766 (9900 whites, 7800 blacks), 1772 (18000 whites, 15000 blacks), 1776 (20500 whites, 19500 blacks). Up until about 1750, practically all farming was done by white farmers working small plots of land. But after 1750, large plantations owned by entrepreneurs and worked by slaves slowly began to be set up, especially in the fertile coastal and river areas. Most Georgians during this period remained small farmers, but many moved out of the plantation areas into the backwoods regions. Rice production became the predominant activity, with large quantities being shipped out. Other exports included indigo, corn, lumber products, cattle, horses, deer skins, tar, turpentine, beef, and pork. Settlement on the frontier was invited by the GA governor and considerable response was being had as Virginians and Carolinians came down the Appalachian valleys and many Scotch-Irish came directly from Ireland. GA was well on its way to becoming a thriving, productive colony at the end of this period of time (1776).

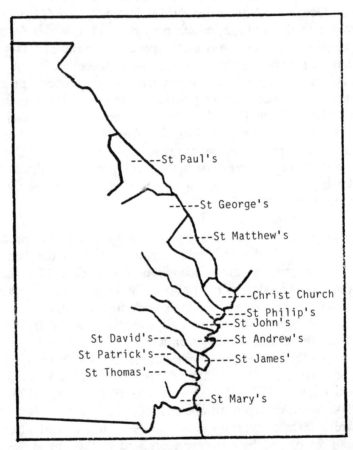

Figure 3. GA Parishes, 1758/1765-1777.

4. The Revolutionary War (1776–82)

As mentioned, the French and Indian War (1754-63) was a conflict that was fought outside GA, but the colony benefited enormously. The Spanish were removed from the southern border and the French from the western. The decade following the end of the war was one of explosive economic expansion in GA. The low country (along the coast and along the Savannah River) was producing rice and indigo on large plots of land which were held by slaveowners. In the back country, with Augusta thriving as its center, settlers were working small and medium-sized farms and were doing lumbering. Savannah prospered as the capital and shipping center of the colony, where publication of a newspaper, the GA Gazette, had begun in 1763. The war had left England badly in debt, and in 1765, they levied document taxes on all the colonies. The colonies resented the action, claiming that as English citizens they should not be taxed except by vote of their representatives. Demonstrations against the taxation were broad spread in the colonies (including GA), and led to repeal of the tax act. However, England held fast to her right to tax the colonies without their concurrence. The thirteen colonies set up a tight communication network, and when the British Parliament passed another tax act in 1768, MA recommended a unified opposition. The GA Lower House of Assembly endorsed the position, and the governor dissolved the Assembly. There followed a series of conflicts between the Lower House on one hand and the governor and the Upper House on the other hand, the former opposing the English, the latter supporting them.

In 1773, several Indian tribes ceded to GA a sizable territory in payment of a debt they owed some traders (see Figure 4). In this same year, the British government repealed taxes on everything except tea, but people in the colonies countered by refusing to receive, buy, or use tea. In Boston this activity one night took the form of a group of rebels throwing a shipload of tea into the harbor. The Parliament reacted in 1774 by closing the port of Boston and revoking MA's charter. An extensive number of rebels (now beginning to be called Patriots) met in Savannah, declared their sympathy with MA, pledged resistance to England, and sent aid to Boston. GA quickly came to be divided in a three fold way: Patriots (against England), Loyalists (for England), and a sizable uncommitted group. The older settlers tended to be Loyalist, the younger generation Patriot. The business men in Savannah first were inclined toward England, but later changed. The

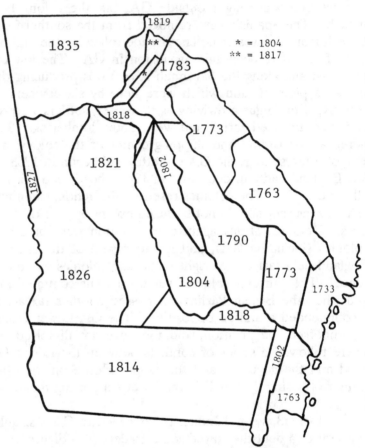

Figure 4. GA Land Cessions

German settlers were usually Loyalist, but the English, Scottish, and Irish settlers of the up-country, as well as the descendants of New Englanders, were generally anti-British. These sympathies produced an excruciating civil conflict in GA. For six years there were to be military battles between Loyalist Georgians and Patriot Georgians, plundering invaders, guerilla warfare, quarreling leaders, hostile Indians, inhabitants in flight, hunger, fire, homelessness, and death. The governor, who was greatly respected, was able to prevent GA from naming delegates to the First Continental Congress, a gathering of representative of the colonies in 1774. In early 1775, British military forces began to arrive in Boston, and in April war broke out in the environs of the city at the towns of Lexington and Concord. Many Georgians organized local anti-British groups, then set up a GA Provisional Congress which created a Council of Safety, all these actions being opposed by the GA royal government.

In a very short time, the GA militia expelled Loyalists, and the Council of Safety acting under the Provincial Congress took charge of the government. In January 1776, the royal governor fled, and another Provincial Congress met, five delegates to the Continental Congress being elected, plans being inaugurated to arm the province, and a government being established (the Provincial Congress, the Council of Safety, trial courts, a president). During August, news of the signing of the Declaration of Independence came to GA, three of the delegates being involved. Thus GA became a state, and a convention was called to adopt a constitution and to establish a permanent government. The convention met in October 1776 and the new constitution (February 1777) called for a governor, an executive council, a unicameral legislature (Assembly), and a court system. The twelve parishes were done away with, and the state was divided into eight counties, the parishes which made up each being listed in parentheses: Wilkes (land ceded in 1773), Richmond (St. Pauls), Burke (St. Georges), Effingham (St. Matthews and part of St. Philips), Chatham (part of St. Philips, Christ Church), Liberty (St. Johns, St. Andrews, St. James), Glynn (St. Davids, St. Patricks), and Camden (St. Thomas, St. Marys). See Figure 5 for the areas involved. The Assembly set up a Superior (trial) Court for each county, authorized the continuation of the minor courts (justices of the peace), and selected those county officials who performed state duties (sheriff, tax collector, justices). GA during 1777 busied itself with fortification construction, stockpiling supplies, and organizing its forces. Loyalists (Tories) and their Indian allies from East FL conducted raids into southern GA, destroying property and stealing cattle.

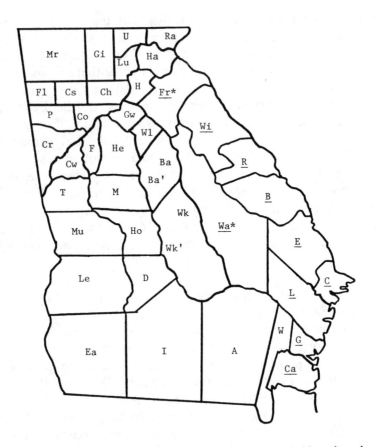

Figure 5. GA's original counties and how the land was distributed. Eight counties formed in 1777 (headright grants): Camden[Ca], Glynn[G], Liberty[L], Chatham[C], Effingham[E], Burke[B], Richmond[R], Wilkes[Wi]. Two counties formed in 1783 (headright and bounty* grants): Franklin[Fr*], Washington[Wa*]. Three counties formed in the 1805 lottery: Wayne[W], Wilkinson[Wk], Baldwin-[Ba]. Counties added to in 1807 lottery: Wilkinson-[Wk'], Baldwin [Ba']. Eight counties formed in 1820 lottery: Walton[Wl], Gwinnett[Gw], Hall[H], Habersham-[Ha], Early[Ea], Irwin[I], Appling[A], Rabun[Ra]. Five counties formed in 1827 lottery: Carroll[Cr], Coweta-[Cw], Troup[T], Muscogee[Mu], Lee[Le]. Nine counties formed in 1832 lottery: Cherokee which was almost immediately split into Cass (renamed Bartow in 1861)[Cs], Cherokee[Ch], Cobb[Co], Floyd[Fl], Gilmer[Gi], Lumpkin-[Lu], Murray[Mr], Paulding[P], Union[U].

Several attempts by GA troops to invade East FL during 1776-8 came to nothing.

In the north during these years (1775-8), the British armies had done very well after having been driven from Boston. They took New York City, Philadelphia, and sizable portions of NJ, NY, and CT. But things then turned, with a large British army being defeated at Saratoga, the abandonment of Philadelphia by the Royal forces, and the regaining of considerable territory in NJ, NY, PA, and CT. This was followed by the entry of France (against the British) into the war. The King's generals decided at this point to invade and conquer SC and GA. On 19 November 1778, a British force from FL invaded GA, but was compelled to retire when reinforcements failed to arrive. Then, on 27 December, a British fleet brought troops to the mouth of the Savannah River. The troops came ashore and defeated the outnumbered defenders of Savannah, the remnant of the GA army fleeing into SC. In short order, Ebenezer fell to the British, then Royal troops from FL took Sunbury (09 January 1779) and Fort Morris, and after forestalling the British advance on Augusta, GA forces finally had to surrender the town. This British takeover resulted in many people switching to the Loyalist side. With Loyalist forces now holding the low country and the chief town of the upcountry, the rural territories of GA fell subject to widespread guerilla warfare, parties of marauding Loyalists, and opportunistic renegades. A large band of these roving Tory militia was defeated in Wilkes County on 13 February 1779 at Kettle Creek. During these months of January and February, a contingent of the Continental Army was being gathered in SC near Savannah. Their presence forced the British evacuation of Augusta, and shortly thereafter a detachment entered GA and camped on Brier Creek, where they waited for more American troops to join them for an attack on the British. Before this could happen, the King's troops surprised them and dealt them a disastrous defeat.

When the British took Savannah (29 December 1778), the state government moved to Augusta, which it had to flee when Augusta fell ten days later. Following this, the government operated somewhat fitfully as it moved around in the back country. A large French fleet appeared off Savannah on 01 September 1779, and most of the British troops in GA (including those in Augusta) were recalled to the defense of the city. On 16 September French and American forces began a three-week seige of Savannah, followed by an unsuccessful assault, with the British remaining in possession of both the city and the state. With the British government seated in Savannah, the badly organized GA state government (now returned to Augusta) fell to quarrelling among themselves, and for a time there were two factions in Augusta, both claiming to have elected a governor. Finally in January 1780, a duly constituted General Assembly elected a chief executive, and shortly thereafter the seat of state government was moved to Heard's Fort (now Washington). In May, Charleston, SC, fell to the British, and large numbers of GA troops were captured, which permitted Augusta to be reoccupied by Loyalist forces. Many upcountry people swore allegiance to the King, but Patriot militia continued guerilla warfare against the Loyalists. After about a year of back country and out-of-state raising of troops, the Continental Army supported by SC and GA forces made an attack upon Augusta in May 1781 and defeated its British defenders. This placed the northern counties of GA back in the possession of the Americans, inhabitants who had fled now returned, and GA state government was reestablished at Augusta. The British still held Savannah, Ebenezer, Sunbury, and an outpost on the Ogeechee River.

It was not long before the Continental Army retook Ebenezer, and shortly afterwards news came that a large British army had been defeated at Yorktown, VA, in October 1781. In January 1782 more Continental troops came into GA, the state governor called for citizens to unite with them and for Loyalist soldiers to desert, the American forces drove the British out of the Ogeechee River post, and hemmed them in at Savannah. Most of GA was now back in Patriot hands. In May 1782, the King ordered the British government to surrender Savannah, and on 21 July this was done, the Americans reoccupying it after three and a half years of Loyalist rule. Many British sympathizers swore allegiance to the victorious Patriots, but sizable numbers left (perhaps 7500), mostly for East FL and the West Indies. The war was over, and in the peace treaties of 1782-3, England recognized the independence of the thirteen states, made the MS River the western boundary of GA, and ceded both East and West FL to Spain. The war left a free GA, but Spain was once again on the southern border, and Indian problems remained. The occupation of the low country (Savannah and its environs) by the British during 1778-82 had driven GA state government into the upcountry, where upcountry leaders took control of the state, causing the coastal region to lose its political dominance.

5. Early statehood (1783-1821)

During the 38 years of early statehood (1783-1821), GA underwent greater changes than at any other time in its history, and all of them are exceptionally important genealogically. The recovery from the ravages of the Revolutionary War were fairly rapid, bringing with it sizable alterations in governmental structure at all levels: national, state, and local. The tide of immigration into the state exhibited an explosive increase with settlers pouring in, which resulted in the Indians being pushed westward and northward. Accompanying this population increase was a very healthy expanding frontier economy with tobacco, rice, and lumber products at its base, but with cotton gradually becoming the chief commodity. All of these changes had profound effects upon the society of the state: the return of many Patriots who fled during the War, the large increase in slaves who came in to farm the cotton, the frontier conflicts with the Indians, the sharp differences between the crude frontier life and the situation in the older areas, and the replacement of the older Episcopalian church influence by Baptists and Methodists.

When the British left GA in 1782, state government was set up in Savannah operating under the state constitution of 1777. The lands and property belonging to British sympathizers were confiscated and sold. Then in November 1783, the Creeks ceded to GA a considerable portion of land north and west of Wilkes County (see Figures 4 and 5). The new territory was divided into the counties of Franklin and Washington, and as a reward to those who served the state in the Revolutionary War, each received a warrant for a tract of the land. In addition to these awards, each head of a family could claim land upon payment of a small fee. A number of tracts were awarded to soldiers from other states (especially VA, NC, SC) who had served GA. Savannah became unsatisfactory as the state capital because of its distance from the frontier areas, and so in 1786, the government was moved to Augusta. Shortly thereafter, the settlements in northeast GA made it necessary for GA and SC to settle the boundary between them, since it had never been defined in that region. This was done by a joint commission in 1789.

Back in 1778, the 13 states which had rebelled against Great Britain had loosely bound themselves together in a written agreement called the Articles of Confederation. This document provided only for a Continental Congress of state delegates, but it had little power over the states. Very quickly after the War it was realized that a permanent union of the 13 states was needed, and a convention was called in 1787 to consider this. They drew up a Constitution which provided for a unification of the 13 states into a federal republic with a central government. On 02 January 1788, GA approved and adopted the Constitution, becoming the fourth state to do so. On 04 March 1789, most states having joined, the new US government was inaugurated. In May 1789, a GA convention met and revised its state constitution to conform to the new federal document. The governor's council was replaced with a state senate, the property qualification to vote was dropped, and the governor's term was lengthened to two years. The court system remained as before, except that the chief justiceship was abolished.

The type of cotton which would grow in mainland GA, the short staple cotton, was such that the lint adheres firmly to the seed, which requires a great deal of hard labor to process. This kept the culture of cotton from being profitable, but the situation was all changed in 1793 when Whitney invented the cotton engine (gin) which very rapidly and effectively removed the fiber. Now cotton could be raised profitably, and it very quickly replaced tobacco as the best money crop in the upcountry. Cotton could be easily grown on large plantations with slave labor and on smaller farms as well. By 1821, cotton was being raised by over 60% of the upcountry farmers and the increase in plantations and slaves had been extraordinary. The success of this venture resulted in a rising demand for the takeover of more Indian lands. Cotton was on its way to dominating the state's economy.

In 1795, GA claimed much of the land which now makes up AL and MS. The legislature in that year sold to four companies 35 million acres in this area around the Yazoo River for less than 1.5 cents per acre. It was soon discovered that bribery had been wanton, and following a tremendous popular protest, the 1796 legislature rescinded its action. The legislature did this in their first session in the town of Louisville, to which the capital had been moved in May 1795. The Yazoo companies challenged the legislative action, as did many people who had purchased land from them, in the courts and the US Congress. In 1802, GA ceded to the US all its western lands (now AL and MS), thereby handing the problem over to the federal government. When the Supreme Court upheld the Yazoo sale, the US government was forced to repurchase the lands from the Yazoo companies. In 1798, the

GA constitution was rewritten, and a document which lasted over half a century was produced. It provided for three separate branches of government: legislative (a senate and a house of representatives making up the general assembly), executive (governor, secretary of state, treasurer, surveyor-general), and judicial (a superior and inferior court required to sit in each county twice a year). The state lines were defined, freedom of the press and jury trial were secured, habeas corpus was not to be suspended, religious freedom was guaranteed, and slave importation was forbidden. The courts in each county were to be served by a clerk and a sheriff, and in the absence of a supreme court, the superior court justices met once a year to take any needed actions. Probate matters were put under the inferior courts, and gradually over the next few decades other county functions were transferred to them. The population in 1776 was about 40000, in 1790 it had more than doubled to about 83000, and by 1800 it had almost doubled again to 163000.

As mentioned, in 1802, GA signed over all her western lands (now AL and MS) to the US government in exchange for some money, several conditions relating to lands, and the agreement that the US would purchase for GA all Indian land within the state. In that year, the US obtained from the Creeks a large section of land west of the Oconee River and a strip extending from the Altamaha River to the St. Mary's River (labelled 1802 in Figure 4). The lands were made into the counties of Baldwin, Wilkinson, and Wayne, were surveyed, and were divided into lots. The lots were distributed in 1805 to the people of the state by a land lottery. Slips of paper bearing lot numbers were put in boxes along with blank slips. Those entitled to draw were: one draw for each unmarried male over 20 years old, two draws for every married white male, two draws for every white widow, one draw for every family of orphans under 21. The drawing was conducted by the government, and the fortunate ones received grants of the lots. Within 12 months the granted land had to be secured by a small fee payment. All land west of the Oconee River was distributed by this procedure as it was gradually acquired from the Indians. The lands east of the Oconee River were distributed by the older plan called the headright system. The old headright system gave to each head of a family a tract of unoccupied land which he selected. Upon paying for a survey, then a small fee for land over 200 acres, 50 acres were granted for each family member and each slave owned by the head of the family, up to 1000 acres. It is important to remember that the Oconee River is the dividing line between the headright system and the land lottery system of land titles. The seaboard settlements had been made by Europeans, but the settlers who came into north and middle GA just before and after the Revolution were native Americans, moving in from VA, MD, NC, and SC. Wilkes County was settled rapidly after the War, 36000 out of the total 83000 Georgians in 1790 living there. It was mostly Virginians and North Carolinians who settled Wilkes County, as had been the case for Burke County. Franklin and Washington Counties were settled mainly by Scotch-Irish people who came from NC and the Anderson District of SC.

The rapid ingress of population brought pressure for moving the capital to the center of the state, so in 1803 a site was selected, and in 1807 the new town of Milledgeville became the capital. Another Creek Indian treaty for land cession was made in 1804, the ceded areas were added to Baldwin and Wilkinson Counties, and were distributed in the land lottery of 1807. Winners in the 1805 land lottery could not participate in this new one, but otherwise the regulations were similar. Transportation during these years was largely by road (wagons and coaches) and by river (poled boats and rafts), with neither being kept up very well. There were very few factories or industrial firms in the state, farming absorbing the activities of most citizens. Savannah was the export-import center of the state with Augusta being the upcountry trade headquarters. As the cotton culture increased, so did the number of slaves, most of them coming in from states to the north of GA. The percentage of blacks in the population increased from 36% in 1790 to 44% in 1820. The disarray that the churches of GA were in after the War persisted for quite some time, with the most notable development being the remarkable growth of Baptists and Methodists. By 1810, the population of GA had reached 250000, with Savannah the largest city (about 5000).

In the first decade of the 1800s, France and England were at war, and American ships trading with either were subject to search or capture by the other. Toward the end of the decade, English battle-ships were stopping American vessels and a growing tide of opinion favoring war was being generated. After a British ship fired shots in Savannah harbor in 1809, GA advocated war, which was declared by the US in June 1812. The conflict came to be known as the War of 1812. The people of GA fortified the coast and built forts on the frontier since many Creek Indians were anxious to take advantage of the situation. On 30 August 1813 Creeks attacked Fort Mims and massacred the occupants, then a general uprising of hostile Creeks and

Seminoles set in. GA troops went after the Seminoles and drove them back into FL, and both TN and GA forces were called out to go against the Creeks. The GA soldiers entered Creek territory and defeated the Indians at their towns of Antosee and Tallassee on 29 November 1813. A second campaign was mounted in January 1814 and a large contingent of Creeks at Hotle Crawle was dispersed. In March of that year Jackson dealt the Creeks an overwhelming defeat at the Battle of Horseshoe Bend in AL. In the peace settlement of 09 August 1814, the Creeks were forced to give up their land in southern GA (see Figure 4). This land was to be organized into Early, Irwin, and Appling Counties. In May of 1814 and January 1815 the British raided some of the GA islands, the last raids occurring after the treaty ending the War had been signed (24 December 1814).   On 26 January 1815, news was received of Jackson's victory over the British at New Orleans, this battle also being fought after the peace treaty. In the peace treaty FL was given back to Spain, which was unfortunate for GA, because the Spanish permitted the area to be a refuge for pirates, outlaws, and hostile Seminole Indians.

In 1817, war with the Seminoles broke out, several forays being made by the Indians and by US troops into each other's territory. In early 1818, over 3000 US soldiers invaded FL, driving the Indians back from the GA border and taking possession of Pensacola, one of their supply bases. In 1817, the Cherokees ceded to the US (and thus to GA) all of their lands east of the Chattahoochee River in the northeastern part of the state (see Figures 4 and 5). This territory was organized into Hall and Habersham Counties. In 1818, the Creeks ceded a tract of land in between the Appalachee and Chattahoochee Rivers (which became Gwinnett and Walton Counties) and a parcel of land lying south of the Ocmulgee River (which was to be added to Irwin and Appling Counties).   Then in 1819, the Cherokees gave up the land resting between the Chattahoochee and the Chestatee Rivers in the far northeastern corner of GA, a piece of land which was to become Rabun County. All of these cessions may be visualized by looking at the 1817, 1818, and 1819 labels on Figure 4 and by viewing Figure 5. Early in 1819, Spain, under pressure to control the FL territories or to surrender them, sold East and West FL to the US. As of 1820, the population of GA had risen to 340000 with Savannah still the largest town (over 8000 people). The Savannah population figure fits in well with the fact that most GA residents lived on farms, a few of them rich planters with many slaves, but most of them small farmers. In the year 1820, the land cessions of 1814, 1817, 1819, and 1820 were distributed in a third GA lottery. The period of early statehood (1783-1821) effectively ended with a Creek-US treaty of January 1821 by which GA obtained a sizable area of land, this being the remaining land between the Flint, Ocmulgee, and Chattahoochee Rivers. Later in the year, the territory was laid out into the Counties of Dooly, Houston, Monroe, Henry, and Fayette, and was distributed in the fourth GA land lottery. See Figures 4 and 5. Nineteen years had now gone by since the agreement of the US in 1802 to obtain all GA Indian lands for the state. Millions of acres were still occupied by Indians, and so the GA government continued pressing for possession of these areas.

6. The middle years (1821-61)

In the early 1820s both the Creeks and the Cherokees resolved not to give up any more land, appealed their cases to the US, but after some hesitation the US agreed that it was obligated to remove all Indians from GA. In February 1825, the Creeks in GA (the Lower Creeks) signed over all their land to GA in exchange for territory west of the MS River. However, the Creeks outside of GA (the Upper Creeks) declared the cession invalid because they were not consulted, and proceeded to murder the GA Creek leader. The US, trying to calm the situation, made a new treaty with the Creeks in which they ceded all but 300000 acres and were to keep possession until the start of 1827. In defiance of the US government, the GA governor ordered the areas surveyed, and informed the US that any US troops sent to enforce the federal position would be met by GA militia. This led to a US program to acquire all GA Creek lands which was finally settled on 15 November 1827, and shortly after the Creeks left GA for the West. These territories were distributed in the fifth GA land lottery (1827), which produced the Counties of Carroll, Coweta, Troup, Muscogee, and Lee (see Figures 4 and 5). Even though only GA residents could participate in the lotteries, many of the winners sold their winnings to settlers or to land brokers who then sold them to settlers.

As of 1829, the GA legislature passed laws extending its jurisdiction over the lands occupied by the Cherokees in northwestern GA. One of the reasons for this was that gold had been discovered in the area, and both Cherokees and illegal white intruders rushed into mining, producing much strife. By 1830, the state population numbered 517000 with slightly less than half being slaves. In 1831, the Cherokee lands were surveyed by GA, and the Counties of Cass (later renamed

Bartow), Cherokee, Cobb, Floyd, Gilmer, Lumpkin, Murray, Paulding, and Union were laid out (see Figures 4 and 5), even though the Indians still possessed the area. Then, in a treaty of December 1835, the Cherokees gave up all their lands in exchange for five million dollars and seven million acres west of the MS River. By this agreement, the Cherokees were to leave and GA was to take over the lands in 1838. The population in 1840 had reached approximately 691000 (408000 white, 283000 black), with the economy continuing to expand and be very prosperous except for a few short periods. The larger towns were Savannah (12000), Augusta (8000), Columbus (4000), and Macon (3500). Prior to 1840 the transportation in GA (on which the economy was quite dependent) was chiefly by water and by ill-maintained wagon roads, with a few canal projects having been proposed, but not many built. All of this was to undergo a notable exchange with the coming of the railroads. The basic transportation needs of GA called for Macon to be connected with Savannah, for Athens, Eatonton, and Madison to be connected with Augusta, and for a line from central GA to the TN River at northwest GA to be laid. The state had begun issuing charters for railroad construction in 1833 and later was to directly provide some funding. By 1840 there were 636 miles of rail in GA, more than in any other state. In 1845 a rail terminal called Terminus was set up in north central GA; it was renamed Marthasville shortly after, then its name changed to Atlanta, a town destined to become the rail center of GA and of much of the southeastern US. By 1861 GA had the best rail system in the deep south with over 1600 miles of track. These railroads steadily reinforced the ever-expanding vigorous economy.

As of the years 1839-40, GA finally had all of its territory, with the northwestern and southwestern portions of the state now open for settlement. The GA legislature established a state supreme court in 1845 with three justices and the power to review the decisions of all other courts. The Mexican state of Texas, which had many US settlers in it, rebelled in 1835 and set up their own government. In the war which ensued, a GA battalion, which went to assist the Texans, was massacred. The Texans, however, prevailed and TX became a free state in 1836, then in 1845 in response to their request, they were admitted to the US. Soon after Mexico declared war on the US. GA sent a volunteer regiment into this theater of war, but it saw no action, even though it was there for 12 months. A sizable number of Georgians who had enlisted in the regular army did see battle action, the war ending with the surrender of Mexico City in 1847 after a series of decisive US victories. In the peace treaty of 1848, the US acquired much territory (CA, UT, NM, NV, TX). In 1849, CA applied for statehood with a constitution prohibiting slavery. Upon the objection of southern states (including GA), a compromise was reached in 1850 by which CA was admitted free (no slavery), but with UT and NM Territories to be allowed to settle the question for themselves. In general, GA had strong sympathies for any measure which would keep the Union from being disrupted, as long as the rights of the slave states were honored. The population of the state in 1850 was about 906000 with 522000 whites and 384000 blacks. Tremendous growth in material prosperity had occurred since 1820, and this was to continue until 1861. Cotton was the chief crop with slave labor doing much of the cultivation, but the production of corn, swine, rice, wheat, tobacco, lumber, and livestock was also very sizable. Industrialization had also made some notable beginnings with cotton gins, flour mills, textile mills, saw mills, mining operations, quarries, and tanneries opening up in many areas. Slavery was an integral part of both the agricultural and the industrial efforts of GA. Education had been slowly advancing, but over 20% of the whites were illiterate as of 1850. There were a few small church colleges and a small ill-supported state college (about 100 students). A medical school had been set up in Augusta in 1828, and in the early 1850s Savannah and Atlanta were to establish similar schools. There were a number of weekly county newspapers, and the larger cities had dailies. The churches had been growing rapidly as GA ceased to be a frontier state, especially Baptist and Methodist, but also Presbyterian, Lutheran, and Episcopalian. There were also comparatively small Catholic and Jewish beginnings.

The disagreements between the northern and southern states over the issue of slavery in new states took another turn in 1854. Congress passed a law giving KS settlers the right to decide whether they would have slavery or not. Both north and south sent settlers in to swing the vote and violence began to break out between them, resulting in a small war. From this time on, the disagreements between the north and the south escalated quite rapidly. In 1858, the US Supreme Court rendered a decision that all western territories were open to slavery and that Congress had no right to decide the question for the people. The fight in the late 1850s over these issues caused a breakup of most previous political alignments in the US. By 1860, most northerners had become Republicans, and most southerners had become Democrats, the dividing issue between them being whether Congress could decide about slavery in the new territories. At the national Democratic Convention held in 1860 in Charleston, more than half the

GA delegation walked out when the convention voted to oppose protection of slave owners in the western territories. In a second convention held in Baltimore shortly thereafter, the delegates split into two groups, and each group nominated a slate of candidates. A third group known as the Constitutional Union Party also put up candidates. GA people voted in the election of 1860 for the tickets of all three of these parties. The split in the Democratic ranks assured the election of Lincoln, the Republican candidate, to the presidency of the country.

Even though GA was reluctant to withdraw from the US, on 20 December 1860 SC seceded, stating that the Congress had violated the Constitution and that the Republican Party would destroy the rights of the individual states. MS, FL, and AL followed SC in short order. On 03 January 1861, GA militia seized Ft. Pulaski (at the mouth of the Savannah River), and then on 19 January a state convention voted to secede. Troops were raised all over the state, and the US forces at the Federal Arsenal in Augusta surrendered. GA had declared herself a free and independent state. As GA left the Union, her population was about 1,057,000, approximately 466000 being slaves. These forty years (1821-61) had been a period of extraordinary progress. GA had come to be a producer of very large quantities of cotton, corn, wheat, and other foodstuffs, and had developed an extensive railroad system.

7. The Civil War and reconstruction (1861-70)

Shortly after secession, GA sent delegates to a deep south state convention in Montgomery, AL, which organized the Confederate States of America on 04 February 1861. When SC Confederate forces on 12 April attacked and forced the surrender of Ft. Sumter (Charleston, SC), Lincoln called for volunteers to suppress the rebellion. These acts inaugurated an all-out war of the northern against the southern states (now including VA, NC, SC, GA, TN, AL, MS, LA, AR, FL, and TX). GA immediately began raising, training, and equipping troops, 25000 being in service by October 1861, a number which reached 120000 by the end of the war. The economy of the state was shifted from cotton to foodstuffs, its industrial production was turned to war goods, and GA's rail system was pressed into increased service.

Early in the Civil War (1861-2), the battles raged a long distance from GA: in VA where the Union armies were attempting to take

Richmond, and in the west along the KY-TN interface and in the MS Valley where the Yankee forces were trying to drive wedges into the south and divide her territory by pushing down the MS River and by moving to Nashville then Chattanooga. GA soldiers fought valiantly in both theaters of war helping to offer a stubborn resistance to the invasions from the north. As these northern campaigns got under way, the Union Navy began developing blockades of the Confederate coastline. In November 1861, a northern naval force captured Port Royal and Hilton Head islands off the SC coast just north of Savannah. Methodically the Yankee Navy moved down the coast so that by March 1862, all of GA's sea islands had been occupied. Then on 11 April, Ft. Pulaski (at the mouth of the Savannah River) was captured, thus closing the port of Savannah.

In September 1863, Union troops captured Chattanooga, TN, just across the northwestern line of GA. When they moved into GA, the Federal forces were defeated and driven back into Chattanooga. After sizable US reinforcements were brought in, the Union troops attacked the Confederates in the battles of Lookout Mountain and Missionary Ridge (23-25 November), sending the southern army in defeat back into GA. In May 1864, a concerted effort to take Richmond was begun by the Federals in VA, and simultaneously a drive toward Atlanta was launched. The numerically-superior northerners outflanked the Rebel forces at Dalton, then inflicted heavy losses on the Confederates at Resaca. A major fight was waged at New Hope Church, then the Yankees were dealt heavy losses at Kennesaw Mountain, but the relentless advance southward resumed. On 09 July Union troops were on the outskirts of Atlanta, on 18 July Confederate attacks were thrown back, and a 40-day seige of the town began. After two more repulsed attacks, the Confederate army evacuated Atlanta on 02 September and Union forces entered the town. The southern army marched north into south central TN, hoping to cut the long Yankee supply lines and to draw them back toward TN. A contingent of Federal forces was sent after the northward moving Confederate army, crushing them at Franklin and Nashville later in the year. The main body of Union troops burned Atlanta then started southeastward for Savannah. They destroyed rail lines, factories, bridges, stored supplies, and food, as they foraged and lived off the land. By 22 November, they reached Milledgeville, then continued on destroying and pillaging, only barely opposed by weak scattered GA militia units. On 13 December the northern troops took Ft. McAllister, and shortly after the 10000 defenders of Savannah left, permitting the Union soldiers to march in on 21 December.

After a two-month rest, the Federal troops moved northward, crossing SC, then entering NC. In VA, the Yankee forces began to close in on Richmond, and on 09 April 1865 the large Confederate army in VA surrendered at Appomattox. On 16 April US forces entered GA from AL and captured Columbus, then moved on to take Macon on 20 April. The war was effectively brought to an end by the surrender of the only sizable remaining Confederate army near Durham Station, NC, on 26 April 1865. GA was left in terrible condition, many men dead, the economy devastated, fields laying idle and unkept, buildings burned, railroads destroyed, unemployment rampant, poverty widespread, industry decimated. The US President appointed a provisional governor, and on 26 October the state accepted all the requirements for readmission into the Union, including rescinding the secession, abolition of slavery, and the writing of a new state constitution. A new state legislature was elected in November, in December they ratified the Thirteenth Amendment to the US Constitution (prohibition of slavery), and GA entered the Union. However, in 1866, the GA legislature refused to ratify the Fourteenth Amendment (full citizenship for blacks), and Congress, who now took over the running of reconstruction, expelled GA and placed the state under military control in March 1867. The new military government arranged for a legislature to be elected which approved the Fourteenth Amendment on 21 July 1868. The military forces left and GA joined the Union again. In elections held in April, a new constitution was ratified and the state capital was moved to Atlanta. Then in September, the legislature of GA expelled 27 black members, whereupon military control in the state was re-established, with GA again losing its statehood. The black legislators were re-seated, and on 02 February 1870, the Fifteenth Amendment (blacks cannot be denied the right to vote) was approved. This permitted the re-entry of GA into the US in July.

During the politically turbulent years of reconstruction (1865-70), the situation was horribly complicated by corruption, exploitation, and unscrupulous activities. Even though there were many honest and charitable leaders on both sides attempting to restore GA, their efforts were often perverted by greedy, dishonest, and/or prejudiced individuals. Some northerners came down to help (the Union League, the Freedman's Bureau), others came to exploit and defraud. Many Georgians were well meaning, but others out of fear or greed or prejudice, practiced deceit, resorted to violence (Ku Klux Klan), and opposed reconstruction measures. It was a terribly mixed-up situation with good and bad on both sides, all of which caused GA to be the last state to be re-admitted to the Union. The major permanent change in GA which the war brought about was a transformation in the social order. The abolition of slavery caused the demise of the plantation system and broke the political grip of the planters on the state. Systems of sales on time, leasing, renting, and share-cropping came to be widely practiced on the smaller farms into which the plantations had been divided. The middle class of people, most of whom had not been slaveholders, began to rise in influence and prosperity.

8. The post—war years (1870—)

Beginning in 1870 GA fairly rapidly began to regain the economic momentum it had lost during the war and reconstruction. Cotton, corn, and forage crop production rose such that in 1910 GA ranked 4th among the states in agricultural output. In a like fashion, the extent of manufacturing increased over six fold, with Atlanta, which had become the capital in 1868, leading the activity. Among the major industries in 1910 were cotton, milling, fertilizer production, lumbering, and cottonseed oil production. Beginning in 1873, there were successful efforts at starting and developing a public school system, such that by 1910 over 70% of children were in attendance. These advances were paralleled by notable expansions of the state higher educational system, with several branches being established, all of which was accompanied by the growth and development of private institutions of higher education, some of which had been established earlier by religious groups. This period (1870-1910) also saw reforms in the prison system, the building of better roads, the restoration and expansion of the railroads, and considerable growth of cities (especially Atlanta, Macon, Rome, Athens, Waycross, and Albany).

In 1894, the people of Cuba rebelled against the oppressive Spanish rule of the island. In agreement with the sympathies of many Americans, the US in 1897 demanded that peace be established in Cuba and sent a battleship into Havana harbor on 15 February 1898. When the ship was wrecked by an explosion, the US raised troops to enforce its insistence that Spain free Cuba. Three GA regiments (the 1st, 2nd, and 3rd) were raised, but only one was sent to Cuba. After land warfare in Cuba, and the naval defeats of Spain in Santiago Bay

(Cuba) and the Philippines, the Spanish sued for peace, and a treaty ending the Spanish-American War was signed in August 1898. Shortly after the turn of the century, the position of Compiler of State Records was established, and this officer began compiling the colonial, revolutionary, and Confederate documents of GA. During the period 1870-1910, the population of GA had continued its upward trend from 1,184,000 (1870) to 1,542,000 (1880) to 1,837,000 (1890) to 2,216,000 (1900) to 2,609,121 (1910).

In the first decade of the 20th century, a number of progressive governmental programs were inaugurated, but many blacks were deprived of the vote in 1908 by legislation requiring literacy tests. The coming of World War I brought prosperity to GA as farmers benefitted from high food prices, and as war-supporting industry grew. The state sent over 93000 men into the conflict during 1917-8. The strong dependency of GA on cotton production caused the 1920s to be devastating times for the state. In the early 1920s, the cotton crops were ruined by boll weevil infestation and the exhaustion of the soil, which had been brought about by overuse and erosion. The state suffered greatly by stagnation or decline in cotton production, political leadership, health care, educational facilities, population, manufacturing, employment, and highway construction. These debilities were continued with the onset of the great national depression in the 1930s. The decade of the 1930s witnessed several attempts at governmental reform which were alternately disabled by short sighted politicians. Beginning in 1942, a new governor began reforms, which were promoted by the prosperity resulting from World War II. Among the reforms were the elimination of the poll tax (enfranchising most blacks) and the introduction of a merit system in government. The most notable events of the 1950s and 1960s centered around federal court decisions which produced a gradual increase in black voting and the desegregation of schools and public facilities. Since these turbulent days, amazing things have occurred in GA. Led by the city of Atlanta, the state has taken giant strides in commerce, agriculture, transportation, education, industry, culture, and recreation. Today it truly deserves its nickname of Empire State of the South.

---

9. Recommended readings

A knowledge of the history of GA and of its local regions is of extreme importance for the tracing of the genealogies of its former inhabitants. This chapter has been a brief treatment of that history. Your next step should be the detailed reading and study of a couple of good one-volumed works. These are recommended:

___R. P. Brooks, HISTORY OF GA, Atkinson, Mentzer, and Co., Boston, MA, 1913.

___J. C. Bonner, THE GA STORY, Oklahoma City, OK, 1958.

___K. Coleman, A HISTORY OF GA, University of GA Press, Athens, GA, 1977.

___K. Coleman, GA HISTORY IN OUTLINE, University of GA Press, Athens, GA, 1978.

___E. M. Coulter, SHORT HISTORY OF GA, University of NC Press, Chapel Hill, NC, 1960.

___L. B. Evans, A HISTORY OF GA, American Book Co., New York, NY, 1908.

___A. Johnson, GA AS COLONY AND AS STATE, Cherokee Publishing Co., Covington, GA, 1938.

___H. H. Martin, GA: A HISTORY, New York, NY, 1977.

___F. L. Mitchell, GA LAND AND PEOPLE, Reprint Co., Spartanburg, SC, 1900.

If you care to go further, or if you need to read more in detail about certain events or regions, you may consult one or more of the following multi-volumed histories of GA. These vary in their usefulness and accuracy, so a bit of caution is called for. The best ones are Jones and Stevens.

___W. G. Cooper, THE STORY OF GA, New York, NY, 1938, 4 volumes, 4th volume biographical.

___W. Grice, GA THROUGH THE CENTURIES, A HISTORY, Lewis Historical Publishing Co., New York, NY, 1965-6, 3 volumes, 2nd and 3rd volumes biographical.

___C. Howell, HISTORY OF GA, Chicago, Il, 1926, 4 volumes, 2nd-4th volumes biographical.

___C. C. Jones, Jr., THE HISTORY OF GA, Boston, MA, 1883, 2 volumes.

___L. L. Knight, A STANDARD HISTORY OF GA AND GEORGIANS, Lewis Historical Publishing Co., Chicago, Il, 6 volumes, 4th-6th volumes biographical.

___W. B. Stevens, A HISTORY OF GA, The Beehive Press, Savannah, GA, 1847/59, 2 volumes.

In order to locate detailed historical works on specific time periods, specific subjects, or specific areas of GA, consult:

___J. E. Simpson, GA HISTORY: BIBLIOGRAPHY, Scarecrow Press, Metuchen, NJ, 1976.

___A. A. Rowland and J. E. Dorsey, A BIBLIOGRAPHY OF WRIT-
INGS ON GA HISTORY, 1900-70, Reprint Co., Spartanburg,
SC, 1978.

___M. J. Kaminkow, US LOCAL HISTORIES IN THE LIBRARY OF
CONGRESS, Magna Carta Book Co., Baltimore, MD, 1975.

___P. W. Filby, A BIBLIOGRAPHY OF AMERICAN COUNTY
HISTORIES, Genealogical Publishing Co., Baltimore, MD,
1985.

___J. E. Dorsey, GA GENEALOGY AND LOCAL HISTORY,
Reprint Co., Spartanburg, SC, 1983.

The most-important state-wide historical periodicals are:

___GA HISTORICAL SOCIETY QUARTERLY, GA Historical
Society, Savannah, GA.

___ATLANTA HISTORICAL JOURNAL, Atlanta Historical Society,
Atlanta, GA.

---

10. GA county formation

In 1733 settlement of the GA colony was begun. As various regions were occupied, they came to be known as towns (population concentrations) or districts (population less concentrated) or were identified as islands or as areas between certain rivers. These designations were largely for location purposes and had little official standing as clear-cut divisions. In 1741, GA was divided into two counties, but the arrangement was revoked very shortly since it did not function. Then in 1758 the 25 subdivisions (towns, districts, islands, regions) were constituted into 8 parishes. The names of these subdivisions and the parishes into which they were incorporated are listed in section 3 of this chapter. The parishes were (reading from north to south): St. Paul's, St. George's, St. Matthew's, Christ Church, St. Philip's, St. John's, St. Andrew's, and St. James'. Turn back to Figure 3 to see exactly where they were located. The extension of the southern boundary of GA in 1763 led to the creation of 4 more parishes in 1765 (reading north to south): St. David's, St. Patrick's, St. Thomas', and St. Mary's (Figure 3). In 1773, sizable territory was ceded to GA by the Creeks and the Cherokees, but the area was not formally included in the parishes because of the onset of the Revolutionary War.

One of the provisions of the constitution of the new state of GA as of 1777 was the establishment of 8 counties: Wilkes (from the ceded land), Richmond (St. Paul's), Burke (St. George's), Effingham (St. Matthew's, part of St. Philip's), Chatham (Christ Church, part of St.

Philip's), Liberty (St. John's, St. Andrew's, St. James'), Glynn (St. David's, St. Patrick's), and Camden (St. Thomas', St. Mary's). The territories involved can be seen in Figure 5. In 1784, the GA legislature voted to set up Houston County way out on the frontier in the area of Muscle Shoals. The surveys were never made and the county was never established, the project being abandoned in 1786. A similar situation applied to Bourbon County which the legislature authorized at the intersection of the Yazoo and MS Rivers in 1785. The act was repealed in 1788 before any lands were granted. Following the cession of Indian land in 1783, Washington and Franklin Counties were created in 1784, this making 10 original counties (original counties being ones which did not come from previously established counties). In 1786, Greene County was split off from Washington County, and by 1800 14 new counties had been taken out of the original 10, so that there were 24 at the turn of the century. As you will remember, the land in these counties was distributed by the headright system or by bounty grants (to soldiers and patriots).

Further Indian cessions of land were made in 1802, and the next year the land lottery system was set up to distribute the lands west of the Oconee River. The first counties to be so distributed were Baldwin, Wilkinson, and Wayne in the lottery of 1805. Five other lotteries took place as further Indian cessions gave GA land: 1807 (more territory for Baldwin and Wilkinson), 1820 (Rabun, Hall, Habersham, Gwinnett, Walton, Early, Irwin, Appling), 1821 (Fayette, Henry, Monroe, Houston, Dooly), 1827 (Carroll, Coweta, Troup, Muscogee, Lee), 1832 (Cherokee which was very soon split into Cass, Cherokee, Cobb, Floyd, Gilmer, Lumpkin, Murray, Paulding, Union). This meant that GA had 40 original counties: 10 as of 1784, then 3 more in 1805, 8 more in 1821, 5 more in 1827, and 9 more in 1832. These original counties can be seen in Figure 5. From them, all other GA counties came, Greene County being the first of these non-original (derivative) counties when in 1786 it was taken out of Washington County.

The net result of the creation of 40 original counties plus the creation of many derivative counties out of them was as follows. There were 8 counties in 1777, 10 in 1784, 11 in 1790, 24 in 1800, 37 in 1810, 47 in 1820, 76 in 1830, 93 in 1840, 95 in 1850/, 132 in 1860 and 1870, 137 in 1880 and 1890 and 1900, 146 in 1910, 155 in 1920, 161 in 1930, and 159 in 1940 and thereafter. The decrease of 2 counties between 1930 and 1940 was due to the merging of Campbell and Milton Counties with Fulton County in the early 1930s. Figure 6 is a map of the current 159 counties of GA. The key to the abbreviations on this map is given at the end of this chapter. Each of these counties will be discussed in detail in Chapter 4, where the counties from which each came and the dates will be given. For example, let us suppose you want to know the history of the land area that is now Bleckley County. In Chapter 4 you will read that Bleckley County was created out of Pulaski County in 1912, which came from Laurens County in 1808, which was taken from Wilkinson County in 1807, which had been created in 1803/5 from Creek Indian cessions of 1802/5.

Not only were new counties created out of older ones, many county boundaries were also changed down through the years. A great deal of detail concerning county creations and line changes, along with maps, is given in the following reference volumes. The first of these is by far the most detailed.

___P. Bryant and I. Shields, GA COUNTIES: THEIR CHANGING BOUNDARIES, GA Department of Archives and History, Atlanta, GA, 1983.

___The GA Historical Society, THE COUNTIES OF THE STATE OF GA, The Society, Savannah, GA, 1981.

___M. R. Hemperley, HANDBOOK OF GA COUNTIES, GA Surveyor General Department, Atlanta, GA, 1980.

The counties shown on the map in Figure 6 are listed below along with their abbreviations to permit you to locate them. Appling(A), Atkinson(At), Bacon(Bc), Baker(Bk), Baldwin(Ba), Banks(Bn), Barrow(Bw), Bartow(Br), Ben Hill(Bh), Berrien(Be), Bibb(Bi), Bleckley(Bl), Brantley(B2), Brooks(Bs), Bryan(By), Bulloch(Bu), Burke(B), Butts(Bt), Calhoun(C3), Camden(Ca), Candler(Cn), Carroll(Cr), Catoosa(Ct), Charlton(C4), Chatham(C), Chattahoochee(Cc), Chattooga(Cg), Cherokee(Ch), Clarke(Cl), Clay(Cy), Clayton(C2), Clinch(Ci), Cobb(Co), Coffee(Ce), Colquitt(Cq), Columbia(Cu), Cook(Ck), Coweta(Cw), Crawford(Cf), Crisp(Cp), Dade(Da), Dawson(Dw), Decatur(De), DeKalb(Dk), Dodge(Do), Dooly(D), Dougherty(Du), Douglas(Dg), Early(Ea), Echols(Ec), Effingham(E), Elbert(El), Emanuel(Em), Evans(Ev), Fannin(Fa), Fayette(F), Floyd(Fl), Forsyth(Fo), Franklin(Fr), Fulton-(Fn), Gilmer(Gi), Glascock(Gl), Glynn(G), Gordon(Go), Grady(Gy), Greene(Gr), Gwinnett(Gw), Habersham(Ha), Hall(H), Hancock(Hn), Haralson(Hl), Harris(Hr), Hart(Ht), Heard(Hd), Henry(He), Houston(Ho), Irwin(I), Jackson(J), Jasper(Ja), Jeff Davis(Jd), Jefferson(Jf), Jenkins(Jk), Johnson(Jo), Jones(Jn), Lamar(La), Lanier(Ln), Laurens

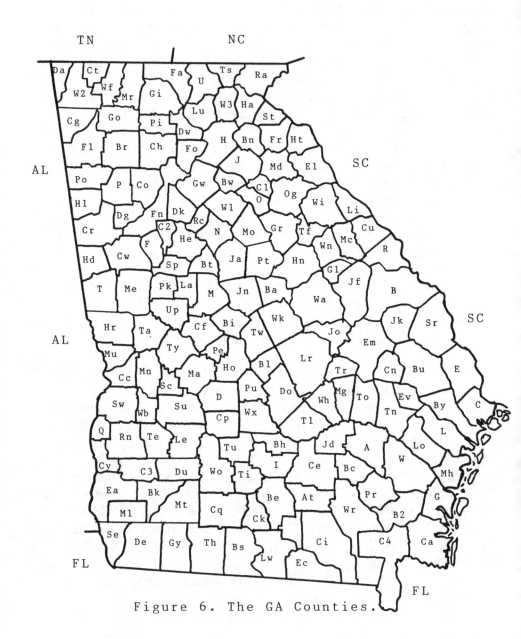

Figure 6. The GA Counties.

(Lr), Lee(Le), Liberty(L), Lincoln(Li), Long(Lo), Lowndes(Lw), Lumpkin(Lu), McDuffie(Mc), McIntosh(Mh), Macon(Ma), Madison(Md), Marion(Mn), Meriwether(Me), Miller(Ml), Mitchell(Mt), Monroe(M), Montgomery(Mg), Morgan(Mo), Murray(Mr), Muscogee(Mu), Newton(N), Oconee(O), Oglethorpe(Og), Paulding(P), Peach(Pe), Pickens(Pi), Pierce(Pr), Pike(Pk), Polk(Po), Pulaski(Pu), Putnam(Pt), Quitman(Q), Rabun(Ra), Randolph(Rn), Richmond(R), Rockdale(Rc), Schley(Sc), Screven(Sr), Seminole(Se), Spaulding(Sp), Stephens(St), Stewart(Sw), Sumter(Su), Talbot(Ta), Taliaferro(Tf), Tattnall(Tn), Taylor(Ty), Telfair(Tl), Terrell(Te), Thomas(Th), Tift(Ti), Toombs(To), Towns(Ts), Treutlen(Tr), Troup(T), Turner(Tu), Twiggs-(Tw), Union(U), Upson(Up), Walker(W2), Walton(Wl), Ware(Wr), Warren(Wn), Washington(Wa), Wayne(W), Webster(Wb), Wheeler(Wh), White(W3), Whitfield(Wf), Wilcox(Wx), Wilkes(Wi), Wilkinson(Wk), Worth(Wo).

LIST OF ABBREVIATIONS

A	=	Agricultural census
CH	=	Court house(s)
FHC	=	Family History Center(s)
FHL	=	Family History Library
G	=	GA State census records
GA	=	Georgia
GDAH	=	GA Department of Archives and History
GHS	=	GA Historical Society (Savannah)
GSU	=	Genealogical Society of UT (Utah)
I	=	Industrial census records
LGL	=	Large genealogical library
LL	=	Local library(-ies)
M	=	Mortality census records
NA	=	National Archives
NAAB	=	National Archives, Atlanta Branch
NAFB	=	National Archives, Field Branch
P	=	Pensioner census, Revolutionary War
R	=	Regular census records
RL	=	Regional library(-ies)
S	=	Slaveowner census records
Su	=	Substitute census records
UGL	=	University of GA Libraries (Athens)
WML	=	Washington Memorial Library (Macon)

Chapter 2

TYPES OF RECORDS

The state of Georgia (GA) is rich in genealogical source material, even though there have been some notable losses of records, especially in certain localities. A great deal of work has been done by many people in accumulating, preserving, photocopying, microfilming, transcribing, abstracting, printing, and indexing records. Among the most important genealogical records of GA are the local governmental county records (birth, court, death, divorce, estate, land, marriage, plat, probate, tax, will, others). Microfilm copies of the major county records for most GA counties organized before 1900 are available in the GA Department of Archives and History (GDAH) in Atlanta. The original records for GA counties remain mostly in the county court houses, although some have been deposited in GDAH, and a few have been destroyed. The Genealogical Society of UT (FHL) in Salt Lake City also has microfilm copies of many GA county records (not as many as GDAH) and these are available on loan through the many local branch libraries (FHC) of the Genealogical Society of UT located throughout the US.

The best overall centralized collection of genealogical material in the state of GA is the GA Department of Archives and History (GDAH) in Atlanta. This repository has an exceptionally large collection of originals or copies of original federal, state, and county governmental records. Included are birth, census, colonial, court, death, divorce, estate, immigration, land, marriage, military, naturalization, tax, and will records. In addition, GDAH has a sizable collection of published volumes which contain genealogical data. Among the types of data included in them are atlas, Bible, biography. birth, cemetery, church, city directory, county history, colonial, court, death, estate, immigration, ethnic, gazetteer, genealogical indexes, genealogical periodicals, land, marriage, military, naturalization, published genealogies, tax, and will. The GDAH also has a well-stocked collection of manuscript materials, including family histories, letters, church records, legal papers, pamphlets, newspaper clippings, and business records. In the same building with the GDAH is the GA Surveyor General Department with its large collection of land records, plat books, land lottery lists, and maps.

The three best collections of published GA genealogical volumes are located in three different cities in GA: Athens, Savannah, and Macon. These repositories have all sorts of data which have been gathered and edited into books which have been printed. Books containing these types of records are available in them: atlas, Bible, biography, birth, cemetery, census, church, city directory, city and county history, colonial, court, death, divorce, emigration, estate, ethnic, gazetteer, genealogical indexes and compilations, immigration, land, map, marriage, military, naturalization, published genealogy, tax, and will. These libraries also have collections of GA genealogical periodicals, manuscripts, and newspapers. The first of these excellent libraries is the University of GA Libraries (UGL) located in Athens. Its particular strengths are biographies, maps, manuscripts, a state and county record collection of over 50000 records, a large family history collection, books on the colony/state of GA, and the largest collection of newspapers available. Of particular note is its Hargett Rare Book and Manuscript Library. The second of these leading libraries is the Washington Memorial Library (WML) which is situated in Macon. Its strength is that it holds the largest collection in GA of books which deal with genealogy. Much of the material is located in its Genealogical and Historical Room. The third of the major genealogically-oriented libraries is the GA Historical Society Library (GHS) in Savannah. Even though their collection is biased toward eastern GA, they have an exceedingly good manuscript collection and particular strength in colonial records.

There is a fairly sizable collection of books and microfilms of GA genealogical materials in the largest genealogical library in the world, namely, the Family History Library (FHL) which is located in Salt Lake City, UT. Not only are the materials available at the library in Salt Lake City, but the microfilms may be borrowed through the numerous branches of the FHL, the Family History Centers (FHC) which are located all over the US. Each Branch Library has microfilm copies of the major indexes (surname, locality, International Genealogical Index, Ancestral File, Integrated AIS Census) which list the holdings of the Main Library in Salt Lake City, and from which microfilms may be ordered.

Many records pertaining to GA which were accumulated by the federal (US) government are available in the National Archives (NA) in Washington, DC. These records include the following types: census, passenger arrival, naturalization, military (service, pension, bounty land), Indian, Black, claims, court, and map. Many of the most useful of these materials have been microfilmed by the NA. Some of the microfilms are available in the GDAH and in the three libraries mentioned above (UGL,

WML, GHS), and many are available in eleven <u>National Archives Field Branches</u> (NAFB), one of which is in Atlanta, the <u>National Archives Atlanta Branch</u> (NAAB). Some of them are also available from your local library, which can borrow them from the AGLL, PO Box 244, Bountiful, UT 84010.

In addition to the above collections, there are GA record collections in a number of <u>large genealogical libraries</u> (LGL) around the country, those nearest GA usually having larger holdings. Other collections, usually with an emphasis on a particular section of GA, are located in several good <u>regional libraries</u> (RL) in larger cities of GA. Finally, <u>local libraries</u> (LL) in the county seats and some other towns often have good materials. These local libraries may be city, county, or private (such as ones sponsored by local historical or genealogical societies). All of the archives, libraries, and repositories mentioned above will be discussed in detail in Chapter 3.

In this chapter, the many types of records which are available for GA genealogical research are discussed. Those records which are essentially <u>national</u> (US) or <u>statewide</u> (GA) in scope will be treated in detail. Records which are basically <u>county</u> records will be described and treated only generally, since detailed lists of them will be given in Chapter 4, where the major local <u>county</u> records available for each of the 159 GA counties will be presented.

2. Bible records

During the past 200 years it was customary for families with religious inclinations to keep vital statistics on their members in the family Bible. These records vary widely, but among the items that may be found are names, dates, and places of birth, christening, confirmation, baptism, marriage, death, and sometimes military service. Although most Bibles containing recorded information probably still remain in private hands, some of the information has been submitted for publication and some has been filed in libraries and archives throughout GA. You should inquire about such records at every possible library in and near your ancestor's county, especially the RL and LL. These repositories will be listed in Chapter 4 under the counties. You should also seek Bible records in the larger archives and libraries in GA: GDAH, UGL, WML, GHS. Also consult the surname and locality indexes at FHC. In these repositories there may be a special Bible record index or a special Bible record file, or as is more often the case, data from Bibles may be listed in indexes or alphabetical files labelled something other than Bible records. The most likely labels are family records, genealogies, manuscripts, names, surnames. Also do not fail to look in the major card index of each of the repositories for the names you are seeking and under the heading Bible records.

Some of the better special indexes and alphabetical files in which GA Bible records may be found are:

__J. E. Dorsey, GA GENEALOGY AND LOCAL HISTORY, A BIBLIOGRAPHY, Reprint Co, Spartanburg, SC, 1983. [Examine all listings under counties you are interested in.]

__DAR of GA, FAMILY BIBLE RECORDS, Volumes 31-61, with master indexes for volumes 31-46, and with indexes for each volume for the others, GDAH, Atlanta, GA.

__INDEX TO BIBLE RECORDS, Microfilm Library, GDAH, Atlanta, GA, look under name, over 3000 cards.

__MAJOR CARD INDEXES and SPECIAL CARD INDEXES, UGL, WML, GHS, FHL, FHC, RL, LL, look under Bible Records and under county.

A number of GA Bible records have been compiled by various organizations and individuals and have been published or put into typescript form. Among those which you should examine are:

__J. H. Austin, GA BIBLE RECORDS, Genealogical Publishing Co., Baltimore, MD, 1985.

__DAR, GA Chapters, HISTORICAL COLLECTIONS, OLD BIBLE RECORDS AND LAND LOTTERIES, Southern Historical Press, Easley, SC, 1969, volume 4.

__DAR, DAR RECORD TRANSCRIPTS, Various Chapters of the DAR, GDAH, Atlanta, GA. [Contain many types of records including Bible records.]

There are also some published and typescript indexes which contain references to GA Bible records:

__INDEXES TO BIBLE AND CEMETERY RECORDS ON FILE IN THE GDAH, Works Progress Administration, Atlanta, GA, 1939.

__E. K. Kirkham, INDEX TO SOME OF THE FAMILY RECORDS OF THE SOUTHERN STATES, Everton Publishers, Logan, UT, 1980.

__J. D. and E. D. Stemmons, THE VITAL RECORD COMPENDIUM, Everton Publishers, Logan, UT, 1979.

Bible records also appear in genealogical articles (especially the GA Genealogist), and in published family genealogies. These two record sources, as well as details on manuscript sources, will be discussed in sections 19, 23, and 32 of this chapter.

3. Biographies

There are numerous major national biographical works which contain sketches on nationally-prominent Georgians of the past. If you suspect or know your ancestor was that well known, you may consult the following master index which gives the sources of over three million biographies located in over 350 national works:

___M. C. Herbert and B. McNeil, BIOGRAPHY AND GENEALOGY MASTER INDEX, Gale Research Co., Detroit, MI, 1980, 3 volumes, with periodic SUPPLEMENTS and computer version BIOBASE.

Numerous good biographical compilations for the state of GA exist. These volumes list persons who have attained state-wide prominence in the fields of law, agriculture, business, politics, medicine, engineering, industry, science, military, manufacturing, teaching, public service, or philanthropy. Included among the better ones are:

___R. Ashford, HISTORICAL SKETCHES AND REMINISCENCES OF GA, Oconee Enterprises, Watkinsville, GA, 1931.

___ATLANTA CENTENNIAL YEARBOOK, 1837-1937, Murphy, Atlanta, GA, 1937.

___J. N. Averitt, GA'S COASTAL PLAIN, Lewis Historical Publishing Co., New York, NY, 1964, volume 3.

___BIOGRAPHICAL SOUVENIR OF THE STATES OF GA AND FL, Southern Historical Press, Easley, SC, 1889 (1976).

___S. Boykin, HISTORY OF THE BAPTIST DENOMINATION IN GA WITH BIOGRAPHICAL COMPENDIUM, Southern Historical Press, Easley, SC, 1881 (1976).

___A. B. Caldwell, HISTORY OF THE AMERICAN NEGRO, GA EDITION, Caldwell, Atlanta, GA, 1920.

___J. H. Campbell, GA BAPTISTS, HISTORICAL AND BIOGRAPHICAL, Ellyson, Richmond, VA, 1847.

___A. D. Candler and C. A. Evans, GA, COMPRISING SKETCHES OF COUNTIES, TOWNS, EVENTS, INSTITUTIONS, AND PERSONS, State Historical Association, Atlanta, GA, 1906, 4 volumes.

___G. H. Cartledge, HISTORICAL SKETCHES, PRESBYTERIAN CHURCHES AND EARLY SETTLERS IN NORTHEAST GA, Mize and Newton, Athens, GA, 1960.

___A. H. Chappell, MISCELLANIES OF GA, HISTORICAL, BIOGRAPHICAL, DESCRIPTIVE, Gilbert Publishing Co., Columbus, GA, 1974.

___K. Coleman and C. S. Gurr, DICTIONARY OF GA BIOGRAPHY, University of GA Press, Athens, GA, 1983, 2 volumes.

___W. G. Cooper, THE STORY OF GA, American Historical Society, New York, NY, 1938, volume 4.

___GA BAPTISTS, EARLY SETTLERS, GA Pioneers, Volumes 2-6, 1965-9.

___F. M. Garrett, ATLANTA AND ENVIRONS, PEOPLE AND EVENTS, Lewis Publishing Co., New York, NY, 1954, volume 3.

___A. H. Gordon, THE GA NEGRO, A HISTORY, Edwards Brothers, Ann Arbor, MI, 1937.

___B. J. W. Graham, BAPTIST BIOGRAPHY, Index Publishing Co., Atlanta, GA, 1917.

___W. Grice, GA THROUGH TWO CENTURIES, 1732-1960, Lewis Publ. Co., West Palm Beach, FL, 1965-6, volumes 2-3.

___H. Ham, REPRESENTATIVE GEORGIANS, BIOGRAPHICAL SKETCHES OF MEN NOW IN PUBLIC LIFE, Savannah, GA, 1887.

___S. G. Hillyer, REMINISCENCES OF GA BAPTISTS, Foote and Davis, Atlanta, GA, 1902.

___C. Howell, THE BOOK OF GA, A WORK FOR PRESS REFERENCE, Biographical Association, Atlanta, GA, 1920.

___C. Howell, HISTORY OF GA, Lewis Publishing Co., Chicago, IL, 1926, volumes 2-4.

___L. L. Knight, ENCYCLOPEDIA OF GA BIOGRAPHY, A. H. Cawston, Atlanta, GA, 1931.

___L. L. Knight, GA'S BICENTENNIAL MEMOIRS AND MEMORIES, The Author, Atlanta, GA, 1931-3, 4 volumes.

___L. L. Knight, GA'S LANDMARKS, MEMORIALS, AND LEGENDS, Byrd Print Co., Atlanta, GA, 1913-4, 2 volumes.

___L. L. Knight, REMINISCENCES OF FAMOUS GEORGIANS, Franklin-Turner, Atlanta, GA, 1907-8, 2 volumes.

___L. L. Knight, A STANDARD HISTORY OF GA AND GEORGIANS, Lewis Publishing Co., Chicago, IL, 1917, volumes 4-6.

___T. W. Loyless, GA'S PUBLIC MEN, 1902-4, Byrd Printing, Atlanta, GA, 1902-4.

___MAKERS OF AMERICA, GA EDITION, Caldwell, Atlanta, GA, 1912, 4 volumes.

___MEMOIRS OF GA, Southern Historical Press, Easley, SC, 1895 (1976), 2 volumes.

___MEN OF GA, Press Association, Atlanta, GA, 1927.

___S. F. Miller, THE BENCH AND BAR OF GA, Lippincott, Philadelphia, PA, 1858.

49

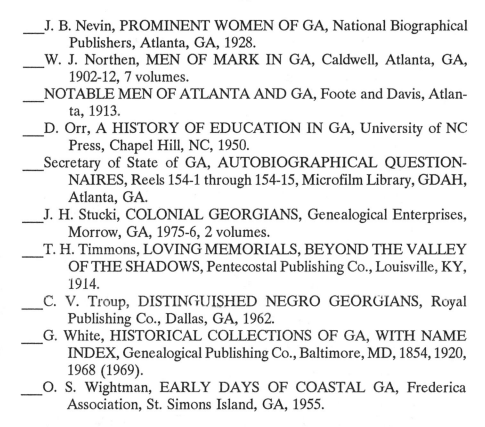

___J. B. Nevin, PROMINENT WOMEN OF GA, National Biographical Publishers, Atlanta, GA, 1928.
___W. J. Northen, MEN OF MARK IN GA, Caldwell, Atlanta, GA, 1902-12, 7 volumes.
___NOTABLE MEN OF ATLANTA AND GA, Foote and Davis, Atlanta, 1913.
___D. Orr, A HISTORY OF EDUCATION IN GA, University of NC Press, Chapel Hill, NC, 1950.
___Secretary of State of GA, AUTOBIOGRAPHICAL QUESTIONNAIRES, Reels 154-1 through 154-15, Microfilm Library, GDAH, Atlanta, GA.
___J. H. Stucki, COLONIAL GEORGIANS, Genealogical Enterprises, Morrow, GA, 1975-6, 2 volumes.
___T. H. Timmons, LOVING MEMORIALS, BEYOND THE VALLEY OF THE SHADOWS, Pentecostal Publishing Co., Louisville, KY, 1914.
___C. V. Troup, DISTINGUISHED NEGRO GEORGIANS, Royal Publishing Co., Dallas, GA, 1962.
___G. White, HISTORICAL COLLECTIONS OF GA, WITH NAME INDEX, Genealogical Publishing Co., Baltimore, MD, 1854, 1920, 1968 (1969).
___O. S. Wightman, EARLY DAYS OF COASTAL GA, Frederica Association, St. Simons Island, GA, 1955.

Not only are there national, state, regional, and professional biographical works for GA, there are also some local (county, city, town) biographical compilations. Some of these are separate books and others are included in county histories (see section 9). Practically all of the above biographical publications are available in UGL, WML, and GHS, along with most of the local volumes. The local publications will also be found in the LL of the places of interest as well as in nearby RL. When you seek biographical compilations in a library, look under these headings in the card catalog(s): US-Biography, GA-Biography, [County Name]-Biography, [City Name]-Biography. Large listings of GA biographical materials will be found in the following volumes. These will be especially helpful for discovering what is available at the local level, where you are more likely to find reference to your ancestor.
___M. J. Kaminkow, US LOCAL HISTORIES IN THE LIBRARY OF CONGRESS, Magna Carta, Baltimore, MD, 1975, 5 volumes.
___J. E. Dorsey, GA GENEALOGY AND LOCAL HISTORY, Reprint Co, Spartanburg, SC, 1983.

___M. Adams, GA LOCAL AND FAMILY HISTORY SOURCES IN
      PRINT, Heritage Research, Clarkston, GA, 1982.
Biographical information is also sometimes found in ethnic publications,
genealogical compilations, genealogical periodicals, manuscripts, military
records, newspapers, published genealogies, regional records, and historical works (state, regional, local). These will all be discussed in later
sections.

      Finally, there are some important finding aids to GA biographical
data which should not be overlooked:
___D. M. Hehir, GA FAMILIES, A BIBLIOGRAPHIC LISTING OF
      BOOKS ABOUT GA FAMILIES, Heritage Books, Bowie, MD,
      1993. 1100 listings.
___K. H. Thomas, BIBLIOGRAPHY OF COMPILATIONS OF
      BIOGRAPHICAL SKETCHES FOR GEORGIANS, GA Life,
      Volume 5 (Summer, 1978), pages 38-9.
___SOURCES OF GA BIOGRAPHY, AN ANNOTATED BIBLIOG-
      RAPHY, Emory University Division of Librarianship, Atlanta,
      GA, 1976.
___CARD INDEX TO PUBLISHED GA BIOGRAPHIES IN GDAH,
      GDAH, Atlanta, GA.
___CARD INDEX TO PUBLIC SERVICE RECORDS, Research Area,
      GDAH, Atlanta, GA.
___BIOGRAPHICAL FILES OF PROMINENT GEORGIANS, Hargett
      Library, UGL, Athens, GA.
___CARD INDEX TO PUBLISHED GA BIOGRAPHIES, Hargett Li-
      brary, UGL, Athens, GA.

4. Birth records There were several early efforts to require
birth registration in GA, the earliest in 1804,
but these failed quite broadly due to non-
compliance. In a few counties and in some
cities, there are a few birth records prior to 1919, when state registration
was required. The counties and the dates are: Carroll(1875),
Chatham(1803-47), Chattooga(1874-6), Clarke(1808-52, 1875-6),
Clayton(1875), Colquitt(1875), Early(1875-7), Emanuel(1822-63),
Jackson(1875), Lumpkin(1875), Miller(1875-6), Oglethorpe(1875-8),
Pulaski(1875), Randolph(1875-7), Richmond(1823-96), Sumter(1875-6),
and Taliaferro(1875-6). The cities and the dates when they began keeping
the records are: Atlanta(1887-), Columbus(1869-), Gainesville(1865-),
Macon(1891-), and Savannah(1890-). The county records are available on

microfilm in the GDAH and the city records are in the County Health Departments. All these records are incomplete.

As mentioned above, GA started requiring births to be recorded with the state in 1919. At first the counties cooperated very well, but in the middle 1920s they did not. It was not until 1928 that the records became 90% complete. They are in the custody of The Vital Records Unit, GA Department of Human Resources, Room 217H, Health Building, 47 Trinity Avenue, Atlanta, GA 30334. Many delayed birth records are available for the time before 1919. GA state law decrees that birth records be severely restricted, they being available only to the individuals themselves, a legal representative of the individual, or to governmental agencies. Since GA is so short on official birth records before 1919, other types of records have to be consulted in attempts to find birth data. Among the better ones are Bible, biography, cemetery, census, church, genealogical periodical, manuscript, military, mortuary, naturalization, newspaper, and published genealogy. These are discussed in other sections of this chapter.

There are a few published or typescript works which contain or lead to birth data compilations. Notable among them are:
__Daughters of the American Revolution, DAR RECORD TYPE-SCRIPTS, The Daughters, Transcripts in GDAH, Atlanta, GA, with INDEX.
__J. D. and E. D. Stemmons, THE VITAL RECORD COMPENDIUM, Everton Publishers, Logan, UT, 1979.
When you are seeking birth date and place information in archives and libraries, be certain to explore all the above-mentioned sources, and don't fail to look under county listings and the following heading in card catalogs: Registers of births, etc.

5. Cemetery records

If you know or suspect that your ancestor was buried in a certain GA cemetery, the best thing to do is to write the caretaker of the cemetery, enclose an SASE, and ask if the tombstone inscriptions and/or the records show your forebear. Gravestones often show names, ages, dates of death and birth, and sometimes family names of wives. Tombstones of children often bear the names or the initials of the parents. In order to locate the caretaker, try writing the local genealogical society, the local historical society, or the

LL. If you do not find your ancestor is buried there, then you should ask the above organizations and the LL about records for other cemeteries in the area. The addresses of these organizations will be given in Chapter 4. As you consider possible burial sites, please remember that most early cemeteries were in conjunction with churches. Therefore, if you know your ancestor's religious affiliation, this could be of help.

Another important cemetery record source is the numerous collections of cemetery records which have been made by the DAR, by the WPA, by state, regional, and local genealogical and historical societies, and by individuals. Some of these have been published, some are in typescript form, and a few are handwritten. A number of them have been microfilmed. Sizable listings of many of those available will be found in:

___J. D. and E. D. Stemmons, THE CEMETERY RECORD COMPEN-DIUM, Everton Publishers, Logan, UT, 1979.

___FHL, FHL CATALOG-LOCALITY SECTION, FHL, Salt Lake City, UT. Available also in FHC. Look under county.

___J. E. Dorsey, GA GENEALOGY AND LOCAL HISTORY, Reprint Co, Spartanburg, SC, 1983, pages 47-376.

___TWENTY-THREE INDEXES TO BIBLE & CEMETERY RE-CORDS IN THE GDAH, Works Progress Administration, Atlanta, GA, 1939.

___Card Catalogs in GDAH (Microfilm Catalog), UGL, WML, GHS, FHL, BFHL, RL, LL.

___T. O. Brooke, GA CEMETERY DIRECTORY AND BIBLIOGRAPHY, Southern Ancestors, Marietta, GA, 1985

The last work is a broadly-based listing of over 10,000 GA cemeteries with the exact locations of published records relating to them. The main collections of GA cemetery records are thus seen to be in the organizations listed in the next-to-last reference. The LL usually have records of cemeteries in their own counties, and RL often have those in their regions. These libraries (LL and RL) are listed under the counties in Chapter 4. In all the libraries, the cemetery records may be located by looking in the card catalog under the surname, the county and/or city, the church, the denomination, the ethnic group, and the cemetery name. Also look under the headings Epitaphs-GA and Cemeteries-GA. Further, you should not forget to inquire if there are special cemetery record indexes. Genealogical periodicals published in or near GA quite frequently carry articles with cemetery data (see later section on genealogical periodicals). Many of these articles are referenced in the book by Dorsey mentioned above. More have probably been published in the GA Genealogical Society Quarterly than in any other GA genealogical journal.

Among the published cemetery record compilations are the following notable works:

___P. R. Baker, NEATH GA SOD, GA Pioneers, Albany, GA, 1970. [Columbia, Glascock, Jefferson, Lincoln, McDuffie, Richmond, Wilkes Counties]

___L. M. Edwards, CEMETERY RECORDS TYPESCRIPTS, Research Area, GDAH, Atlanta, GA, 5 volumes. [Bryant, Bulloch, Candler, Effingham, Emanuel, Evans, Jenkins, Liberty, Screven, Tattnall Counties]

___C. Wilson, ANNALS OF GA, Braid Hutton, Savannah, GA, 1933, Volume 3. [Camden, Chatham, Effingham, Liberty, McIntosh Counties]

___Daughters of the American Revolution, DAR RECORD TYPE-SCRIPTS, The Daughters, Transcripts in GDAH, Atlanta, GA.

___F. M. Garrett, MANUSCRIPT PAPERS, Atlanta Historical Society, Atlanta, GA. [Carroll, Cherokee, Clayton, Cobb, DeKalb, Douglas, Fayette, Forsyth, Fulton, Gwinnett, Hall, Henry, Newton, Paulding, Pike, Rockdale, Spalding, Walton Counties]

___Mrs. P. W. Meldrim, SOME EARLY EPITAPHS IN GA, Seeman Printing Co., Durham, NC, 1925.

___CEMETERY RECORDS OF GA, Genealogical Society of UT, Salt Lake City, UT, 1946-52, 16 volumes. Also on microfilm at FHL.

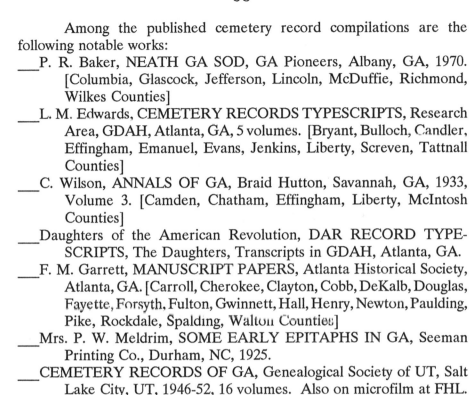

6. Census records

Excellent ancestor information is available in seven types of census reports which have been accumulated for GA: some early lists which serve as substitutes (Su) before there were censuses or for lost censuses, regular (R), agricultural (A), industrial (I), mortality (M), the special 1840 Revolutionary War pension census (P), slaveowner censuses (S), and a few surviving GA state censuses (G) for certain counties.

There are a number of early lists which provide sizable listings of GA residents before regular federal censuses were taken and other lists which serve as substitute censuses (Su) for the lost 1790, 1800, and 1810 GA censuses. Among the most important of these are:

___(1732-82) A. D. Candler, L. L. Knight, and W. Northen, THE COLONIAL RECORDS OF GA, 1732-82, 39 volumes in all, Volumes 1-19 and 21-6 published by State Printers of Atlanta in 1904-16, Volumes 20 & 27-8 published by University of GA Press of Athens in 1975-82, others in typescript in GDAH in Atlanta, with TYPESCRIPT INDEX TO VOLUMES 1-19 & 20-6 in

GDAH, and INDIVIDUAL TYPESCRIPT OR INCLUDED INDEXES IN OTHER VOLUMES.

___(1732-41) E. M. Coulter and A. B. Sayre, A LIST OF EARLY SETTLERS OF GA, 1732-41, Genealogical Publishing Co., Baltimore, MD, 1949(1983).

___(1733-55) P. Bryant, ENTRY OF CLAIMS FOR GA LANDHOLDERS, 1733-55, State Printing Office, Atlanta, GA, 1975.

___(1741-54) G. White, HISTORICAL COLLECTIONS OF GA, WITH NAME INDEX, Genealogical Publishing Co., Baltimore, MD, 1854(1969), pages 32-7.

___(1755-75) P. Bryant and M. R. Hemperley, ENGLISH CROWN GRANTS IN GA, 1755-75, GDAH, Atlanta, GA, 1972-4, 10 volumes, more to come, with F. S. Hodges, MASTER INDEX, typescript in GDAH.

___(1756-1815) INDEX TO THE HEADRIGHT AND BOUNTY LAND GRANTS OF GA, 1756-1909, Southern Historical Press, Easley, SC, 1970.

___(1789-1817) Taylor Foundation, AN INDEX TO GA TAX DIGESTS, 1789-1817, Reprint Co., Spartanburg, SC, 1986. [75,000 persons]

___(1790-1818) R. Blair, SOME EARLY TAX DIGESTS OF GA, Southern Historical Press, Easley, SC, 1926(1971).

___(1790) M. DeLamar and E. Rothstein, THE RECONSTRUCTED 1790 CENSUS OF GA, Genealogical Publishing Co., Baltimore, MD, 1976(1985).

___(1790) Delwyn Associates, SUBSTITUTES FOR GA'S LOST 1790 CENSUS, The Associates, Albany, GA, 1975.

___(1791-1809) Automated Archives, CD151: US CENSUS INDEX SERIES, GREAT LAKES, SOUTH, AND MID-ATLANTIC, on CD-ROM, Automated Archives, Orem, UT, 1994. Contains about 35,000 GA entries. Also available on floppy disks.

___(1802) V. S. and R. V. Wood, THE 1805 GA LAND LOTTERY, Channing Books, Marion, MA, 1964. [Those who had been in GA for at least one year and who registered for the lottery in March 1803.]

___(1810-1819) Automated Archives, CD150: US CENSUS INDEX SERIES, MID-ATLANTIC, SOUTHERN, MID-WEST,, on CD-ROM, Automated Archives, Orem, UT, 1994. Contains GA entries for Franklin, Hancock, Lincoln, Pulaski, and Richmond Counties. Also available on floppy disks.

Even though the 1800 census for GA was lost (as were the 1790 and 1810), the 1800 data for Oglethorpe County were found in the county records. They have been published in:

___M. B. Warren, 1800 CENSUS OF OGLETHORPE COUNTY, The Author, Athens, GA, 1965.

Regular census records (R) are available for practically all of GA in 1820, 1830, 1840, 1850, 1860, 1870, 1880, 1900, 1910 and 1920. The main exception is the absence of the data for Franklin, Rabun, and Twiggs Counties and for part of Columbia County in the 1820 census. The 1890 census for the entire US was almost completely destroyed. Small portions exist for Muscogee County, and some data for Washington County are in the county records. The 1840 census and all before it listed the head of the household plus a breakdown of the number of persons in the household according to sex and age brackets. Beginning in 1850, the names of all persons were recorded along with age, sex, occupation, real estate, marital, and other information, including the state or country of birth. With the 1880 census and thereafter, the birth places of the mother and father of each person are also shown. Chapter 4 lists the regular census records available for each of the GA counties.

Microfilms of the original GA census records (1820-1920) are available as follows:

___US Bureau of the Census, FOURTH CENSUS OF THE US, 1820, GA, The National Archives, Washington, DC, Microfilm M33, Rolls 6-10.

___US Bureau of the Census, FIFTH CENSUS OF THE US, 1830, GA, The National Archives, Washington, DC, Microfilm M19, Rolls 16-21.

___US Bureau of the Census, SIXTH CENSUS OF THE US, 1840, GA, The National Archives, Washington, DC, Microfilm M704, Rolls 37-53.

___US Bureau of the Census, SEVENTH CENSUS OF THE US, 1850, GA, The National Archives, Washington, DC, Microfilm M432, Rolls 61-87.

___US Bureau of the Census, EIGHTH CENSUS OF THE US, 1860, GA, The National Archives, Washington, DC, Microfilm M653, Rolls 111-141.

___US Bureau of the Census, NINTH CENSUS OF THE US, 1870, GA, The National Archives, Washington, DC, Microfilm M593, Rolls 134-184.

___US Bureau of the Census, TENTH CENSUS OF THE US, 1880, GA, The National Archives, Washington, DC, Microfilm T9, Rolls 133-172.

__US Bureau of the Census, ELEVENTH CENSUS OF THE US, 1890, Muscogee County (Columbus), GA, The National Archives, Washington, DC, Microfilm M407, Roll 3.

__US Bureau of the Census, TWELFTH CENSUS OF THE US, 1900, GA, The National Archives, Washington, DC, Microfilm T623, Rolls 178-230.

__US Bureau of the Census, THIRTEENTH CENSUS OF THE US, 1910, GA, The National Archives, Washington, DC, Microfilm T624, Rolls 170-220.

__US Bureau of the Census, FOURTEENTH CENSUS OF THE US, 1920, GA, The National Archives, Washington, DC, Microfilm T625, Rolls 233-286.

Indexes have been printed and/or put on computer disks for the 1820, 1830, 1840, 1850, 1860 and 1870 GA census records. These volumes are:

__GA Historical Society, INDEX TO THE US CENSUS OF GA FOR 1820, Genealogical Publishing Co., Baltimore, MD, 1969.

__R. V. Jackson and G. R. Teeples, GA 1820 CENSUS INDEX, Accelerated Indexing Systems, Bountiful, UT, 1976.

__Automated Archives, CD154: US CENSUS INDEX SERIES, GREAT LAKES, SOUTH, AND MID-ATLANTIC, 1820-1829,,on CD-ROM, Automated Archives, Orem, UT, 1994. Contains GA entries. Also available on floppy disks.

__Delwyn Associates, INDEX TO HEADS OF FAMILIES, 1830 CENSUS OF GA, The Associates, Albany, GA, 1974.

__R. V. Jackson and G. R. Teeples, GA 1830 CENSUS INDEX, Accelerated Indexing Systems, Bountiful, UT, 1976.

__A. K. Register, INDEX TO THE 1830 CENSUS OF GA, Genealogical Publishing Co., Baltimore, MD, 1974(1982).

__Automated Archives, CD148: US CENSUS INDEX SERIES, GREAT LAKES, SOUTH, AND MID-ATLANTIC, 1830-1839, on CD-ROM, Automated Archives, Orem, UT, 1994. Contains GA entries. Also available on floppy disks.

__R. V. Jackson and G. R. Teeples, GA 1840 CENSUS INDEX, Accelerated Indexing Systems, Bountiful, UT, 1977, with ADDITIONS AND CORRECTIONS TO THE AIS 1840/50 CENSUS INDEXES, typescript, GDAH, Atlanta, GA.

__E. Sheffield and B. Woods, 1840 INDEX TO GA CENSUS, The Authors, Baytown, TX, 1971.

__F. T. Ingmire, GA 1840 CENSUS INDEX, by county, Ingmire Publications, San Antonio, TX, 1986.

___Automated Archives, CD152: US CENSUS INDEX SERIES, SOUTHERN STATES, 1840-1849, on CD-ROM, Automated Archives, Orem, UT, 1994. Contains GA entries. Also available on floppy disks.

___R. V. Jackson, G. R. Teeples, and D. Schaefermeyer, GA 1850 CENSUS INDEX, Accelerated Indexing Systems, Bountiful, UT, 1976, with ADDITIONS & CORRECTIONS TO THE AIS 1840/50 CENSUS INDEXES, typescript, GDAH, Atlanta, GA, and K. H. Thomas, CORRECTIONS TO AIS 1850 GA CENSUS INDEX, GA Genealogical Society Quarterly, Volume 16(1980) pages 181-2.

___R. C. Otto, 1850 CENSUS OF GA, INDEX TO HEADS OF FAMILIES IN 25 COUNTIES, The Compiler, Savannah, GA, 1975.

___Automated Archives, CD45: US CENSUS INDEX SERIES, SOUTHERN STATES, 1850, on CD-ROM, Automated Archives, Orem, UT, 1994. Contains GA entries. Also available on floppy disks.

___R. V. Jackson and G. R. Teeples, GA 1860 CENSUS INDEX, Accelerated Indexing Systems, North Salt Lake City, UT, 1986.

___F. T. Ingmire, GA 1860 CENSUS AND CENSUS INDEX, by county, Ingmire Publications, San Antonio, TX, 1991.

___A. Acord, M. S. Anderson, and others, AN INDEX TO THE 1860 GA FEDERAL CENSUS, Family Tree, LaGrange, GA, 1986.

___Automated Archives, CD26: US CENSUS INDEX SERIES, AL, AR, FL, GA, LA, AND SC, 1860, on CD-ROM, Automated Archives, Orem, UT, 1994. Also available on floppy disks.

___INDEX TO 1870 GA CENSUS, American Genealogical Lending Library, Bountiful, UT, 1994.

___1870 GA CENSUS INDEX, Precision Indexing, Bountiful, UT, 1990.

No complete state indexes exist for 1880, but a few counties have been indexed. These include Banks, Clayton, Douglas, Emanuel, Forsyth, Hart, Heard, Johnson, Montgomery, Tattnall, Walker, Washington, and Wayne. The indexes can be found in GDAH as published works, typescripts, or articles in GA genealogical periodicals.

In addition to the above bound volume indexes, there is a microfilm index to the 1880 census which contains only those families with a child under ten. There are also complete microfilm indexes to the 1900, 1910 and 1920 censuses. All four of these indexes are arranged according to a code called Soundex. Librarians and archivists can show you how to use this code. The indexes are:

___US Bureau of the Census, INDEX (SOUNDEX) TO THE 1880 POPULATION SCHEDULES: GA, National Archives, Washington, DC, Microfilm T744, Rolls 1-86. [Only families with a child under 10]

___US Bureau of the Census, INDEX (SOUNDEX) TO THE 1900 POPULATION SCHEDULES: GA, National Archives, Washington, DC, Microfilm T1040, Rolls 1-211.

___US Bureau of the Census, INDEX (SOUNDEX) TO THE 1910 POPULATION SCHEDULES: GA, National Archives, Washington, DC, Microfilm T1263, cities of Atlanta, Augusta, Macon, and Savannah indexed on Rolls 149-174, rest of GA on Rolls 1-148.

___US Bureau of the Census, INDEX (SOUNDEX) TO THE 1920 POPULATION SCHEDULES: GA, National Archives, Washington, DC, Microfilm M1557. Rolls 1-200.

There is also a microfilm alphabetical index to the few surviving census records of 1890, including the small number of listings from Muscogee County (Columbus):

___US Bureau of the Census, INDEX TO THE ELEVENTH (1890) CENSUS OF THE US, National Archives, Washington, DC, Microfilm M496, Rolls 1-2.

The indexes listed in the previous paragraphs are exceptionally valuable as time-saving devices. However, few indexes of any sort are perfect, and therefore, you need to exercise a little caution in using them. If you do not find your ancestor in them, do not conclude that he or she is not in the state. This may mean only that your forebear has been accidentally omitted or that the name has been misspelled, misread, or misprinted. Once you have located a name in the indexes, you can go directly to the reference in the census microfilms and read the entry. When indexes are not available (partly for 1880), it is necessary for you to go through the census listings entry-by-entry. This can be essentially prohibitive for the entire state, so it is needful for you to know the county in order to limit your search. Both the census records and the indexes are available in GDAH and FHL (through FHC) and some are available in UGL, WML, GHS, LGL, and RL. Ones pertaining to specific counties may be in LL. Both the NA and the NAFB (including NAAB) also have the microfilms and the printed indexes. The NAFB are located in or near Boston (Waltham), New York, Philadelphia, Atlanta (East Point), Chicago, Kansas City, Fort Worth, Denver, San Francisco (San Bruno), Los Angeles (Laguna Niguel), and Seattle. Their exact addresses and telephone numbers can be obtained from the telephone directories in these cities. Also, the microfilmed census records and the microfilmed indexes may be borrowed through interlibrary loan [from AGLL, PO Box

244, Bountiful, UT 84010 or Census Microfilm Rental Program, PO Box 2940, Hyattsville, MD 20784]. There is a charge of a few dollars per roll.

Agricultural census records (A), also known as farm and ranch census records, are available for 1850, 1860, 1870, and 1880 for GA. The 1850 records are partial, the data for Quitman through Wilkinson Counties being missing. These records list the name of the owner, size of farm or ranch, value of the property, crops, livestock, and other details. If your ancestor was a farmer (quite likely), it will be worthwhile to seek him in these records. No indexes are available, but you will probably know the county, so your entry-by-entry search should be fairly easy. The original records are in the Duke University Library, Durham, NC. The GDAH has microfilm copies:
___1850/60/70/80 AGRICULTURAL CENSUS RECORDS, Microfilm copies, GDAH, Atlanta, GA.

Industrial census records (I), also known as manufactures census records, are available for 1820, 1850, 1860, 1870, and 1880. The records list manufacturing firms which produced articles having an annual value of $500 or more (for the 1850-80 periods). Given in the later records are the name of the firm, the owner, the product(s), the machinery, number of employees, and other details. Indexes accompany the 1820 microfilmed records, but the others are unindexed. The 1820 records are on NA microfilms, the 1850-80 original records are in the Duke University Library, Durham, NC, and the GDAH has microfilm copies of the 1820 and 1850-1880 data.
___US Bureau of the Census, RECORDS OF THE 1820 CENSUS OF MANUFACTURES, The National Archives, Washington, DC, Microfilm M279, Rolls 1-27.
___1880 MANUFACTURES CENSUS RECORDS, Microfilm copy, GDAH, Atlanta, GA.
___US Bureau of the Census, NON-POPULATION CENSUS SCHED-ULES, 1850/60/70/80 FOR GA, The National Archives, Washington, DC, Microfilm T1137, Rolls 1-27.

Mortality census records (M) are available for the one year periods of 01 June (1849, 1859, 1869, 1879) to 31 May (1850, 1860, 1870, 1880). The records give information on persons who died in the year preceding the 1st of June of each of the census years 1850, 1860, 1870, and 1880. The data contained in the compilations include name, age, sex, occupation, place of birth, and other information. A microfilm copy of the records is available in GDAH, as well as NA and FHL:

___US Bureau of the Census, MORTALITY CENSUS SCHEDULES FOR GA, The National Archives, Washington, DC, Microfilm T655, Rolls 7-12, 1850/60/70 records indexed, 1880 records unindexed.

The 1850 and 1860 records have been made available in published form:

___1850 GA MORTALITY SCHEDULES, Ingmire Publications, St. Louis, MO, 1984.

___R. V. Jackson, MORTALITY SCHEDULE, GA, 1850, Accelerated Indexing Systems, Bountiful, UT, 1979.

___A. C. Shaw, 1850 GA MORTALITY SCHEDULES OR CENSUS, The Author, Jacksonville, FL, 1971.

___R. V. Jackson, MORTALITY SCHEDULE, GA, 1860, Accelerated Indexing Systems, North Salt Lake City, UT, 1986.

___Automated Archives, CD164: DEATH RECORD SERIES, #1, MORTALITY RECORDS 1850-1880, on CD-ROM, Automated Archives, Orem, UT, 1994. Contains about 9900 GA entries for 1850-1860. Also available on floppy disks.

Most of these are available in GDAH, UGL, WML, GHS, and in some LGL and RL.

Revolutionary War pensioners (P) were included in a special federal census taken in 1840. The compilation was an attempt to list all pension holders, however there are some omissions and some false entries. The list and an index have been published as:

___US Census Office, SIXTH CENSUS, 1840, A CENSUS OF PEN-SIONERS FOR REVOLUTIONARY OR MILITARY SER-VICES, Genealogical Publishing Co., Baltimore, MD, 1841(1967).

This volume, or other reprints of the 1840 data, is available in GDAH, UGL, WML, GHS, FHL(FHC), in most LGL, in many RL, and in some LL.

The 1850 and 1860 regular census records contain names of slaveowners (S) along with the number of slaves owned. Not many slave names are given, but there are a few. The records for GA are on microfilm as follow:

___US Bureau of the Census, SEVENTH CENSUS OF THE US, 1850, GA, The National Archives, Washington, DC, Microfilm M704, Rolls 88-96, by county.

___US Bureau of the Census, EIGHTH CENSUS OF THE US, 1860, The National Archives, Washington DC, Microfilm M653, Rolls 142-153, by county.

The colony and state of GA conducted a number of colony or <u>GA state</u> censuses (G). The records for 1738/40/50/56 are in the British Public Record Office in London, England, under the file numbers CO5/711/44, CO5/643/20, and CO5/645/71. The data for 1753 are in:

___E. B. Greene and V. D. Harrington, AMERICAN POPULATION BEFORE THE FEDERAL CENSUS OF 1790, The Authors, New York, NY, 1932.

All these are numbers only, no names are given. Beginning in 1786, state censuses which give names were taken approximately on a seven-year cycle up to 1869. However, not many of these records survive. Most of them have been published with a few being only on microfilm. Included among them are these for the following counties: Bartow or Cass(1834), Bulloch(1866), Chatham(1845/52), Cherokee(1834), Cobb(1834), Columbia(1859/79), Dooly(1845), Forsyth(1834/45), Gilmer(1834), Greene(1798), Jasper(1852), Laurens(1838), Lumpkin(1834/8), Murray(1834), Newton(1838), Paulding(1838), Richmond(1852), Taliaferro(1827), Tattnall(1838), Terrell(1859), Union(1834), Warren(1845). All of these will be found in GDAH, in books, typescripts, microfilms, or periodicals. About all that they list is the head of the household and the number of people in the household. Some are:

___GA STATE CENSUS RECORDS, 1838-45, Genealogical Society of UT, 1957/61, 2 reels of microfilm.

___B. S. Townsend, INDEX TO SEVEN STATE CENSUS REPORTS FOR COUNTIES IN GA, Taylor Foundation, Atlanta, GA, 1975.

7. Church records The charter of the colony of SC provided for the admission of all Protestant sects of the Christian Faith, even though the official colonial religion was Anglican (Episcopalian or Church of England). Roman Catholics were excluded because of the Spanish threat from FL. People of various denominations came in early years: Anglican(1733), Lutheran(1734), Presbyterian(1735), Moravian(1735/6), Jewish(1733/6), Baptist(1765), and after the Revolution: Methodist(1785) and Roman Catholic(1792). Organized religion, however, did not prosper in colonial GA. Even though most of the immigrants were religious, holding to the basic tenets of Christianity, they did not affiliate with any particular church. And, as a result, only a few church buildings were erected, only a few ministers could be supported, and only a small number of congregations were organized. The Revolutionary War left this small number of churches utterly in disarray, and recovery afterwards did not set in very quickly.

Beginning in the 1780s, the Baptists, and then a little later, the Methodists started to increase dramatically. This was largely due to the frontier activities of the Baptist farmer-preachers and the Methodist circuit-riding ministers. The GA Baptist Association was organized in 1784, and in 1788 the first GA Methodist Conference was set up. Very quickly these two denominations became the strongest in the state, remaining so today. Other denominations grew more slowly, chiefly in towns in the older (non-frontier) parts of the state. In spite of this notable expansion, GA had many unchurched people in the first half of the 19th century (1800-50), less than one-fourth of the inhabitants belonging in 1820/30. However, continued growth occurred, such that by 1860 there were 1141 Baptist churches, 1035 Methodist, 129 Presbyterian, 27 Union, 25 Episcopalian, 15 Christian (Disciples), 9 Lutheran, 8 Catholic, 3 Universalist, and one Jewish.

As did the Revolution, the Civil War had devastating effects on organized religion, with the conflict leaving destroyed or run-down church buildings, scattered congregations, and few ministers. Most denominations which had severed connections with their northern counterparts, including the Baptists and Methodists, did not reunite. Church membership, especially among the two predominant groups (Baptist and Methodist), began to increase slowly as the post-war reconstruction proceeded, then rose rapidly among both whites and blacks, who worshipped in segregated churches. The centers of rural social life were these Baptist and Methodist churches with these denominations also being the largest in the towns and cities. However, in the larger towns and cities, there were usually other churches, particularly Presbyterian and Episcopalian, and occasionally Lutheran, Catholic, and Jewish.

The records of GA churches often prove useful since they sometimes contain vital data (birth, marriage, death) and often locate your ancestor. There are two major weaknesses, however, which accrue to them. The first is that in the early days not too many Georgians were church members. The second is that the major churches during most of GA's history have been the Baptist and the Methodist, and these denominations (unlike many others) did not usually record birth, marriage, and death data in their official records. About all that will be found in most of their records are minutes of congregational meetings, lists of officers, admissions, dismissals, and sometimes membership lists. Even so, you must not fail to seek church records which relate to your progenitors, since they could be surprisingly informative. Some of the church records of GA have been inventoried, some copied into books, periodicals, and manuscripts, some have been microfilmed, some have been deposited in denominational, state, local, or private archives (or libraries), but most remain in the individual churches. The major places where they may be found are in the churches themselves, in denominational archives (listed later), in LL, RL, GDAH, UGL, WML, GHS, and FHL, and in some GA college and university archives.

Some major listings of GA church records and some finding aids to assist you in locating them are:

___J. E. Dorsey, GA GENEALOGY AND LOCAL HISTORY, A BIBLIOGRAPHY, Reprint Co, Spartanburg, SC, 1983, pages 47-376. Listings of many published and manuscript church records by county.

___M. Adams, GA LOCAL AND FAMILY HISTORY SOURCES IN PRINT, Heritage Research, Clarkston, GA, 1982.

___J. D. And E. D. Stemmons, VITAL RECORD COMPENDIUM, Everton Publishers, Logan, UT, 1979, pages 35-44.

___GA Historical Records Survey, INVENTORY OF THE CHURCH AND SYNAGOGUE ARCHIVES OF GA: BAPTISTS, Atlanta Assn. of Baptist Churches, Atlanta, GA, 1941, 2 volumes.

___E. K. Kirkham, A SURVEY OF AMERICAN CHURCH RECORDS BEFORE THE CIVIL WAR, Everton Publishers, Logan, UT, 1978, 2 volumes.

___GA PIONEERS GENEALOGICAL MAGAZINE, Mary Carter, Albany, GA, 1964-, Volume 1-, check all issues.

___Card indexes in GDAH, UGL, WML, GHS, FHL(FHC), RL, LL in your ancestor's county, and in denominational archives. Look under county, church name, and denominational name. Also ask about special indexes, listings, finding aids, and inventories.

These volumes, articles, and indexes list many published and microfilmed church records, and church record surveys, inventories, and sources. Keep them in mind as we now go about describing exactly how to find possible church records on your progenitors.

Should you have the good fortune to know or strongly suspect your ancestor's church, you can write directly. Send an SASE, a check for $5, your forebear's name, and the pertinent dates. Request a search of the records or information on the location of the records if the church no longer has them. If they neither have them nor know where the records are, dispatch an inquiry to the GA or the national denominational repository, enclose an SASE, and ask them if they know where the records are. Also consult all the materials in the previous paragraph to try to locate the records.

If, as is often the case, you know your ancestor's county but not his church, you will need to dig a little deeper. First, you need to examine the indexes of the compiled church records of the pertinent county. Many of these can be located by using the aids listed in the second paragraph above. If you know or can guess the denomination, this might narrow your search, but do not too easily overlook other denominations. Should you still not find what you are seeking, examine maps of your progenitor's county which show churches, and observe those churches near your forebear's property. Suitable maps for this purpose are listed in section 17 of this chapter, especially those maps available from the US Geological Survey. Then investigate these nearby churches, seeking their records by using the items listed in the fifth paragraph of this section, and by writing to them (SASE). Letters to LL (listed later), to local genealogical or historical societies (listed later), and to denominational repositories concerning churches in your ancestor's part of the county and the records of these churches should be dispatched.

Important archives or church information centers for the major denominations in GA include:

___(Baptist) GA Baptist Historical Society Collection, Stetson Library, Mercer University, Macon, GA 31201. Baptist church minutes, newspapers, association records, minister lists, indexes. Marriage and death index to state Baptist newspaper, The Christian Index (1828-).

___(Catholic) Savannah Diocesan Archives, 302 East LIberty St., Savannah, GA 31402. Archdiocese of Atlanta, 680 W. Peachtree st., Atlanta, GA 30308.

___(Jewish) American Jewish Archives, 3101 Clifton Avenue, Cincinnati, OH 45220.

___(Methodist) Library, Candler School of Theology, Emory University, Emory, GA 30338. United Methodist Museum, PO Box 408, Saint Simon's Island, GA 31522. Methodist church records, conference minutes, minister lists, newspapers.

___(Presbyterian) Historical Foundation of the Presbyterian and Reformed Churches, Assembly Drive, PO Box 847, Montreat, NC 28757.

___(Episcopal) Diocesan Office, 2744 Peachtree Rd., NW, Atlanta, GA 30363 or 611 E. Bay, Savannah, GA 31401.

___(Lutheran) Library, Lutheran Southern Seminary, 4201 North Main Street, Columbia, SC 29203.

___(Quaker) Friends Historical Collection, Library, Guilford College, Guilford, NC 27410.

Addresses of headquarters and/or repositories of other denominations may be obtained from:

___YEARBOOK OF AMERICAN AND CANADIAN CHURCHES, Abingdon Press, Nashville, TN, latest edition.

Your research into your forebear's religious affiliation will be enhanced and placed in context by the use of some volumes which give details on the histories of GA churches:

___(Baptist) S. Boykin, HISTORY OF THE BAPTIST DENOMINA-TION IN GA, Southern Historical Press, Easley, SC, 1881 (1976). Over 600 biographies of ministers and leaders.

___(Baptist) J. H. Campbell, GA BAPTISTS, HISTORICAL AND BIOGRAPHICAL, Ellyson, Richmond, VA, 1847.

___(Baptist) D. C. Dodd, MARCHING THROUGH GA, A HISTORY OF FREE WILL BAPTISTS IN GA, The Author, Colquitt, GA, 1977.

___(Baptist) GA BAPTISTS, EARLY SKETCHES, GA Pioneers, Volumes 2-6, 1965-9.

___(Baptist) B. J. W. Graham, BAPTIST BIOGRAPHY, Index Printing Co., Atlanta, GA, 1917.

___(Baptist) S. G. Hillyer, REMINISCENCES OF GA BAPTIST, Foote and Davis, Atlanta, GA, 1902.

___(Baptist) J. Mercer, A HISTORY OF THE GA BAPTIST ASSOC-IATION, GA Baptist Historical Society, Washington, GA, 1838(1980).

___(Baptist) M. K. Overby, GA BAPTIST CHURCH RECORDS, GA Genealogist, State Records 2-50.

___(Baptist) M. K. Overby, OBITUARIES PUBLISHED BY THE CHRISTIAN INDEX, 1822-99, GA Baptist Historical Society, Macon, GA, 1975/82, 2 volumes.

___(Baptist) M. K. Overby, MARRIAGES PUBLISHED IN THE CHRISTIAN INDEX, 1822-55, GA Baptist Historical Society, Macon, GA, 1971.

___(Baptist) B. D. Ragsdale, STORY OF GA BAPTISTS, Foote and Davis, Atlanta, GA, 1932-8, 3 volumes.

___(Methodist) E. Brewer, A STUDY OF THE CHURCHES AND COUNTIES OF THE NORTH GA CONFERENCE OF THE

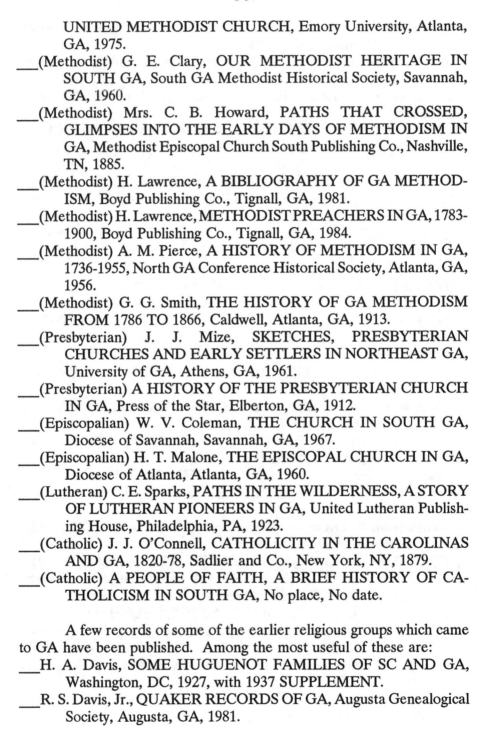

UNITED METHODIST CHURCH, Emory University, Atlanta, GA, 1975.

___(Methodist) G. E. Clary, OUR METHODIST HERITAGE IN SOUTH GA, South GA Methodist Historical Society, Savannah, GA, 1960.

___(Methodist) Mrs. C. B. Howard, PATHS THAT CROSSED, GLIMPSES INTO THE EARLY DAYS OF METHODISM IN GA, Methodist Episcopal Church South Publishing Co., Nashville, TN, 1885.

___(Methodist) H. Lawrence, A BIBLIOGRAPHY OF GA METHODISM, Boyd Publishing Co., Tignall, GA, 1981.

___(Methodist) H. Lawrence, METHODIST PREACHERS IN GA, 1783-1900, Boyd Publishing Co., Tignall, GA, 1984.

___(Methodist) A. M. Pierce, A HISTORY OF METHODISM IN GA, 1736-1955, North GA Conference Historical Society, Atlanta, GA, 1956.

___(Methodist) G. G. Smith, THE HISTORY OF GA METHODISM FROM 1786 TO 1866, Caldwell, Atlanta, GA, 1913.

___(Presbyterian) J. J. Mize, SKETCHES, PRESBYTERIAN CHURCHES AND EARLY SETTLERS IN NORTHEAST GA, University of GA, Athens, GA, 1961.

___(Presbyterian) A HISTORY OF THE PRESBYTERIAN CHURCH IN GA, Press of the Star, Elberton, GA, 1912.

___(Episcopalian) W. V. Coleman, THE CHURCH IN SOUTH GA, Diocese of Savannah, Savannah, GA, 1967.

___(Episcopalian) H. T. Malone, THE EPISCOPAL CHURCH IN GA, Diocese of Atlanta, Atlanta, GA, 1960.

___(Lutheran) C. E. Sparks, PATHS IN THE WILDERNESS, A STORY OF LUTHERAN PIONEERS IN GA, United Lutheran Publishing House, Philadelphia, PA, 1923.

___(Catholic) J. J. O'Connell, CATHOLICITY IN THE CAROLINAS AND GA, 1820-78, Sadlier and Co., New York, NY, 1879.

___(Catholic) A PEOPLE OF FAITH, A BRIEF HISTORY OF CATHOLICISM IN SOUTH GA, No place, No date.

A few records of some of the earlier religious groups which came to GA have been published. Among the most useful of these are:

___H. A. Davis, SOME HUGUENOT FAMILIES OF SC AND GA, Washington, DC, 1927, with 1937 SUPPLEMENT.

___R. S. Davis, Jr., QUAKER RECORDS OF GA, Augusta Genealogical Society, Augusta, GA, 1981.

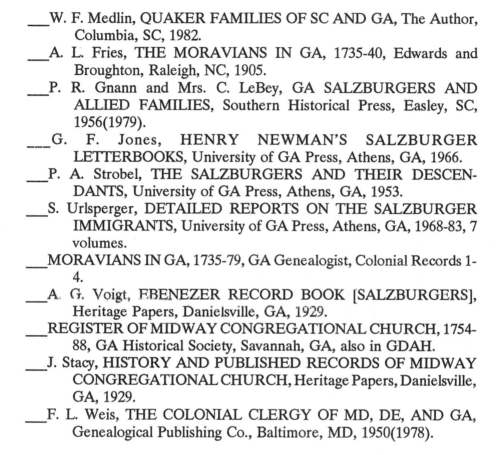

___W. F. Medlin, QUAKER FAMILIES OF SC AND GA, The Author, Columbia, SC, 1982.

___A. L. Fries, THE MORAVIANS IN GA, 1735-40, Edwards and Broughton, Raleigh, NC, 1905.

___P. R. Gnann and Mrs. C. LeBey, GA SALZBURGERS AND ALLIED FAMILIES, Southern Historical Press, Easley, SC, 1956(1979).

___G. F. Jones, HENRY NEWMAN'S SALZBURGER LETTERBOOKS, University of GA Press, Athens, GA, 1966.

___P. A. Strobel, THE SALZBURGERS AND THEIR DESCEN-DANTS, University of GA Press, Athens, GA, 1953.

___S. Urlsperger, DETAILED REPORTS ON THE SALZBURGER IMMIGRANTS, University of GA Press, Athens, GA, 1968-83, 7 volumes.

___MORAVIANS IN GA, 1735-79, GA Genealogist, Colonial Records 1-4.

___A. G. Voigt, EBENEZER RECORD BOOK [SALZBURGERS], Heritage Papers, Danielsville, GA, 1929.

___REGISTER OF MIDWAY CONGREGATIONAL CHURCH, 1754-88, GA Historical Society, Savannah, GA, also in GDAH.

___J. Stacy, HISTORY AND PUBLISHED RECORDS OF MIDWAY CONGREGATIONAL CHURCH, Heritage Papers, Danielsville, GA, 1929.

___F. L. Weis, THE COLONIAL CLERGY OF MD, DE, AND GA, Genealogical Publishing Co., Baltimore, MD, 1950(1978).

As you search for your ancestor's church records, please bear in mind that they might be in a wide variety of places. The original, transcribed, microfilmed, and/or published records may be in the local church, local libraries or archives, regional libraries or archives, state libraries or archives, or denominational archives, or even in private hands. Inquire at all these repositories, especially LL, RL, FHL(FHC), GHS, WML, UGL, AND GDAH. When seeking church records in a library or archives card catalog, you should look under the county name, the church name, and the denomination name. Church records are often found in several other sources, which are discussed in different sections of this chapter: cemetery, city and county histories, colonial, DAR, ethnic, genealogical indexes and compilations, genealogical periodicals, manuscripts, mortuary, newspaper, published genealogies, regional records, and WPA records.

Records of religious groups also appeared in denominational periodicals. Data from these publications have been abstracted for GA Baptists, Lutherans, Methdists, Presbyterians, and Quakers. They are listed in Section 31.

8. City directories

During the middle 19th century several larger cities in GA began publishing city directories. These volumes usually appeared erratically at first, but then began to come out regularly (annually) later on. They usually list heads of households and workers plus their home addresses and their occupations, and sometimes the names and addresses of their places of employment. Businesses, professions, institutions, churches, and organizations are also usually listed.

Notable among the GA city directories are those of the following cities. For each of these cities, the earliest and a few of the succeeding directories are listed, then afterwards a date from which publication became fairly regular (annually): Atlanta(1859/60/7/70/2, 1874-), Savannah(1848/9/50/2/8/9/60/7/70/1/2/4/5,1877-). For each of the following cities, the earliest directory is listed: Augusta(1841), Columbus(1859). There are also two regional directories which contain business listings only, one covering GA(1850), and the other covering the South(1854), including GA.

Many of the directories mentioned in the previous paragraph have been microfilmed, quite a few of them through the 1901 volume. The microfilms and/or the original directories should be sought in the Library of Congress, GDAH, UGL, WML, GHS, FHL, RL, and LL. Other GA cities also issued directories, usually at starting dates later than the above ones, but you should not fail to look for them, especially in RL and LL in the pertinent places.

The telephone was invented in 1876-7, underwent rapid development, and became widespread fairly quickly. By the late years of the century, telephone directories were coming into existence. Older issues can often be found in LL, and as the years have gone on, they have proved to be ever more valuable genealogical sources.

9. City and county histories

Histories for many GA counties and numerous GA cities have been published. These volumes usually contain biographical data on leading citizens, details about early settlers, histories of organizations, businesses, trades, and churches, and often lists of clergymen, lawyers, physicians, teachers, governmental officials, farmers, military men, and other groups. Several works which list many of these histories are:

___M. J. Kaminkow, US LOCAL HISTORIES IN THE LIBRARY OF CONGRESS, Magna Carta, Baltimore, MD, 1975, 4 volumes.

___P. W. Filby, BIBLIOGRAPHY OF COUNTY HISTORIES IN AMERICA, Genealogical Publishing Co., Baltimore, MD, 1985.

___J. E. Dorsey, GA GENEALOGY AND LOCAL HISTORY, Reprint Co, Spartanburg, SC, 1983.

___M. L. Adams, GA LOCAL AND FAMILY HISTORY SOURCES IN PRINT, Heritage Research, Clarkston, GA, 1982.

___A. R. Rowland and J. E. Dorsey, A BIBLIOGRAPHY OF THE WRITINGS ON GA HISTORY, 1900-70, Reprint Co, Spartanburg, SC, 1978.

___J. E. Simpson, GA HISTORY, A BIBLIOGRAPHY, Scarecrow Press, Metuchen, NJ, 1976.

___W. S. Yenawise, CHECKLIST OF SOURCE MATERIALS FOR COUNTIES OF GA, GA Historical Quarterly, Volume 32, September 1948, pages 179-229, with C. Hart, SUPPLEMENT, GDAH, Atlanta, GA.

Most of the GA volumes in these bibliographies can be found in GDAH, UGL, WML, GHS, and the Library of Congress in Washington, DC, and some are available in LGL. RL and LL are likely to have those relating to their particular areas. In Chapter 4, you will find listed under the counties recommended county histories. In libraries, the easiest way to find local histories is to look under the names of the county, city, and town. Your attention also needs to be directed to two volumes which contain valuable historical sketches on GA's counties and cities:

___A. D. Candler and C. A. Evans, GA, COMPRISING SKETCHES OF COUNTIES, TOWNS, EVENTS, INSTITUTIONS, AND PERSONS, State Historical Association, Atlanta, GA, 1906, 4 volumes.

___G. White, HISTORICAL COLLECTIONS OF GA, Pudney and Russell, New York, NY, 1855. [Contains name index]

In addition, there are abundant historical materials on counties and cities in GDAH. They may be located by looking in:

___COUNTIES FILE and CITIES FILE, Microfilm Library, GDAH, Atlanta, GA, also look at the LOOSE GA COUNTY RECORDS, Inventory Notebooks, Law Wing, GDAH, Atlanta, GA.

10. Colonial records

The colonial period for GA extended from 1733 until 1776, during which time the area was a colony of Great Britain. Many other sections in this chapter describe specific types of records relating to colonial GA, particularly sections 3, 5-7, 9, 11-12, 15-18, 22-23, 25, 31-36. This section presents the most important colonial records, and is made up of two sub-sections, one dealing with general reference materials to all the colonies (including GA), and a second dealing with reference materials and records of colonial GA.

Among the most important genealogical materials relating to all the colonies are the following. They should be consulted for your colonial GA ancestor. However, some of the volumes must be used with care since some of the information in them is not from original sources and is therefore often inaccurate.

___F. A. Virkus, THE ABRIDGED COMPENDIUM OF AMERICAN GENEALOGY, Genealogical Publishing Co., Baltimore, MD, 1968(1925-42), 7 volumes. [425,000 names of colonial people]

___G. M. MacKenzie and N. O. Rhoades, COLONIAL FAMILIES OF THE USA, Genealogical Publishing Co., Baltimore, MD, 1966(1907-20), 7 volumes. [125,000 names]

___H. Whittemore, GENEALOGICAL GUIDE TO THE EARLY SETTLERS OF AMERICA, Genealogical Publishing Co., Baltimore, MD, 1967(1898-1906).

___T. P. Hughes and others, AMERICAN ANCESTRY, Genealogical Publishing Co., Baltimore, MD, 1968(1887-9), 12 volumes.

___BURKE'S DISTINGUISHED FAMILIES OF AMERICA, Burke's Peerage, London, England, 1948.

___C. E. Banks, PLANTERS OF THE COMMONWEALTH, Genealogical Publishing Co., Baltimore, MD, 1972.

___G. R. Crowther, III, SURNAME INDEX TO 65 VOLUMES OF COLONIAL AND REVOLUTIONARY PEDIGREES, National Genealogical Society, Washington, DC, 1975.

___M. B. Colket, Jr., FOUNDERS OF EARLY AMERICAN FAMILIES, Order of Founders and Patriots of America, Cleveland, OH, 1975.

___H. K. Eilers, NSDAC BICENTENNIAL ANCESTOR INDEX, National Society Daughters of American Colonists, Ft. Worth, TX, 1976.

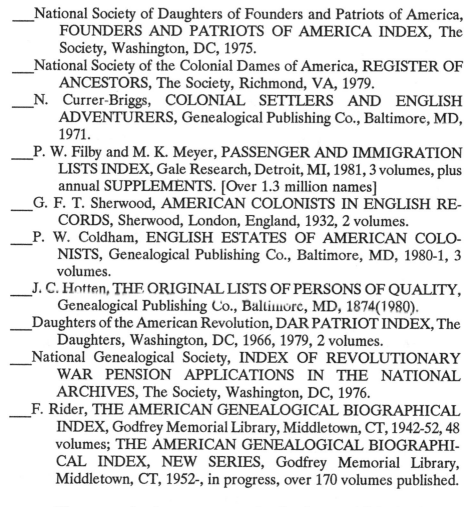

___National Society of Daughters of Founders and Patriots of America, FOUNDERS AND PATRIOTS OF AMERICA INDEX, The Society, Washington, DC, 1975.

___National Society of the Colonial Dames of America, REGISTER OF ANCESTORS, The Society, Richmond, VA, 1979.

___N. Currer-Briggs, COLONIAL SETTLERS AND ENGLISH ADVENTURERS, Genealogical Publishing Co., Baltimore, MD, 1971.

___P. W. Filby and M. K. Meyer, PASSENGER AND IMMIGRATION LISTS INDEX, Gale Research, Detroit, MI, 1981, 3 volumes, plus annual SUPPLEMENTS. [Over 1.3 million names]

___G. F. T. Sherwood, AMERICAN COLONISTS IN ENGLISH RE-CORDS, Sherwood, London, England, 1932, 2 volumes.

___P. W. Coldham, ENGLISH ESTATES OF AMERICAN COLO-NISTS, Genealogical Publishing Co., Baltimore, MD, 1980-1, 3 volumes.

___J. C. Hotten, THE ORIGINAL LISTS OF PERSONS OF QUALITY, Genealogical Publishing Co., Baltimore, MD, 1874(1980).

___Daughters of the American Revolution, DAR PATRIOT INDEX, The Daughters, Washington, DC, 1966, 1979, 2 volumes.

___National Genealogical Society, INDEX OF REVOLUTIONARY WAR PENSION APPLICATIONS IN THE NATIONAL ARCHIVES, The Society, Washington, DC, 1976.

___F. Rider, THE AMERICAN GENEALOGICAL BIOGRAPHICAL INDEX, Godfrey Memorial Library, Middletown, CT, 1942-52, 48 volumes; THE AMERICAN GENEALOGICAL BIOGRAPHI-CAL INDEX, NEW SERIES, Godfrey Memorial Library, Middletown, CT, 1952-, in progress, over 170 volumes published.

There are also important record collections, published volumes, and typescript and published indexes relating specifically to colonial GA. Among the most useful of the original records for looking up your ancestors who came to GA before 1776 are the following. As you consider them, it is essential that you remember that during GA's colonial history there were no record-keeping counties or other political sub-divisions. All records were kept at the colony level and were recorded at Savannah.

___COLONIAL CONVEYANCE(DEED) BOOKS C1, C2, S, U, V, X1, CC1, CC2, DD, 1750-98, GDAH, Atlanta, GA, Microfilm Reels 40-19/20/1/2/3/5, indexed.

___COLONIAL LAND BOOKS, GDAH, Atlanta, GA: CLAIMS BOOK M(U3), 1755-7, Microfilm Reel 40-43, indexed; FIATS FOR GRANTS BOOKS L, T, BB, 1755-76, Microfilm Reel 40-44;

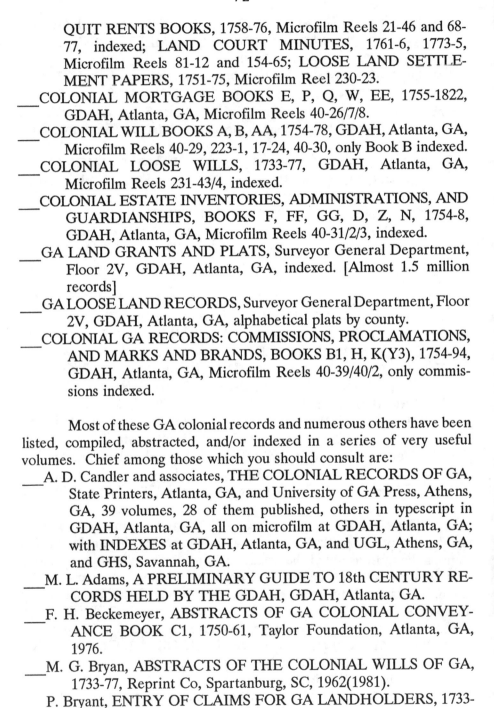

QUIT RENTS BOOKS, 1758-76, Microfilm Reels 21-46 and 68-77, indexed; LAND COURT MINUTES, 1761-6, 1773-5, Microfilm Reels 81-12 and 154-65; LOOSE LAND SETTLE-MENT PAPERS, 1751-75, Microfilm Reel 230-23.

___COLONIAL MORTGAGE BOOKS E, P, Q, W, EE, 1755-1822, GDAH, Atlanta, GA, Microfilm Reels 40-26/7/8.

___COLONIAL WILL BOOKS A, B, AA, 1754-78, GDAH, Atlanta, GA, Microfilm Reels 40-29, 223-1, 17-24, 40-30, only Book B indexed.

___COLONIAL LOOSE WILLS, 1733-77, GDAH, Atlanta, GA, Microfilm Reels 231-43/4, indexed.

___COLONIAL ESTATE INVENTORIES, ADMINISTRATIONS, AND GUARDIANSHIPS, BOOKS F, FF, GG, D, Z, N, 1754-8, GDAH, Atlanta, GA, Microfilm Reels 40-31/2/3, indexed.

___GA LAND GRANTS AND PLATS, Surveyor General Department, Floor 2V, GDAH, Atlanta, GA, indexed. [Almost 1.5 million records]

___GA LOOSE LAND RECORDS, Surveyor General Department, Floor 2V, GDAH, Atlanta, GA, alphabetical plats by county.

___COLONIAL GA RECORDS: COMMISSIONS, PROCLAMATIONS, AND MARKS AND BRANDS, BOOKS B1, H, K(Y3), 1754-94, GDAH, Atlanta, GA, Microfilm Reels 40-39/40/2, only commissions indexed.

Most of these GA colonial records and numerous others have been listed, compiled, abstracted, and/or indexed in a series of very useful volumes. Chief among those which you should consult are:

___A. D. Candler and associates, THE COLONIAL RECORDS OF GA, State Printers, Atlanta, GA, and University of GA Press, Athens, GA, 39 volumes, 28 of them published, others in typescript in GDAH, Atlanta, GA, all on microfilm at GDAH, Atlanta, GA; with INDEXES at GDAH, Atlanta, GA, and UGL, Athens, GA, and GHS, Savannah, GA.

___M. L. Adams, A PRELIMINARY GUIDE TO 18th CENTURY RE-CORDS HELD BY THE GDAH, GDAH, Atlanta, GA.

___F. H. Beckemeyer, ABSTRACTS OF GA COLONIAL CONVEY-ANCE BOOK C1, 1750-61, Taylor Foundation, Atlanta, GA, 1976.

___M. G. Bryan, ABSTRACTS OF THE COLONIAL WILLS OF GA, 1733-77, Reprint Co, Spartanburg, SC, 1962(1981).

___P. Bryant, ENTRY OF CLAIMS FOR GA LANDHOLDERS, 1733-55, State Printing Office, Atlanta, GA, 1975.

___E. M. Coulter and A. B. Saye, A LIST OF EARLY SETTLERS OF GA, 1732-41, Genealogical Publishing Co., Baltimore, MD, 1949(1983).

___G. G. Davidson, EARLY RECORDS OF GA: WILKES COUNTY, Southern Historical Press, Easley, SC, 1936(1968), Volume 1, pages 2-29.

___W. H. Dumont, COLONIAL GA GENEALOGICAL DATA, 1748-53, National Genealogical Society, Washington, DC, 1971.

___GA GENEALOGICAL MAGAZINE, has published many of the above Colonial GA records in Issues 4-45.

___M. R. Hemperley and P. Bryant, ENGLISH CROWN GRANTS IN GA, 1755-75, GA Surveyor General Department, Atlanta, GA, 1972-6, 10 volumes, with TYPESCRIPT INDEX at GDAH, Atlanta, GA, only 8 volumes indexed in it.

___IMMIGRANTS FROM GREAT BRITAIN TO THE GA COLONY, Genealogical Enterprises, Morrow, GA, 1970.

___INDEX TO GA COLONIAL CONVEYANCES AND CONFIS-CATED LAND RECORDS, 1750-1804, Taylor Foundation, Atlanta, GA, 1981.

___INDEX TO THE HEADRIGHT AND BOUNTY GRANTS IN GA FROM 1756-1909, Southern Historical Press, Easley, SC, 1970.

___INDEX TO PROBATE RECORDS OF COLONIAL GA, 1733-78, Taylor Foundation, Atlanta, GA, 1983.

___J. H. Stucki, COLONIAL GEORGIANS, Genealogical Enterprises, Morrow, GA, 1975-6, 2 volumes.

___G. F. Walker, ABSTRACTS OF GA COLONIAL BOOK J, 1755-62, Taylor Foundation, Atlanta, GA, 1978. Bonds, bills of sale, deeds of gift, powers of attorney.

___M. B. Warren, GA GOVERNOR AND COUNCIL JOURNALS, 1753-, Heritage Papers, Danielsville, GA, 1992-, several volumes.

___M. B. Warren, GA LAND OWNERS MEMORIALS, 1758-76, Heritage Papers, Danielsville, GA, 1988.

___GENERAL INDEX TO THE GA GAZETTE, 1763-1845, GHS, Savannah, GA.

Other sources of early original GA records are the two following manuscript collections:

___LOOSE GA COLONIAL RECORDS, Telamon Cuyler Collection, UGL, Athens, GA, especially the COLLECTION OF GA LAND GRANTS.

___LOOSE GA COLONIAL RECORDS, Manuscript Division, Perkins Library, Duke University, Durham, NC.

All the published works mentioned in the previous paragraph are available in GDAH, UGL, WML, and GHS, and some of them will be found in RL and LL in GA. There are also some other books of general use for locating forebears in colonial GA:

___COLONIAL GA MARRIAGES, 1760-1810, Ingmire Publications, St. Louis, MO, 1986.

___L. L. Knight, GA's BICENTENNIAL MEMOIRS AND MEMORIES, The Author, Atlanta, GA, 1931-3, 4 volumes.

___National Society of the Colonial Dames of America, REGISTER OF THE GA SOCIETY, COLONIAL DAMES OF AMERICA, Waverly Press, Baltimore, Md, 1937.

___Mrs. H. Peterson, ROSTER OF MEMBERS, REGISTER OF COLONIAL ANCESTORS, AND HISTORY OF THE GA SOCIETY OF THE DAUGHTERS OF AMERICAN COLONISTS, The Society, Atlanta, Ga, 1968.

___THE STORM CLOUDS GATHER, GA IN TURMOIL BEFORE THE REVOLUTION, The GA Genealogist, Colonial Records 1-10.

___S. B. G. Temple and K. Coleman, GA JOURNEYS, 1732-54, University of GA Press, Athens, GA, 1961.

Quite a number of other references to colonial records of GA are found in:

___J. E. Dorsey, GA GENEALOGY AND LOCAL HISTORY, A BIBLIOGRAPHY, Reprint Co, Spartanburg, SC, 1983, pages 28-33.

---

11. Court records

In 1733, when GA was first settled, the trustees set up two basic types of courts. One was the Courts of Conscience which were presided over by justices of the peace and dealt with minor civil and a few minor criminal matters. The other was the Town Court of Savannah which handled all other law and equity cases in the colony. This court sat chiefly in Savannah, but also went into other towns as the need arose. All records, however, were kept in Savannah. The courts were assisted by bailiffs, constables, tithingmen, and recorders or clerks. When the Royal Governor took over in 1754, he established a General Court which handled civil matters and also sat as a Court of Oyer and Terminer to deal with criminal cases. Four other courts, which were staffed largely by other governmental officers, were set up: a Court of Chancery (equity matters), a Court of Ordinary (estate matters), a Court of Vice-Admiralty (maritime matters), and a Court of Errors (appeals from the General Court). The Courts of Conscience continued as they had in the Trustee Period. Assistance to the courts was given by an attorney-general, a provost marshall to act as a sheriff, a customs officer, land surveyors, a receiver of quit rents, a register of deeds, plus clerks and record custodians. Fortunately, many of the more genealogically significant records were saved, including ones dealing with bonds, claim entries, commissions, estates, deeds, land grants, land plats, land settlements, marks and brands, mortgages, proclamations, quit rents, and wills. Unfortunately, a number of records were lost, even though some of them have been discovered recently in several archival repositories. Most of the existing colonial records have been listed in the previous section, and further mention of them as well as others, will be made in sections to come (14-15, 22-23, 25, 30, 34-35).

Following the turmoil during and after the Revolution, GA officials reorganized the court system. The General Assembly arranged for each county to have three basic courts: Courts of Justices of the Peace, an Inferior Court, and a Superior Court. The Courts of Justices of the Peace functioned mainly in minor civil matters, continuing the work of the Courts of Conscience. The Inferior Court acted in three ways: as the conductor of county affairs, as a court of law for lesser civil and some criminal cases, and as the manager of estate matters. The Inferior Court thus recorded minor civil cases, wills, estate administrations, estate inventories, guardianships, county affairs, sometimes land lottery records, and marriages. The Superior Court handled civil and criminal matters, land matters, voter registration, professional registration, naturalizations, sometimes land lottery records, and sometimes assisted the Inferior Court in managing the county. In 1868, the Inferior Court was abolished, its county governing power going to a County Commission, its civil and criminal tasks going to the Superior Court, and its estate functions going to a newly created Court of Ordinary. In 1846, a GA Supreme Court was set up, and in 1907, a GA State Court of Appeals was constituted.

Please do not forget that all GA court records prior to the Revolution were kept on the colony level, because there were no counties and therefore no county courts. Many of these records have been listed in the previous section which deals with colonial records. In using these records, which are located in GDAH, you must not overlook the very important civil and criminal case records. Researchers often go to the estate and land records, but forget that numerous early Georgians were involved in law suits, a very valuable genealogical source. After the Revolution, court records of importance were kept by both state courts (Supreme Court, Court of Appeals), and by the county courts (Superior,

Inferior, Ordinary). The records of many of the more important Superior Courts during 1805-43 and the records of the GA Supreme Court from 1846 onwards are abstracted in two sets of books:

___T. U. P. Charlton, GA DECISIONS, REPORTS OF CASES IN THE SUPERIOR COURTS OF GA, 1805-43, Franklin Turner, Atlanta, GA, 1907.

___J. M. Kelly and successors, GA REPORTS OF CASES IN THE SUPREME COURT OF GA, 1846-, Jenkins, New York, NY, and other publishers.

A very convenient way to find out if your progenitor appealed a court case to one of these higher courts is to look him or her up in a very good index to the records of the GA District Superior Courts, GA Supreme Court, GA Court of Appeals, and US Federal Courts in GA:

___GA DIGEST, 1792-1942, West Publishing Co., St. Paul, MN, 1942, Volumes 22-23. [Use both volumes since the indexes differ.]

The detailed case files for the cases abstracted in the GA REPORTS OF CASES IN THE SUPREME COURT OF GA are in the GDAH. They often contain good genealogical data:

___LOOSE GA STATE SUPREME COURT PAPERS, 1846 to past 1900, Inventories in the Law Wing, GDAH, Atlanta, GA.

The county courts (Superior, Inferior, Ordinary, other Special Courts) and county governments kept many records of exceptional value. Included were amnesty oaths(1867), apprentice, bastardy, birth, Confederate, Court of Ordinary minutes, death, deed and mortgage, estate(administration, annual return, appraisement, bond, guardian, inventory, 12-month support), free persons of color, homestead exemption, Inferior Court minutes, jury, Land Court, land lottery, lunacy, marriage, naturalization, Ordinary index, pauper, registration, school, slave importation, state census, Superior Court records, Superior Court minutes, tax, tavern, voter, and will. All of these should be carefully searched for their content of family historical information. Many of these are in GDAH and FHL(FHC). Chapter 3 will discuss these repositories and Chapter 4 will contain detailed lists of what is available for each of the GA counties which were organized before 1900.

12. DAR records

The GA Chapters of the Daughters of the American Revolution (DAR) have rendered genealogists a very valuable service. Over many years, they have copied, abstracted, and/or indexed a vast array of GA family history records. They have published some in books, some in their magazine, and many are in typescript or manuscript form. The DAR materials include many sorts of records: Bible, church, cemetery, census, court, family, genealogies, land lottery, marriage, newspaper, school, tax, and will. They are particularly heavy on church, cemetery, and will records. Many of the materials are in various GA libraries (UGL, WML, GHS, RL), but the best collection is in GDAH (over 300 volumes). Records for over 90 GA counties will be found there. A partial listing of them is given in:

___M. G. Bryan, CATALOG OF THE GA SOCIETY DAR LIBRARY IN GDAH, GDAH, Atlanta, GA.

The DAR compilations include three published sets:

___DAR, HISTORICAL COLLECTIONS OF THE JOSEPH HABERSHAM CHAPTER, Genealogical Publishing Co., Baltimore, MD, 1967, 3 volumes.

___DAR, HISTORICAL COLLECTIONS OF THE GA CHAPTERS, Byrd, Atlanta, GA, 1926-49, 5 volumes.

___DAR of GA, MEMBERSHIP ROLL AND REGISTER OF ANCESTORS, 1946 issue by N. Brawner, 1976 issue by G. M. Drew, The Society, Atlanta, GA.

These nine volumes and the large number of typescripts and manuscripts of the DAR are listed by county in the following excellent finding aid:

___J. E. Dorsey, GA GENEALOGY AND LOCAL HISTORY, Reprint Co, Spartanburg, SC, 1983.

You should examine the listings under the counties for each county in which you had or suspect you had ancestors. This volume also lists many other sources of records: genealogical periodicals, special collections in UGL, manuscripts and typescripts in GDAH, plus many others. In the GDAH, there is another useful finding aid for the DAR typescript materials:

___DAR COMPILATIONS CARD FILE, 1965-, GDAH, Atlanta, GA.

13. Death records

There were several early efforts, the earliest in 1804, to require death registration in GA, but these failed quite broadly due to non-compliance. In a few counties and in some cities there are a few death records prior to 1919, when state registration was required. The counties and the dates are: Carroll(1875), Chatham(1803-47, with index to 1733-), Chattooga(1875-6), Clarke(1875-6), Colquitt(1875), Early(1875), Elbert(1875-8), Greene(1811-33), Jackson(1875), Jefferson(1875), Lumpkin(1875), McIntosh(1875), Miller(1875-6), Talbot(1875), and Taliaferro(1875-6). The cities and the dates when they began keeping records are: Atlanta(1896-), Columbus(1890-), Gainesville(1909-), Macon(1882-), and Savannah (1803-). The county records are available, along with those for Gainesville, in the GDAH, and the city records are in the corresponding County Health Departments. All these records are incomplete.

As mentioned above, GA started requiring deaths to be recorded with the state in 1919. At first the counties cooperated very well, but in the middle 1920s they did not. In 1922, the records became 90% complete which they continued to be except for the period 1925-8. Anyone can purchase a death certificate if the year and county of death are provided to The Vital Records Unit, GA Department of Human Resources, Room 217H, Health Building, 47 Trinity Avenue, Atlanta, GA 30334. Since GA is so short on death records before 1919, other types of records have to be consulted in attempts to find death data. Among the better ones are Bible, biography, cemetery, census, church, genealogical periodical, manuscript, military, mortuary, newspaper, published genealogy, and above all, will and estate records. These are discussed in other sections of this chapter.

There are a few published or typescript works which contain or lead to death data compilations. Notable among these are:
___J. E. Dorsey, GA GENEALOGY AND LOCAL HISTORY, A BIBLIOGRAPHY, Reprint Co, Spartanburg, SC, 1983. [Look under counties.]
___DAR, DAR RECORD TYPESCRIPTS, in GDAH, Atlanta, GA, with INDEXES. [Look in card file of them in GDAH.]
___J. D. and E. D. Stemmons, THE VITAL RECORD COMPENDIUM, Everton Publishers, Logan, UT, 1979.
When you are seeking death date and place information in archives and libraries, be certain to explore all the above mentioned sources, and don't fail to look under county listings and the following heading in card catalogs: Registers of births, deaths, etc.

14. Divorce records

In the Southern English colonies, including GA, the influence of the Church of England (which strongly opposed divorce) during the pre-Revolutionary period was such that civil divorce laws were not in effect. Marital discord was usually either borne or settled by separation or desertion. Divorce by petition to the Legislature was permitted, but seldom used. After the Revolution, divorce could be obtained 1798-1835 from the Legislature or could be granted by the Superior Court from 1798 to the present. Early on, two separate juries had to hear the case at different times and had to concur in their verdicts. Also during the period 1798-1949, second marriages required a court petition. Therefore, to seek a divorce record, you need to search the Legislative records until 1835 and the Superior Court records in the pertinent county from 1798 forward. A useful article has been published listing the approximately 300 divorces approved by the GA Legislature during the years 1798-1833:

___C. Hart, GENEALOGICAL INFORMATION FOUND IN LEGIS-LATIVE ACTS, DIVORCES, GA Genealogical Society Quarterly, Volume 1, Number 3, 1965, pages 9-19, and Volume 6, Number 3, page 298.

A further listing of legislative divorces and separations is given in:

___R. S. Davis, Jr., GA BLACK BOOK II, Southern Historical Press, Easley, SC, 1987.

You should also look in GDAH in the General Name Index and the notebook entitled GA DIVORCE (the latter in the Microfilm Library). Also be sure and consult Section 31 for the newspaper abstract volumes, a few of which contain divorces. In 1952, a law requiring all divorces to be reported to a state office was passed, but records are not available through that office. All records after 1835 must be sought in the Superior Court records in the county of interest.

15. Emigration and immigration

Since GA was one of the thirteen original colonies, many early settlers came in (immigrated) and many of them or their descendants moved out (emigrated) chiefly to the west (into what is now AL and MS, and beyond). There are a number of good volumes available which list immigrants to the areas that became the US. You should consult these volumes because they include both people who came directly to GA and people who came to some other colony or state and then to GA. The first set of volumes is an index to well over a million listings. These references have been abstracted from many published lists. Each listing gives the full name of the immigrant, the names of accompanying relatives, ages, the date and port of arrival, and the source of the information. The volumes in the set are:

___P. W. Filby and M. K. Meyer, PASSENGER AND IMMIGRATION LISTS INDEX, Gale Research Co., Detroit, MI, 1981-7, 8 volumes, further annual volumes being published.

Do not fail to look for every possible immigrant ancestor of yours in this very large index. Also of importance for locating passengers or passenger lists are:

___ H. Lancour, R. J. Wolfe, and P. W. Filby, BIBLIOGRAPHY OF SHIP PASSENGER LISTS, 1538-1900, Gale Research Co., Detroit, MI, 1981.

___ US National Archives and Records Service, GUIDE TO GENEA-LOGICAL RESEARCH IN THE NATIONAL ARCHIVES, The Service, Washington, DC, 1982, pages 41-57.

___ A. Eakle and J. Cerny, THE SOURCE, Ancestry Publishing Co., Salt Lake City, UT, 1984, pages 453-516.

___ P. W. Coldham, BONDED PASSENGERS TO AMERICA, 1615-1775, Genealogical Publishing Co., Baltimore, MD, 1981-3, 9 volumes.

___ R. J. Dickson, ULSTER IMMIGRATION TO COLONIAL AMER-ICA, 1718-75, Ulster-Scot Historical Foundation, Belfast, Ireland, 1976.

___ C. Boyer, SHIP PASSENGER LISTS, THE SOUTH, 1538-1825, The Author, Newhall, CA, 1980.

Then, you can look into some works (microfilms and books) dealing especially with immigration to GA. Among these are:

___ National Archives and Records Service, A SUPPLEMENTAL INDEX TO PASSENGER LISTS OF VESSELS ARRIVING AT ATLANTIC AND GULF PORTS, 1820-74, The Service, Washington, DC, Microfilm M334, 188 rolls. [Indexes Savannah 1820-3/25-6/31 and Charleston 1820-9.]

___ National Archives and Records Service, COPIES OF LISTS OF PASSENGERS ARRIVING AT MISCELLANEOUS PORTS ON THE ATLANTIC AND GULF COASTS, 1820-73, The Service, Washington, DC, Microfilm M575, 16 rolls. [Includes Darien 1823/5, Savannah 1820-2/24-6/31/47-51/65-7, and Charleston 1820-8.]

___ National Archives and Records Service, INDEX TO PASSENGERS OF VESSELS ARRIVING AT PORTS IN AL, FL, GA, AND SC, 1890-1924, The Service, Washington, DC, Microfilm T517, 26 rolls.

___ S. Urlsperger, DETAILED REPORTS ON THE SALZBURGER EMIGRANTS WHO SETTLED IN AMERICA, University of GA Press, Athens, GA, 1968, 2 volumes.

___ L. D. Cofer, QUEENSBORO OR THE IRISH TOWN AND ITS CITIZENS, The Author, Louisville, GA, 1977.

___E. M. Coulter and A. B. Saye, A LIST OF EARLY SETTLERS OF GA, 1732-41, Genealogical Publishing Co., Baltimore, MD, 1949(1983).

___C. Cunningham, MIGRATIONS, ACTUAL AND IMPLIED [FROM NC TO GA], The Author, Raleigh, NC, 1968.

___G. G. Davidson, EARLY RECORDS OF GA, WILKES COUNTY, Southern Historical Press, Easley, SC, 1967. [Persons coming into GA from NC, SC, and VA, 1773-5.]

___P. Gnann, GA SALZBURGER AND ALLIED FAMILIES, The Author, Savannah, GA, 1970.

___G. F. Jones, THE GERMANS OF COLONIAL GA, Genealogical Publishing Co., Baltimore, MD, 1986.

___IMMIGRATION AND EMIGRATION TO AND FROM GA, see GA Genealogical Magazine, especially issues of 1963-8/74/77-81; GA Genealogical Society Quarterly, especially issues of 1961/8/78; GA Genealogist, Our People, issue 7; GA Pioneers, issues of 1976. [Includes those coming from NC, SC, and VA.]

___Genealogical Enterprises, IMMIGRANTS FROM GREAT BRITAIN TO THE GA COLONY, The Enterprises, Morrow, GA, 1970.

___C. H. Hamlin, THEY WENT THATAWAY [VA TO GA], Genealogical Publishing Co., Baltimore, MD, 1974.

___F. M. Hawes, NEW ENGLANDERS IN THE GA CENSUS OF 1850, Typescript, GDAH, Atlanta, GA.

___H. B. Johnston, Jr., NORTH CAROLINIANS TO GA, GA Genealogical Magazine, Numbers 40-54, 1971-4.

___G. Raffalovich, A BIBLIOGRAPHY OF BOOKS AND ARTICLES RELATING TO IMMIGRATION TO GA, The Author, No place, 1938.

___J. Stephenson, SCOTCH-IRISH MIGRATION TO SC, REV. WILLIAM MARTIN AND HIS FIVE SHIPLOADS OF IMMIGRANTS, The Author, Washington, DC, 1971.

___W. C. Stewart, GONE TO GA, 1810-20, National Genealogical Society, Washington, DC, 1965.

___A. G. Voight, EBENEZER RECORD BOOK, The Author, Savannah, GA, 1929.

In addition to the above works, do not overlook the materials referenced in several other sections of this chapter: church records, city and county histories, colonial records, ethnic records, genealogical periodicals, naturalization records, published genealogies, and regional records. Of particular value are the earlier land records (crown grants, headright grants, bounty grants, and entries of claims) as described later in the section on land records.

In addition to works on immigration, there are also several volumes on _emigration_, that is, movements out of GA to settle areas mainly to the west. Among those which might help you in your search for a migratory GA progenitor are:

___H. Askew, 1850 CENSUS OF TX OF ALL PERSONS BORN IN GA, GA Genealogical Society Quarterly, Volume 8, Number 1, pages 1-62.

___D. A. Avant, FL PIONEERS AND THEIR AL, GA, NC, SC, MD, AND VA ANCESTORS, Southern Historical Press, Easley, SC, 1979.

___M. G. Bryan and W. Dumont, PASSPORTS ISSUED BY GOVERN-ORS OF GA, 1785-1820, National Genealogical Society, Washington, DC, 1959/64, 2 volumes.

___EMIGRATION AND IMMIGRATION FROM AND TO GA, see GA Genealogical Magazine, especially issues of 1963-8/74/77-81; GA Genealogical Society Quarterly, especially issues of 1961/8/78; GA Genealogist, Our People, Issue 7; GA Pioneers, issues of 1976. [Includes Georgians going to AL, AR, CA, LA, MS, NC, TN.]

___D. W. Potter, PASSPORTS OF SOUTHEASTERN PIONEERS, 1770-1832, The Author, Nashville, TN, 1982.

Numerous other emigration and immigration listings, especially ones published in periodicals, are referenced in the following works:

___O. K. Miller, MIGRATION, EMIGRATION, IMMIGRATION, Everton Publishers, Logan, UT, 19774/81, 2 volumes.

___J. E. Dorsey, GA GENEALOGY AND LOCAL HISTORY, A BIBLIOGRAPHY, Reprint Co, Spartanburg, SC, 1983, pages 15-16.

Finally, do not forget to look in the card catalogs of GDAH, UGL, WML, and GHS for immigration and emigration records.

16. Ethnic records

A brief review of the history of GA will indicate that the main ethnic groups which entered early GA were the English and Scots plus several small varied groups (Jews, Salzburgers, Moravians, other Germans, Italians, Swiss, French, and Welsh). During the formative years of the colony and continuing into the following century, many blacks were brought in and large numbers of Indians occupied much of the territory. Just before and after the Revolution, GA's frontier country was settled by native Americans coming in from states to the north of GA, many of these people having had Scotch-Irish origins. A number of these groups are treated in other sections of this chapter, particularly the sections on church records and emigration and immigration. This section will describe some finding aids, sources, and records on several major ethnic groups which are not treated elsewhere.

Finding aids, sources, and record compilations for <u>blacks</u> in GA are:

___MICROFILM RECORDS: BLACK HISTORY [A BIBLIOGRA-PHY], GDAH, Atlanta, GA, 1977.

___RECORDS OF BLACK AMERICANS in National Archives and Records Service, GENEALOGICAL RESEARCH IN THE NA, The Service, Washington, DC, 1982, Chapter 12.

___J. Cerny, BLACK ANCESTRAL RESEARCH in A. Eakle and J. Cerny, THE SOURCE, Ancestry Publishing Co., Salt Lake City, UT, 1984, Chapter 19.

___CARD INDEX TO PROMINENT BLACKS and LARGE COLLEC-TION OF BLACK HISTORY BOOKS, Arnett Library, Atlanta University, Atlanta, GA.

___NEWSLETTER OF AFRICAN-AMERICAN FAMILY HISTORY ASSOCIATION, The Association, 2077 Bent Creek Way, SW, Atlanta, GA 30B11.

___A. B. Caldwell, HISTORY OF THE AMERICAN NEGRO, GA EDITION, Caldwell, Atlanta, GA, 1920.

___A. H. Gordon, THE GA NEGRO, A HISTORY, Edwards Brothers, Ann Arbor, MI, 1937.

___J. Martin, SLAVE BILLS OF SALE PROJECT, African-American Family History Association, Atlanta, GA, 1986, 2 volumes.

___L. P. and M. S. Terrell, BLACKS IN AUGUSTA, A CHRONOLO-GY, Preston Publishers, Augusta, GA.

___C. V. Troup, DISTINGUISHED NEGRO GEORGIANS, Royal Publishing Co., Dallas, GA, 1962.

___O. S. Wightman, EARLY DAYS OF COASTAL GA, Frederica Association, St. Simons Island, GA, 1955.

___L. A. Windley, RUNAWAY SLAVE ADVERTISEMENTS, Greenwood Press, Westport, CT, 1983, Volume 4.

For the <u>Indians</u> (Creeks and Cherokees), the following finding aids, reference sources, books, and record compilations should be looked into:

___R. S. Davis, Jr., GUIDE TO NATIVE AMERICAN (INDIAN) RESEARCH SOURCES AT GDAH, The Author, Jasper, GA, 1985.

___Works Progress Administration, CHEROKEE INDIAN LETTERS, and CREEK INDIAN LETTERS, The Administration, typescript in the GDAH, Atlanta, GA.

___RECORDS OF AMERICAN INDIANS in National Archives and Records Service, GENEALOGICAL RESEARCH IN THE NA, The Service, Washington, DC, 1982, Chapter 11.

___G. J. Nixon, RECORDS RELATING TO NATIVE AMERICAN RE-SEARCH, in A. Eakle and J. Cerny, THE SOURCE, Ancestry Publishing Co., Salt Lake City, UT, 1984, Chapter 17.

___INDIAN SOURCE MATERIAL IN THE GDAH, Office of Indian Affairs, GDAH, Atlanta, GA, 1985.

___National Archives Atlanta Branch, SOURCES FOR INDIAN RESEARCH, The Branch, East Point, GA, 1981.

___INDIAN RECORD ARTICLES in GA Genealogical Society Quarterly, Volumes 3/5/8-9(1967-73), and GA Genealogist, State Records 1-60.

___PANTON, LESLIE, AND COMPANY PAPERS, FL Historical Society, Gainesville, FL, 26 reels of microfilm indexed. Records of a very large Indian trading company.

___D. W. Silar, THE EASTERN CHEROKEES, A CENSUS OF THE CHEROKEE NATION IN NC, TN, AL, AND GA IN 1851, Polyanthos Press, Cottonport, LA, 1972.

___J. E. Dorsey, GA GENEALOGY AND LOCAL HISTORY, A BIBLIOGRAPHY,Reprint Co, Spartanburg, SC, 1983, pages 35-6.

___M. Warren, MARRIAGES AND DEATHS, 1820-30, ABSTRACTED FROM EXTANT GA NEWSPAPERS (INCLUDING THE CHEROKEE PHOENIX), Heritage Papers, Danielsville, GA, 1972.

___M. B. Warren, WHITES AMONG THE CHEROKEES, Heritage Papers, Danielsville, GA, 1988.

___D. K. Hampton, CHEROKEE RESERVES, Baker Publishing Co., Oklahoma City, OK, 1980. [Cherokees settling in OK following the 1817/8 treaties.]

___L. Hays, INDIAN TREATIES, CESSIONS OF LAND IN GA, 1705-1837, WPA, Atlanta, GA, 1941.

___JOURNAL OF CHEROKEE STUDIES, Museum Complex, PO Box 770A, Cherokee, NC 28719.

___J. W. Jordan, CHEROKEE BY BLOOD, RECORDS OF EASTERN CHEROKEE ANCESTRY IN THE US COURT OF CLAIMS, 1906-10, Heritage Books, Bowie, MD, 1987-94, numerous volumes.

━━━━━━━━━━━━━━━━━━━━━━━━━━━━━━━

17. Gazetteers, atlases, and maps

━━━━━━━━━━━━━━━━━━━━━━━━━━━━━━━

Detailed informa-
tion regarding
GA geography is
exceptionally
useful to the genealogical searcher, especially with regard to land records.
These records usually mention locations in terms requiring an understanding of local geographical features. Several sorts of geographical aids are
valuable in this regard: gazetteers, atlases, and maps. Gazetteers are
volumes which list geographical features (towns, villages, crossroads,
settlements, districts, rivers, streams, creeks, hills, mountains, valleys,
coves, lakes, ponds), locate them, and sometimes give a few details
concerning them. An atlas is a collection of maps in book form. Among
the better gazetteer-type materials for GA are:

___J. H. Goff, PLACE NAMES OF GA, University of GA Press, Athens,
    GA, 1975,

___K. K. Krakow, GA PLACE NAMES, Winship Press, Macon, GA,
    1975.

___A. Sherwood, A GAZETTEER OF GA, 1827, Cherokee Publishing
    Co., Atlanta, GA, 1860(1970).

___A. D. Candler and C. A. Evans, GA, COMPRISING SKETCHES OF
    COUNTIES, TOWNS, EVENTS, INSTITUTIONS, AND
    PERSONS, State Historical Association, Atlanta, GA, 1906, 4
    volumes.

___M. R. Hemperley, A MAP OF GA'S EARLY ROADS AND
    TRAILS, CIRCA 1730-1850, GA Surveyor General Department,
    Atlanta, GA, 1979.

___M. R. Hemperley, CITIES, TOWNS, AND COMMUNITIES OF GA
    BETWEEN 1847 AND 1962, Southern Historical Press, Easley,
    SC, 1980.

___M. R. Hemperley, THE JOHN H. GOFF COLLECTION, A GUIDE,
    GA Surveyor General Department, Atlanta, GA, with the Goff
    Collection on forts, ferries, and roads.

___C. C. Jones, Jr., THE DEAD TOWNS OF GA, Reprint Co,
    Spartanburg, SC, 1878(1974).

___L. L. Knight, GA'S LANDMARKS, MEMORIALS, AND LEGENDS,
    Byrd Print Co., Atlanta, GA, 1913-4, 2 volumes.

___G. White, STATISTICS OF THE STATE OF GA, Reprint Co,
    Spartanburg, SC, 1849(1972).

Few atlases are available for GA counties, but three pre-1900 atlases for
GA cities were published: Atlanta(1893), Atlanta(1893), Macon(1878).
The above volumes will be found in GDAH, UGL, WML, GHS, and some
of them can be located in RL and LL. A useful atlas for the state is:

___J. C. Bonner, ATLAS FOR GA HISTORY, Duplicating Department, Milledgeville, GA, 1969.

The best collections of GA maps useful for genealogical research are in the GA Surveyor General Department, in UGL, and in GHS. Useful volumes describing many maps available in these and in other collections are:

___GA Historical Records Survey, CLASSIFIED INVENTORY OF GA MAPS, The Survey, East Point, GA, 1941.

___J. G. Blake, PRE-19TH CENTURY MAPS IN THE COLLECTION OF THE GA SURVEYOR GENERAL DEPARTMENT, The Department, Atlanta, GA, 1975.

___M. Johnsen, 19TH CENTURY MAPS IN THE COLLECTION OF THE GA SURVEYOR GENERAL DEPARTMENT, The Department, Atlanta, GA, 1981.

We will now draw your attention to several specialized types of maps which can assist you as you attempt to locate your progenitor's land and as you look for streams, roads, bridges, churches, cemeteries, towns, and villages in the vicinity. The sources of these maps or reference books to them will now be listed and then the maps will be described.

___B. M. and F. W. Hall, HALL'S ORIGINAL COUNTY MAP OF GA, GDAH, Atlanta, GA, 1898.

___Map Room, GA Department of Transportation, 2 Capital Square, Atlanta, GA 30334. [Place to purchase GA county maps.]

___Branch of Distribution, Topographic Maps of GA, US Geological Survey, 503 National Center, 12201 Sunrise Valley Drive, Reston, VA 22092. Phone 1-800-872-6277.

___R. W. Stephenson, LAND OWNERSHIP MAPS, Library of Congress, Washington, DC, 1967. [County maps showing names of land owners on them.]

___J. R. Hebert, PANORAMIC MAPS OF ANGLO-AMERICAN CITIES IN THE LIBRARY OF CONGRESS, The Library, Washington, DC, 1974.

___J. Sutherland, SANBORN [FIRE INSURANCE] MAPS HELD BY THE MAP COLLECTION, UGL, Athens, GA, 1981.

___Library of Congress, FIRE INSURANCE [SANBORN] MAPS IN THE LIBRARY OF CONGRESS, The Library, Washington, DC, 1981, pages 106-19. [Pre-1900 maps of 78 GA cities and towns, much detail.]

___W. Thorndale and W. Dollarhide, MAP GUIDE TO THE US
FEDERAL CENSUSES OF GA, American Genealogical Lending
Library, Bountiful, UT, 1985.

The first reference in the list is to Hall's map. It is important to
genealogists for tracing counties as they developed in GA. The map is
available for purchase from the GDAH. The second item above is the
address to which you may write in order to buy good GA county maps
which show considerable detail. The third reference is the address of the
Geological Survey Office from which highly detailed maps of GA can be
purchased. The Survey has mapped the entire state and has issued a
series of hundreds of excellent maps, each covering a very small area. Ask
them for the free Index of Topographic Maps of GA, then from it order
the maps which are of interest to you. The maps you will want are called
Topographic Quadrangle Maps. The fourth item refers you to a list of
county maps which show the names of land owners on them. Such maps
are available for the following counties in the pre-1900 era:
Chatham(1816/75), Cherokee(1895), Clarke(1893), Coffee(1891), Floyd
(1895), Fulton(1872), Hart(1889), Jefferson(1879), Oglethorpe(1894),
Paulding(1896), Walker(1893), Washington(1897), and Whitfield(1879).
The fifth reference is a book which lists GA city and town panoramic
maps which are available from the Library of Congress. These maps are
careful depictions of cities as they would appear from a balloon flying
above them. For the time before 1900, these are available: Albany(1885),
Atlanta(1871/92), Columbus(1886), Macon(1887), Quitman(1885), Talla-
poosa(1892), Thomasville(1885/96), and Valdosta(1885). The sixth and
seventh items refer to volumes which list city and town maps which were
drawn for fire insurance purposes. The earliest ones for GA date back to
1885. The eighth listing is a folder which contains maps showing counties
in each of the years in which a federal census was taken. The maps are
valuable aids in using the census records.

---

18. Genealogical indexes

There are a number of indexes
and compilations for the colony
and state of GA which list very
large numbers of names. These
are of considerable utility because they may save you going through many
small volumes and detailed records, especially in the early stages of your
search for GA ancestors. The nation-wide indexes and compilations of
this sort include:

___SURNAME INDEX and INTERNATIONAL GENEALOGICAL
INDEX at FHL, Salt Lake City, UT, also available at FHC. [See

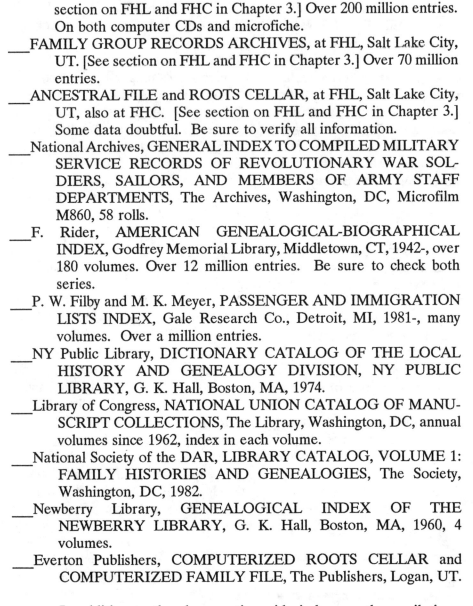

section on FHL and FHC in Chapter 3.] Over 200 million entries. On both computer CDs and microfiche.
__FAMILY GROUP RECORDS ARCHIVES, at FHL, Salt Lake City, UT. [See section on FHL and FHC in Chapter 3.] Over 70 million entries.
__ANCESTRAL FILE and ROOTS CELLAR, at FHL, Salt Lake City, UT, also at FHC. [See section on FHL and FHC in Chapter 3.] Some data doubtful. Be sure to verify all information.
__National Archives, GENERAL INDEX TO COMPILED MILITARY SERVICE RECORDS OF REVOLUTIONARY WAR SOL-DIERS, SAILORS, AND MEMBERS OF ARMY STAFF DEPARTMENTS, The Archives, Washington, DC, Microfilm M860, 58 rolls.
__F. Rider, AMERICAN GENEALOGICAL-BIOGRAPHICAL INDEX, Godfrey Memorial Library, Middletown, CT, 1942-, over 180 volumes. Over 12 million entries. Be sure to check both series.
__P. W. Filby and M. K. Meyer, PASSENGER AND IMMIGRATION LISTS INDEX, Gale Research Co., Detroit, MI, 1981-, many volumes. Over a million entries.
__NY Public Library, DICTIONARY CATALOG OF THE LOCAL HISTORY AND GENEALOGY DIVISION, NY PUBLIC LIBRARY, G. K. Hall, Boston, MA, 1974.
__Library of Congress, NATIONAL UNION CATALOG OF MANU-SCRIPT COLLECTIONS, The Library, Washington, DC, annual volumes since 1962, index in each volume.
__National Society of the DAR, LIBRARY CATALOG, VOLUME 1: FAMILY HISTORIES AND GENEALOGIES, The Society, Washington, DC, 1982.
__Newberry Library, GENEALOGICAL INDEX OF THE NEWBERRY LIBRARY, G. K. Hall, Boston, MA, 1960, 4 volumes.
__Everton Publishers, COMPUTERIZED ROOTS CELLAR and COMPUTERIZED FAMILY FILE, The Publishers, Logan, UT.

In addition to the above nation-wide indexes and compilations, there are a sizable number of large indexes and compilations dealing exclusively with GA. Among the most notable of these are:
__SUBSTITUTE CENSUS INDEXES and REGULAR CENSUS INDEXES FOR GA, listed in Section 6, this Chapter. [Millions of entries.]

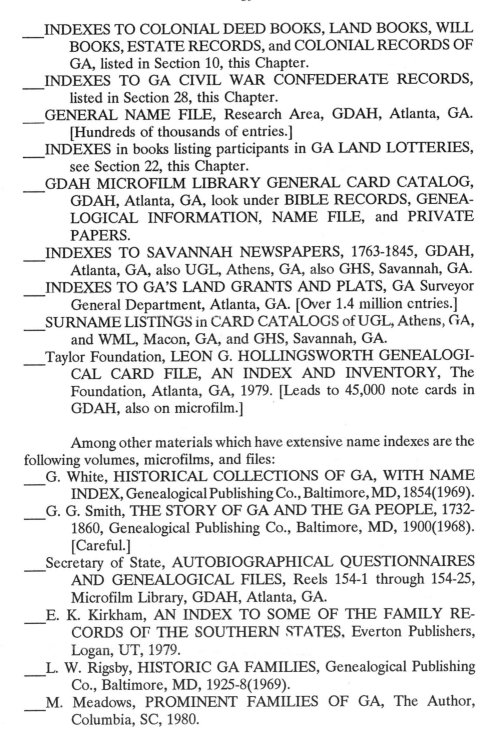

___INDEXES TO COLONIAL DEED BOOKS, LAND BOOKS, WILL BOOKS, ESTATE RECORDS, and COLONIAL RECORDS OF GA, listed in Section 10, this Chapter.

___INDEXES TO GA CIVIL WAR CONFEDERATE RECORDS, listed in Section 28, this Chapter.

___GENERAL NAME FILE, Research Area, GDAH, Atlanta, GA. [Hundreds of thousands of entries.]

___INDEXES in books listing participants in GA LAND LOTTERIES, see Section 22, this Chapter.

___GDAH MICROFILM LIBRARY GENERAL CARD CATALOG, GDAH, Atlanta, GA, look under BIBLE RECORDS, GENEALOGICAL INFORMATION, NAME FILE, and PRIVATE PAPERS.

___INDEXES TO SAVANNAH NEWSPAPERS, 1763-1845, GDAH, Atlanta, GA, also UGL, Athens, GA, also GHS, Savannah, GA.

___INDEXES TO GA'S LAND GRANTS AND PLATS, GA Surveyor General Department, Atlanta, GA. [Over 1.4 million entries.]

___SURNAME LISTINGS in CARD CATALOGS of UGL, Athens, GA, and WML, Macon, GA, and GHS, Savannah, GA.

___Taylor Foundation, LEON G. HOLLINGSWORTH GENEALOGICAL CARD FILE, AN INDEX AND INVENTORY, The Foundation, Atlanta, GA, 1979. [Leads to 45,000 note cards in GDAH, also on microfilm.]

Among other materials which have extensive name indexes are the following volumes, microfilms, and files:

___G. White, HISTORICAL COLLECTIONS OF GA, WITH NAME INDEX, Genealogical Publishing Co., Baltimore, MD, 1854(1969).

___G. G. Smith, THE STORY OF GA AND THE GA PEOPLE, 1732-1860, Genealogical Publishing Co., Baltimore, MD, 1900(1968). [Careful.]

___Secretary of State, AUTOBIOGRAPHICAL QUESTIONNAIRES AND GENEALOGICAL FILES, Reels 154-1 through 154-25, Microfilm Library, GDAH, Atlanta, GA.

___E. K. Kirkham, AN INDEX TO SOME OF THE FAMILY RECORDS OF THE SOUTHERN STATES, Everton Publishers, Logan, UT, 1979.

___L. W. Rigsby, HISTORIC GA FAMILIES, Genealogical Publishing Co., Baltimore, MD, 1925-8(1969).

___M. Meadows, PROMINENT FAMILIES OF GA, The Author, Columbia, SC, 1980.

___L. L. Knight, GA'S LANDMARKS, MEMORIALS, AND LEGENDS, Byrd Print Co., Atlanta, GA, 1913-4, 2 volumes.

___INDEX TO GA POOR SCHOOL AND ACADEMY RECORDS, 1826-50, Taylor Foundation, Atlanta, GA, 1981.

___R. S. Davis, Jr., THE GA BLACK BOOK, MORBID, MACABRE, AND DISGUSTING RECORDS OF GENEALOGICAL VALUE, Southern Historical Press, Easley, SC, 1982/81, 2 volumes. Prison, asylum, murder, and divorce records.

___R. S. Davis, Jr., A RESEARCHER'S LIBRARY OF GA HISTORY, GENEALOGY, AND RECORD SOURCES, Southern Historical Press, Easley, SC, 1987/91, 2 volumes. About 30,000 names.

___CARD FILE OF GENEALOGICAL EXCHANGE CARDS, Research Area, GDAH, Atlanta, GA.

___J. H. Austin, THE GEORGIANS, GENEALOGIES OF PIONEER FAMILIES, Genealogical Publishing Co., Baltimore, MD, 1984.

Most of the volumes mentioned in this section are available in GDAH, UGL, WML, and GHS.

---

19. Genealogical periodicals

Several genealogical periodicals and some historical periodicals carrying genealogical data or aids have been or are being published for GA. These journals and newsletters contain genealogies, local history data, genealogical records, family queries and answers, book reviews, and other pertinent information. If you had a GA progenitor, you will find it of great value to subscribe to one or more of the state-wide periodicals, as well as any periodicals published in the region, county, or city where he/she lived. Periodicals pertinent to GA research may be divided into three classes: (1) those that have state-wide coverage, (2) those that have regional coverage, and (3) those that cover individual counties or cities.

Chief among the periodicals which have a state-wide coverage of GA are:

___FAMILY PUZZLERS, weekly, 1964-, Heritage Papers, Danielsville, GA.

___GA GENEALOGICAL MAGAZINE, quarterly, 1961-, Southern Historical Press, Easley, SC.

___GA GENEALOGICAL SOCIETY QUARTERLY, 1964-, GA Genealogical Society, Atlanta, GA.

___GA GENEALOGICAL SURVEY, 1891-, Nancy J. Crowell, Riverdale, GA.

___GA GENEALOGIST, quarterly, 1970-, Heritage Papers, Danielsville, GA.

___GA HISTORICAL QUARTERLY, GA Historical Society, Savannah, GA.

___GA PIONEERS, quarterly, 1964-, GA Pioneers, Albany, GA.

___GENEALOGICAL AND HISTORICAL NEWS FOR GA, bimonthly, 1985-, The News, Cumberland Gap, TN.

___GENEALOGICAL GAZETTE, Genealogical Society for the Blind and Physically Handicapped, Atlanta, GA.

___NEWSLETTER OF THE GA ASSOCIATION OF HISTORIANS, The Association, GDAH, Atlanta, GA.

___SOUTHERN GENEALOGIST'S EXCHANGE QUARTERLY, 1957 ff., A. C. Shaw, Jacksonville, FL, and J. D. Wells, Hampton, GA. [Name index in each issue.]

___THEY WERE HERE, GA GENEALOGICAL RECORDS, quarterly, 1965-, F. A. Wynd, Albany, GA.

There are a number of indexes to some of these volumes which can save you considerable time in your research.

___S. E. Lucas, Jr., MASTER INDEX TO THE GA GENEALOGICAL MAGAZINE, NUMBERS 1-46(1961-72), Southern Historical Press, Easley, SC, 1973.

___J. E. Dorsey, GA GENEALOGY AND LOCAL HISTORY, A BIBLIOGRAPHY, Reprint Co, Spartanburg, SC, 1983. [Lists pertinent articles from many genealogical journals, look under county headings.]

___M. B. Warren, GA BIBLIOGRAPHY OF ARTICLES IN PRINT IN GENEALOGICAL MAGAZINES THROUGH AUGUST 1967, Heritage Papers, Danielsville, GA, 1967.

___INDEXES TO GA GENEALOGICAL PERIODICALS (Family Puzzlers, GA Genealogical Magazine, GA Life, GA Historical Quarterly to 1932, Collections of the GA Historical Society to 1932, and others), Research Area, GDAH, Atlanta, GA.

The regional journals, newsletters, and magazines which will be useful to you if your ancestors come from the areas of interest are:

___ANCESTORING, biannual, 1980-, Augusta Genealogical Society, Augusta, GA. [For the Richmond County area.]

___ANCESTORS UNLIMITED, quarterly, 1979-, Ancestors Unlimited, Jonesboro, GA. [Clayton, Fayette, and Henry County area.]

___ARMCHAIR RESEARCHER, quarterly, 1980-, Joel D. Wells, Hampton, GA. [Area southwest of Atlanta.]

___CENTRAL GA GENEALOGICAL SOCIETY QUARTERLY, 1979-, The Society, Warner Robins, GA.

___FOXFIRE, Foxfire, Rabun Gap, GA. [History and folklore of North GA.]

___HEARD HERITAGE, quarterly, 1976-, Lynda S. Eller, Lanett, AL. [Heard County area.]

___HUXFORD GENEALOGICAL SOCIETY QUARTERLY, The Society, Homerville, GA. [The Wiregrass or South GA area.]

___GENEALOGICAL SOCIETY OF ORIGINAL MUSCOGEE COUNTY NEWSLETTER, bimonthly, 1980-, The Society, Columbus, GA.

___NORTH GA JOURNAL, Northeast GA Historical and Genealogical Society, Dahlonega, GA.

___NORTHWEST GA HISTORICAL AND GENEALOGICAL SOCIETY QUARTERLY, 1968-, The Society, Rome, GA.

___WEST CENTRAL GA GENEALOGICAL SOCIETY NEWSLETTER, quarterly, 1982-, The Society, LaGrange, GA.

___WHITFIELD-MURRAY COUNTY HISTORICAL QUARTERLY, 1977-, Whitfield-Murray Historical and Genealogical Society, Dalton, GA.

Finally, there are several important county and city genealogical and/or historical periodicals which will be meaningful to your progenitor research if your forebears lived there. Among them are:

___ATLANTA HISTORICAL JOURNAL, Atlanta Historical Society, Atlanta, GA.

___CARROLL COUNTY GENEALOGICAL QUARTERLY, 1980-, Carroll County Genealogical Society, Carrollton, GA.

___COWETA COUNTY GENEALOGICAL SOCIETY MAGAZINE, The Society, Newnan, GA.

___DOUGLAS COUNTY GENEALOGY, quarterly, 1978-, Joe Braggett, Douglasville, GA.

___FAMILY TREE, quarterly, 1979-, Cobb County Genealogical Society, Marietta, GA.

___FORSYTH COUNTY GENEALOGICAL AND HISTORICAL SOCIETY QUARTERLY, The Society, Rome, GA.

___GWINNETT HISTORICAL SOCIETY NEWSLETTER, 1975-, The Society, Lawrenceville, GA.

___HARRIS COUNTY, GA, AND HER PEOPLE, quarterly, Family Tree Publications, LaGrange, GA.

___LOWNDES COUNTY HISTORICAL SOCIETY NEWSLETTER, The Society, Valdosta, GA.

___PAPERS OF THE ATHENS HISTORICAL SOCIETY, The Society, Athens, GA.

___RICHMOND COUNTY HISTORY, quarterly, Richmond County Historical Society, Augusta, GA.

___SOUTHERN ECHOES, monthly, Augusta Genealogical Society, Augusta, GA.

___SOUTHERN ROOTS AND SHOOTS, quarterly, Delta Genealogical Society, Rossville, GA.

___TROUP COUNTY, GA, AND HER PEOPLE, The Family Tree, La-Grange, GA.

The best sources for GA genealogical periodicals are the GDAH, UGL, WML, and GHS. Pertinent local periodicals will be found in RL and LL. The largest number of indexes is located in GDAH.

Not only do articles pertaining to GA genealogy appear in the above publications, they are also printed in other genealogical periodicals. The best way to locate these articles is through indexes to the major genealogical periodicals. These indexes are:

___For periodicals published 1858-1952, consult D. L. Jacobus, INDEX TO GENEALOGICAL PERIODICALS, Genealogical Publishing Co., Baltimore, MD, 1973.

___For periodicals published 1847-1985, then annually 1986-present, consult Allen County Public Library Foundation, PERIODICAL SOURCE INDEX (PERSI), Allen County Public Library Foundation, Fort Wayne, IN, 1986-.

___For periodicals published 1962-9 and 1974-present, consult the annual volumes by various editors, E. S. Rogers, G. E. Russell, L. C. Towle, and C. M. Mayhew, GENEALOGICAL PERIODICAL ANNUAL INDEX, various publishers, most recently Heritage Books, Bowie, MD, 1962-9, 1974-present.

These index volumes should be sought in GDAH, UGL, WML, GHS, and GSU(available through FHC), most LGL, some RL, and a few LL. In them, you ought to consult all GA listings, then all listings under the counties which concern you, as well as listings under family names (if included in the indexes).

20. Genealogical societies

In the state of GA various societies for the study of genealogy, the discovery of hereditary lineages, the accumulation of data, and the publication of the materials have been organized. The resident members of these societies are generally very knowledgeable about the background, the early families, and the available records of their areas of concern. By consulting them, you can often save valuable time as they guide you in your work, and as you make use of their record compilations and collections. The local societies are also the best organizations to contact in order to find if someone else is working or has worked on your family lines. It is advisable for all GA researchers to join the state-wide organization as well as the local organizations in the area(s) of their interest. All correspondence with such societies should be accompanied by an SASE.

The major state-wide society for genealogical research in GA is:
___GA GENEALOGICAL SOCIETY, PO Box 38066, Atlanta, GA 30334.
Among other societies in GA which are active at the present time are the following locally-oriented ones:
___ALPHARETTA OLD MILTON COUNTY GA HISTORICAL AND GENEALOGICAL SOCIETY, 10 South Main St., Alpharetta, GA 30201.
___ANCESTORS UNLIMITED GENEALOGICAL SOCIETY, PO Box 490336, College Park, GA 30349.
___AUGUSTA GENEALOGICAL SOCIETY, PO Box 3743, Augusta, GA 30904.
___CARROLL COUNTY GENEALOGICAL SOCIETY, PO Box 576, Carrollton, GA 30117.
___CENTRAL GA GENEALOGICAL SOCIETY, PO Box 2024, Warner Robins, GA 31099.
___COBB COUNTY GENEALOGICAL SOCIETY, PO Box 1413, Marietta, GA 30064.
___COWETA COUNTY GENEALOGICAL SOCIETY, Highway 54, Route 1, Sharpsburg, GA 30277.
___DELTA GENEALOGICAL SOCIETY, 504 McFarland Avenue, Rossville, GA 30741.
___FORSYTH COUNTY HISTORICAL AND GENEALOGICAL SOCIETY, PO Box 762, Cummings, GA 30130.
___GA GENEALOGICAL RESEARCHERS ASSOCIATION, 225 Johnson, #43A, Forest Park, GA 30050.
___GENEALOGICAL SOCIETY OF THE ORIGINAL MUSCOGEE COUNTY, 120 Bradley Drive, Columbus, GA 31906.
___HUXFORD GENEALOGICAL SOCIETY, PO Box 595, Homerville, GA 31634.
___MUSCOGEE GENEALOGICAL SOCIETY, PO Box 761, Columbus, GA 31902.

___NORTHEAST GA HISTORICAL AND GENEALOGICAL
SOCIETY, PO Box 907039, Gainesville, GA 30501.

___NORTHWEST GA HISTORICAL AND GENEALOGICAL
SOCIETY, PO Box 5063, Rome, GA 30161.

___ORANGEBURG GERMAN-SWISS GENEALOGICAL SOCIETY,
PO Box 367, Columbus, GA 31902.

___RICHARD RATCLIFF GENEALOGICAL SOCIETY, Rt. 5, Box
454, Tocca, GA 30577.

___SAVANNAH RIVER VALLEY GENEALOGICAL SOCIETY, Hart
County Library, Benson St., Hartwell, GA 30643.

___SOUTH GA GENEALOGICAL SOCIETY, PO Box 602,
Thomasville, GA 31798.

___SOUTHWEST GA GENEALOGICAL SOCIETY, PO Box 4672,
Albany, GA 31706.

___WEST CENTRAL GA GENEALOGICAL SOCIETY, PO Box 2291,
LaGrange, GA 30241.

___WEST GA GENEALOGICAL SOCIETY, PO Box 1051, LaGrange,
GA 30241.

___WHITFIELD-MURRAY HISTORICAL AND GENEALOGICAL
SOCIETY, 715 Chattanooga Avenue, Dalton, GA 30720.

Two highly-specialized genealogical societies with national appeal
are located in GA:

___AFRICAN-AMERICAN FAMILY HISTORICAL ASSOCIATION,
PO Box 115268, Atlanta, GA 30310.

___NATIONAL SOCIETY OF COMPUTER GENEALOGISTS, 2815
Clearview Place, Atlanta, GA 30340.

21. Historical societies

In addition to its genealogical societies, GA has many historical societies, foundations, and associations. These societies engage in various activities including the maintenance of libraries, archives, and museums, the publication of newsletters, journals, pamphlets, and books, the collection and indexing of records, and the preservation and upkeep of historic sites. Some of the historical societies have genealogical interests and some do not, but they are all of potential importance to family searchers, since historical orientation is indispensible to genealogy. Below are some of the larger historical societies of GA. Write to those that are in your ancestors' region, ask about their activities, and request membership information. The major state-wide GA historical society is a very old organization which maintains a notable library and archive. It will be discussed in detail in Chapter 3, because it has very large holdings of genealogical materials.

___GA HISTORICAL SOCIETY, 501 Whitaker St., Savannah, GA.

The GA historical organizations listed below are arranged by county. The county appears in parentheses before the organization name if the county is not obvious from the title.

___HISTORICAL SOCIETY OF ALMA, BACON COUNTY, PO Box 2026, Alma, GA 31510.

___(Baldwin County) OLD CAPITAL HISTORICAL SOCIETY, PO Box 4, Milledgeville, GA 31601.

___(Bibb County) MIDDLE GA HISTORICAL SOCIETY, 935 High St., Macon, GA 31207.

___(Bibb County) GA BAPTIST HISTORICAL SOCIETY, Mercer University Library, Macon, GA 31207.

___(Camden County) GUALE HISTORICAL SOCIETY, PO Box 398, St. Marys, GA 31558.

___CARROLL COUNTY HISTORICAL SOCIETY, PO Box 160, Carrollton, GA 30117.

___CHARLTON COUNTY HISTORICAL SOCIETY, Route 3, Box 142C, Folkston, GA 31537.

___(Chatham County) COASTAL HERITAGE SOCIETY, 1 Fort Jackson Rd., Savannah, GA 31402.

___(Chatham County) GA SALZBURGER SOCIETY, 9375 Whitfield Ave., Savannah, GA 31406.

___CHATOOGA COUNTY HISTORICAL SOCIETY, 200 S. Commerce St., Summerville, GA 30747.

___CHEROKEE COUNTY HISTORICAL SOCIETY, PO Box 1287, Canton, GA 30114.

___COLQUITT COUNTY HISTORICAL SOCIETY, Moultrie, GA 31768.

___COWETA CHATTER GENEALOGICAL & HISTORICAL SOCIETY, Highway 54, Rt. 1, Sharpsburg, GA 30277.

___NEWNAN-COWETA (County) HISTORICAL SOCIETY, 30 Temple Ave., Newnan, GA 30263.

___DEKALB (County) HISTORICAL SOCIETY, Old Courthouse, Decatur, GA 30030.

___EARLY COUNTY HISTORICAL SOCIETY, 255 North Main, Blakeley, GA 31723.

___EMANUEL (County) HISTORIC PRESERVATION SOCIETY, PO Box 1101, Swainsboro, GA 30401.

___FAYETTE COUNTY HISTORICAL SOCIETY, PO Box 241, Fayetteville, GA 30214.

___FORSYTH COUNTY GENEALOGICAL & HISTORICAL SOCIETY, PO Box 762, Cummings, GA 30130.

___(Fulton County) ATLANTA HISTORICAL SOCIETY, 3101 St. Andrews Dr., NW. Atlanta, GA 30305.

___(Glynn County) COASTAL GA HISTORICAL SOCIETY, 600 Beachview, St. Simons Island, GA 31522.

___(Glynn County) HISTORICAL SOCIETY OF THE SOUTH GA CONFERENCE, UNITED METHODIST CHURCH, PO Box 407, St. Simons Island, GA 31522.

___GORDON COUNTY HISTORICAL SOCIETY, 102 Court St., Calhoun, GA 30701.

___GRIFFIN HISTORICAL PRESERVATION SOCIETY, PO Box 196, Griffin, GA 30224.

___GWINNETT COUNTY HISTORICAL SOCIETY, PO Box 261, Lawrenceville, GA 30246.

___HARALSON COUNTY HISTORICAL SOCIETY, Courthouse Square, Buchanan, GA 30113.

___JOHNSON COUNTY HISTORICAL SOCIETY, PO Box 86, Wrightsville, GA 31096.

___BARNESVILLE-LAMAR COUNTY HISTORICAL SOCIETY, 888 Thomaston Rd., Barnesville, GA 30204.

___LAURENS COUNTY HISTORICAL SOCIETY, Bellevue and Academy, Dublin, GA 31021.

___LEE COUNTY HISTORICAL SOCIETY, PO Box 393, Leesburg, GA 31763.

___LIBERTY COUNTY HISTORICAL SOCIETY, PO Box 797, Hinesville, GA 31313.

___LOWNDES COUNTY HISTORICAL SOCIETY, 305 West Central Ave., Valdosta, GA 31601.

___(Macon County) ANDERSONVILLE NATIONAL HISTORICAL SITE, Highway 49, Andersonville, GA 31711.

___(McDuffie County) WRIGHTSBORO QUAKER COMMUNITY FOUNDATION, 633 Hemlock Dr., Thomson, GA 30824.

___(McIntosh County) FORT KING GEORGE HISTORIC SITE, Fort King George Dr., Darien, GA 31305.

___MONROE COUNTY HISTORICAL SOCIETY, PO Box 401, Forsyth, GA 31629.

___WHITFIELD-MURRAY (Counties) HISTORICAL SOCIETY, 715 Chattanooga Ave., Dalton, GA 30720.

___(Muscogee County) HISTORIC COLUMBUS FOUNDATION, 700 Broadway, Columbus, GA 31901.

___(Newton County) OXFORD HISTORICAL SHRINE SOCIETY, PO Box 243, Oxford, GA 30267.

___EATONTON-PUTNAM COUNTY HISTORICAL SOCIETY, PO Box 331, Eatonton, GA 31024.

___NORTHEAST GA HISTORICAL & GENEALOGICAL SOCIETY, PO Box 907039, Gainesville, GA 30501.

___NORTHWEST GA HISTORICAL & GENEALOGICAL SOCIETY, PO Box 5063, Rome, GA 30161.

___RANDOLPH COUNTY HISTORICAL SOCIETY, PO Box 456, Cuthbert, GA 31740.

___RICHMOND COUNTY HISTORICAL SOCIETY, 2500 Walton Way, Augusta, GA 30910.

___ROCKDALE COUNTY HISTORICAL SOCIETY, PO Box 351, Conyers, GA 30207.

___(Spalding County) GRIFFIN HISTORICAL AND PRESERVATION SOCIETY, 406 North Hill St., Griffin, GA 30223.

___STEWART COUNTY HISTORICAL COMMISSION, PO Box 818, Lumpkin, GA 31815.

___TALIAFERRO COUNTY HISTORICAL SOCIETY, Monument St., Crawfordsville, GA 30631.

___TATTNALL COUNTY HISTORICAL SOCIETY, Reidsville, GA 30453.

___THOMAS COUNTY HISTORICAL SOCIETY, 725 North Dawson St., Thomasville, GA 31792.

___TREUTLEN COUNTY HISTORICAL SOCIETY, County Courthouse, Soperton, GA 30457.

___(Troup County) CHATTAHOOCHIE VALLEY HISTORICAL SOCIETY, 1213 Fifth Ave., West Point, GA 31833.

___UPSON COUNTY HISTORICAL SOCIETY, PO Box 363, Thomaston, GA 30286.

___WALKER COUNTY HISTORICAL SOCIETY, PO Box 707, Lafayette, GA 30728.

___WHITE COUNTY HISTORICAL SOCIETY, Town Square, Cleveland, GA 30528.

___WHITFIELD-MURRAY (Counties) HISTORICAL SOCIETY, 715 Chattanooga Ave., Dalton, GA 30720.

___WASHINGTON-WILKES (County) HISTORICAL FOUNDATION, 308 East Robert Toombs Ave., Washington, GA 30673.

More complete lists of GA historical organizations of various sorts are provided in these publications:

___ S. Flocks, DIRECTORY OF GA HISTORICAL ORGANIZATIONS AND RESOURCES, GDAH, Atlanta, GA, latest edition.

___ DIRECTORY, HISTORICAL SOCIETIES AND AGENCIES IN THE USE AND CANADA, American Association for State and Local History, Nashville, TN, latest edition.

---

22. Land records

One of the most important types of GA genealogical records is that type which deals with land. This is so because throughout most of its history a very large fraction of the GA population was made up of land owners. In addition, from its beginnings into the 1830s, land was widely available and either free or inexpensive. There are basically seven categories of land records in GA: (1) trustee leases and grants, 1733-55, (2) royal headright grants, 1755-75, (3) state headright grants, roughly 1783-1909, (4) state Revolutionary War bounty grants, (5) state land lottery grants, 1805-32, (6) colonial conveyances such as deeds, mortgages, and land court records, 1755-77/87, and (7) county conveyances such as deeds, mortgages, and land court records, 1777/87-present. Three basic types of land records are involved in these seven categories: trustee leases, grants of various sorts, and conveyances (deeds, mortgages, and other records of land transfers). The word grant refers to the transfer of land from the colony or the state to the first private owner. A deed represents the conveyance (or transfer) of land from one private owner to another.

The trustee leases and grants refer to the 1733-55 period when all land in GA was controlled by the Trustees (see section 2, Chapter 1). Land was given to new settlers, but it could not be sold; it could only be passed on to male heirs. These regulations were abolished in about a decade, and land began to be granted both to charity settlers in small amounts and to entrepreneurs in large amounts for plantations. These plantation developers brought white servants over on indentures (contracts to work 4-7 years to pay back their transportation costs). The royal headright grants relate to parcels of land given by the Royal Colonial Government during 1755-75 under a headright system. That is, a settler received 200 acres plus 50 acres more for each family member and each slave he brought in.

State headright grants were lands given under a headright system by the state of GA from approximately 1783 through 1909. State Revolutionary War bounty grants were gifts of land (250 or 287.5 acres) to those who fought for GA during the war (both Georgians and non-

Georgians) and to those citizens of the new state who remained loyal to the Revolutionary cause. At first (1781) grants were 250 acres, then (1784) 287.5 acres. State land lotteries were held in 1805, 1807, 1820, 1821, 1827, and two in 1832. In these lotteries land tracts were given to residents of GA through lotteries which they could enter free. Winners could receive land they won by the payment of a small grant fee. In the various lotteries, extra chances were sometimes given to certain persons such as orphans, military veterans, widows, and others. Before the Revolution (from before 1755 to 1777/87), colonial conveyances (transfers of land from one private owner to another) were all recorded in Savannah. All deeds, mortgages, land court records, and other land transfer documents were handled at the colony level. However, after the Revolution (1777/87 to the present), such transfers or conveyances were carried out and recorded in the counties (county conveyances). That is, before the War for Independence, deeds and other land documents representing private transfers are to be found at the colony level, after the War at the county level.

In section 10 of Chapter 1, where GA county formation was treated, the distribution of colony/state land through grants during 1733-1909 was described. A map illustrating this was presented as Figure 5. You should carefully review that map. This will show you that the land which rested in the eight easternmost original counties was distributed by headright grants. These original counties were Camden, Glynn, Liberty, Chatham, Effingham, Burke, Richmond, and Wilkes. The land which was involved in the next two original counties (Franklin and Washington) was given by both headright and bounty grants. And all the rest of GA land was granted in the land lotteries.

Now, let us indicate where these important and voluminous records can be found and how you can go about using the available indexes to find your ancestor(s) in them. All colonial and state grant and lottery records are in the GA Surveyor General Department which is located in the same building as the GDAH. Microfilm copies of many of them are in GDAH. Included in these records are the grant and lottery documents, recorded and loose plats (surveys), military and civilian bounty certificates, and miscellaneous loose papers. Keys to this massive collection are a number of published volumes which contain much of the data and index practically all of it. For the Trustee Period, you should consult:

__P. Bryant, ENTRY OF CLAIMS FOR GA LANDHOLDERS, 1733-
   55, State Printing Office, Atlanta, GA, 1975.

___COLONIAL LAND BOOKS: CLAIMS BOOK M(U3), 1755-7, Microfilm Reel 40-43, GDAH, Atlanta, GA, indexed.

For grants and related land records of the Royal Colony and the state until 1909, the following items should be used. Some of them also contain information on the previous Trustee Period. The first item below is particularly important because it is a published index to this vast set of records which refers to over 61000 names.

___S. E. Lucas, Jr., INDEX TO THE HEADRIGHT AND BOUNTY LAND GRANTS OF GA, 1756-1909, Southern Historical Press, Easley, SC, 1970(1981).

___M. B. Warren, GA GOVERNOR AND COUNCIL JOURNALS, 1753-, Heritage Papers, Danielsville, GA, 1992-, several volumes. Petitions for land grants.

___M. B. Warren, GA LAND OWNERS MEMORIALS, 1758-76, Heritage Papers, Danielsville, GA, 1988.

___R. S. Davis, Jr., WILKES COUNTY PAPERS, 1773-1833, Southern Historical Press, Easley, SC, 1979. Early frontier settlers, pp. 3-21.

___G. G. Davidson, EARLY RECORDS OF GA, WILKES COUNTY, Burke Company, Macon, GA, 1932, Volume 1. Early frontier settlers, pp. 2-29.

___GA LAND GRANTS AND PLATS, 1755-1909, originals and indexes to them, GA Surveyor General Department, in building with GDAH, Atlanta, GA.

___LOOSE LAND RECORDS FOR GA, originals, GA Surveyor General Department, in building with GDAH, Atlanta, GA.

___GA COLONIAL AND STATE LAND GRANTS AND PLATS, 1755-1906, microfilms, look under Surveyor General Department listings in GA Official Records Card Catalog, Microfilm Library, Atlanta, GA.

___GA LAND MEMORIALS, QUIT RENTS, AND LAND COURT MINUTES, microfilms, look under Colony in GA Official Records Card Catalog, Microfilm Library, GDAH, Atlanta, GA.

___M. R. Hemperley and P. Bryant, ENGLISH CROWN GRANTS IN GA, 1755-75, GA Surveyor General Department, Atlanta, GA, 1972-6, 10 volumes, with MASTER INDEX, Taylor Foundation, Reprint Co., Greenville, SC, 1989.

___M. R. Hemperley, MILITARY CERTIFICATES OF GA, Southern Historical Press, Easley, SC, 1983.

___R. Blair, REVOLUTIONARY WAR SOLDIERS RECEIPTS FOR GA BOUNTY GRANTS, Foote and Davis,, Atlanta, GA, 1928.

___REVOLUTIONARY WAR BOUNTY GRANTS IN FRANKLIN AND WASHINGTON COUNTIES, original record book in GA

Surveyor General Department, in same building with GDAH, Atlanta, GA; published in GA Genealogist, Franklin County Records 1-17, Washington County Records 1-60.

___COLONIAL LAND BOOKS, microfilm copies in GDAH, Atlanta, GA: FIATS FOR GRANTS BOOKS L, T, BB, 1755-6, Microfilm Reel 40-44; QUIT RENTS BOOKS, 1758-76, Microfilm Reels 21-46 and 68-77, indexed; LAND COURT MINUTES, 1761-6, 1773-5, Microfilm Reels 81-12 and 154-65; LOOSE LAND SETTLE-MENT PAPERS, 1751-75, Microfilm Reel 230-23.

___BOUNTY LAND WARRANTS, CREEK INDIAN WAR, 1798-1804, GA Genealogist, State Records 1-16.

___G. G. Davidson, EARLY RECORDS OF GA, WILKES COUNTY, Southern Historical Press, Easley, SC, 1936(1968), volume 1, pages 2-29.

In addition to distributing its land by headright and bounty grants (which we have just discussed), GA gave land in a series of lotteries held in 1805/07/20/21/27/32 (two in 1832). The original records of the winners and some of the losers are located in the GA Surveyor General Department:

___GA LAND LOTTERY RECORDS, GA Surveyor General Department, in the same building with GDAH, Atlanta, GA.

These records have been copied, published, and indexed in a series of useful volumes. The 1805 listings give the names of all persons who participated in the lottery, both winners and losers, but the other listings (1807/20/21/27/32/33) give only the winners. Quite often county records can be found which list all applicants, so in some counties both winners and losers can be identified. These county records will be listed in Chapter 4. Here are the published lists:

___V. S. and R. V. Wood, 1805 GA LAND LOTTERY, Channing Books, Marion, MA, 1964. [Over 25000 registrants.]

___S. E. Lucas, Jr., 1807 LAND LOTTERY OF GA, Southern Historical Press, Easley, SC, 1968. [Over 12000 winners.]

___S. E. Lucas, Jr., 1820 AND 1821 LAND LOTTERIES OF GA, Southern Historical Press, Easley, SC, 1973.

___S. E. Lucas, Jr., THE 1820 LAND LOTTERY OF GA, Southern Historical Press, Easley, SC, 1986.

___S. E. Lucas, Jr., THE 1821 LAND LOTTERY OF GA, Southern Historical Press, Easley, SC, 1986.

___M. L. Houston, 1827 LAND LOTTERY OF GA, Southern Historical Press, Easley, SC, 1928(1981), with K. H. Thomas, CORREC-TIONS, GA Genealogical Society Quarterly, Volume 16, 1980, page 116. [Over 15000 winners.]

___J. F. Smith, 1832 CHEROKEE LAND LOTTERY, Southern Historical Press, Easley, SC, 1838(1968). [Over 20000 winners.]

___M. M. Richardson, 1832 CHEROKEE LAND LOTTERY, INDEX TO REVOLUTIONARY SOLDIERS, THEIR WIDOWS, AND ORPHANS WHO WERE FORTUNATE DRAWERS, Heritage Papers, Danielsville, GA, 1969.

___M. B. Warren, ALPHABETICAL INDEX TO GA'S 1832 GOLD LOTTERY, Heritage Papers, Danielsville, GA, 1981.

___S. E. Lucas, Jr., 1832 GOLD LOTTERY OF GA, Southern Historical Press, Easley, SC, 1879(1981). [Over 39000 winners.]

___R. S. Davis, Jr., THE 1833 LAND LOTTERY OF GA, Southern Historical Press, Easley, SC, 1991.

___R. S. Davis, Jr., and S. E. Lucas, Jr., GA LAND LOTTERY PAPERS, 1805-1914, Southern Historical Press, Easley, SC, 1979. [Claims of heirs of winners; over 3000 individuals.]

___A. M. Hitz, AUTHENTIC LIST OF ALL LAND LOTTERY GRANTS MADE TO VETERANS OF THE REVOLUTIONARY WAR BY GA, GA Surveyor General Department, Atlanta, GA, 1966.

If you care to read in detail the qualifications for participating in the lotteries, they are accurately discussed in:

___R. S. Davis, Jr., RESEARCH IN GA, Southern Historical Press, Easley, SC, 1981, pages 184-95.

As you will recall, the land records we have now considered (headright grants, bounty grants, lottery grants) all refer to the transfer of land from the GA colony or state to the first private landowner. We will now deal with land records which relate to transfers of land from one private person to another. These records consist mainly of deeds and mortgages, but other types may be involved. Such conveyance records (as they are called) were kept in Savannah for the entirety of GA before 1777. After this date they were kept in the individual counties, although there was some overlap in the decade just following 1777, with full changeover to county record keeping not occurring until 1787. The record books themselves are on microfilm as follows:

___COLONIAL CONVEYANCE (DEED) BOOKS C1, C2, S, U, V, X1, CC1, CC2, DD, 1750-98, GDAH, Atlanta, GA, Microfilm Reels 40-19/20/21/22/23/25, indexed.

___COLONIAL MORTGAGE BOOKS E, P, Q, W, EE, 1755-1822, GDAH, Atlanta, GA, Microfilm Reels 40-26/27/28.

Some of these records have been copied and indexed in several published volumes which can be very helpful:

___ F. H. Beckemeyer, ABSTRACTS OF GA COLONIAL CONVEY-ANCE BOOK C1, 1750-61, Taylor Foundation, Atlanta, GA, 1975. [Land transactions 1733-61 as recorded 1750-61.]

___ INDEX TO GA COLONIAL CONVEYANCES AND CONFIS-CATED LAND RECORDS, 1750-1804, Taylor Foundation, Atlanta, GA, 1981.

___ GA GENEALOGICAL MAGAZINE has published many of the colonial conveyance records in Issue Numbers 4, 6-8, 10-13, 22-30, 42, 44-45.

As mentioned above, after 1777/87 the keeping of land conveyance records was handled in the counties. In Chapter 4, the counties will be listed and the dates for which microfilmed conveyance records (deeds, land court records, land lottery records, mortgages) for each will be listed. The microfilms can be found in GDAH, along with numerous loose county records. Many of the microfilms are also in FHL, and therefore available through FHC. As you search deed, mortgage, and other land records for land grants, sales, and purchases involving your forebears, please don't forget that sometimes land transfers were made by a will or the settlement of an intestate estate, in which case there is usually no deed or mortgage record.

23. Manuscripts

One of the most useful and yet one of the most unused sources of genealogical data are the various manuscript collections relating to GA. These collections will be found in state, regional, and private archives, museums, and repositories located in numerous places in and out of GA, including universities, colleges, and church agencies. Manuscript collections consist of all sorts of records of religious, educational, patriotic, business, social, civil, professional, governmental, and political organizations; documents, letters, memoirs, notes, and papers of early settlers, ministers, politicians, business men, educators, physicians, dentists, lawyers, judges, farmers, and genealogists; records of churches, cemeteries, mortuaries, schools, corporations, and industries; works of artists, musicians, writers, sculptors, photographers, architects, and historians; and records, papers, letters, and reminiscences of participants in various wars, as well as records of military organizations and campaigns.

There are several important national-level catalogs of manuscript repositories and their contents which will lead you to manuscript materials, both in GA and outside GA, which could refer to your GA ancestors. These are:

___US Library of Congress, THE NATIONAL UNION CATALOG OF MANUSCRIPT COLLECTIONS, The Library, Washington, DC, annual volumes since 1962-, index in each volume, also cumulative indexes; by names, places and historical periods, be sure and also look for names under the general heading GENEALOGY.

___P. M. Hamer, A GUIDE TO ARCHIVES AND MANUSCRIPTS IN THE US, Yale University Press, New Haven, CT, 1961.

___US National Historical Publications and Boards Commission, DIRECTORY OF ARCHIVES AND MANUSCRIPT REPOSITORIES IN THE US, The Commission, Washington, DC, 1978.

___National Society of the Daughters of the American Revolution, LIBRARY CATALOG, FAMILY HISTORIES AND GENEALOGIES, The Society, Washington, DC, 1982.

___H. Cripe and D. Campbell, AMERICAN MANUSCRIPTS, 1763-1815, Scholarly Resources, Wilmington, DE, 1977.

The major sources of manuscripts relating to GA are GDAH, UGL, and GHS. There are smaller, but important, collections in the Atlanta Historical Society (3099 Andrews Drive, Atlanta, GA), the Emory University Library (Emory, GA 30338), and the Reese Library of Augusta College (2500 Walton Way, Augusta, GA 30904). The two best collections of GA manuscripts outside of GA are in the Perkins Library of Duke University (Durham, NC 27706) and the Wilson Library of the University of NC (Chapel Hill, NC 27514). In addition, there are the archives and repositories of the major GA religious groups. These were listed in section 7 of this chapter. Among the more valuable manuscript listings and finding aids for GA materials are the following:

___G. McAninch, DIRECTORY OF GA ARCHIVES AND MANUSCRIPT REPOSITORIES, GA Historical Records Board, Atlanta, GA, 1983.

___S. Flocks, DIRECTORY OF GA'S HISTORICAL ORGANIZATIONS AND RESOURCES, GDAH, Atlanta, GA, latest edition.

___GENERAL NAME FILE, VERTICAL SUBJECTS FILE, AND MANUSCRIPTS FILES, Research Area, GDAH, Atlanta, GA. [Includes records of governors, convicts, physicians, Loyalists, military men, state asylum, voters, national guard, and loose county records.]

___INDEXES, GUIDES, AND CATALOGS TO STATE AND PRIVATE MANUSCRIPT COLLECTIONS, GDAH, Atlanta, GA. [Includes Bible, cemetery, church, Civil War, city, county, genealogical, Indian, newspaper, and personal records.]

___M. L. Adams, A PRELIMINARY GUIDE TO 18TH-CENTURY RECORDS HELD BY THE GDAH, GDAH, Atlanta, GA.

___LEON S. HOLLINGSWORTH GENEALOGICAL COLLECTION (45000 NOTE CARDS ON GA FAMILIES), Microfilm Library, GDAH, Atlanta, GA, also available from Taylor Foundation, Atlanta, GA, 1981, to be used with LEON S. HOLLINGS-WORTH GENEALOGICAL CARD FILE INDEX, Taylor Foundation, Atlanta, GA, 1979.

___M. L. Adams, INDEX TO GA ARCHIVE, Society of GA Archivists, Heritage Research, Atlanta, GA, 1978. [Covers volumes 1-5, 1973-7. Also see individual issues after 1977.]

___P. Spalding, THE BOOK OF [MANUSCRIPT] ACCESSIONS, GA DEPOSITORIES, 1973-80, GA Historical Society, Savannah, GA, 1981.

___TELAMON CUYLER COLLECTION, Hargett Library, UGL, Athens, GA. [Over 50000 records.]

___LECONTE GENEALOGICAL COLLECTION, Hargett Library, UGL, Athens, GA. [Very large collection of materials on GA families.]

___LYMAN C. DRAPER COLLECTION, Microfilm Section, UGL, Athens, GA. [Exceptionally large collection of materials on the American frontier and the South about the time of the American Revolution and after.]

___MANUSCRIPT CATALOG, Hargett Library, UGL, Athens, GA.

___GHS, A COMPREHENSIVE CATALOG OF THE MANUSCRIPTS IN THE GHS, The Society, Savannah, GA.

___A. Dees and A. S. Britt, Jr., SELECTED 18TH-CENTURY MANUSCRIPTS, GHS, Savannah, GA, 1980.

___L. M. Hawes and K. E. Oswald, CHECKLIST OF 18TH-CENTURY MANUSCRIPTS IN THE GHS, The Society, Savannah, GA, 1976.

___D. L. Cook, GUIDE TO THE MANUSCRIPT COLLECTIONS OF THE ATLANTA HISTORICAL SOCIETY, The Society, Atlanta, GA, 1976.

___Atlanta Historical Society, FRANKLIN MILLER GARRETT PAPERS, The Society, Atlanta, GA. [Manuscripts containing cemetery records for many counties.]

___Woodruff Library, Emory University, A GUIDE TO MANUSCRIPT SOURCES IN THE SPECIAL COLLECTIONS DEPARTMENT FOR ATLANTA, The Library, Atlanta, GA, 1978.

___INDEX TO THE CHRISTIAN INDEX, 1828-, manuscript, GA Baptist Historical Society Collection, Stetson Memorial Library, Mercer University, Macon, GA.

___A. R. Rowland and V. E. deTreville, LIBRARY OF RICHMOND COUNTY HISTORICAL SOCIETY, Reese Library, Augusta, GA, 1978.

___GUIDE TO THE CATALOGUED COLLECTIONS IN THE MANUSCRIPT DEPARTMENT OF THE PERKINS LIBRARY, DUKE UNIVERSITY, Clio Books, Santa Barbara, CA, 1980.

___THE SOUTHERN HISTORICAL COLLECTION: GUIDE TO MANUSCRIPTS, 1970, with SUPPLEMENTARY GUIDE TO MANUSCRIPTS, 1970-5, Wilson Library, Chapel Hill, NC, 1970/5.

The books mentioned in the two previous paragraphs will be found in GDAH, UGL, WML, GHS, and in many other large genealogical libraries. If you find in these volumes materials which you suspect may relate to your progenitor, write to the appropriate repository asking for details. Don't forget to send an SASE and to ask for names of searchers if you cannot go in person. In almost all of the above-mentioned archives, there are special indexes, catalogs, and other finding aids to facilitate your searches. In some cases, there are several indexes, not just one, so you need to be careful to make sure that you examine all of them.

24. Marriage records

The state of GA first required marriages to be registered in the counties in 1804, but compliance was quite lax, especially in the years shortly after that date. Prior to 1804, some counties permitted those who wished to do so to record their marriages. The practice in GA was for the marriage to be recorded in the county of residence of the bride. The record showed the names of the groom and bride, the date, and the official who performed the ceremony. Marriages were registered by the Inferior Court until 1868, then by the Probate Court or Ordinary. These marriage records will be found in the GA county courthouses, and microfilm copies of those for most counties formed before 1900 are available in GDAH. Many of these are also in FHL (available through FHC). The marriage records are usually indexed. The dates for which these microfilmed records exist for the various counties are given under the counties in Chapter 4.

Quite a number of early GA marriage records have been compiled and are available in published form. Among the most useful of these are:

___COLONIAL GA MARRIAGES, 1760-1810, Ingmire Publications, St. Louis, MO, 1986.

___J. T. Maddox and M. Carter, 37000 EARLY GA MARRIAGES, and 40000 EARLY GA MARRIAGES, and EARLY GA MARRIAGE ROUNDUP, GA Pioneers, Albany, GA, 1975-7, 3 volumes.

___M. Carter, EARLY GA MARRIAGES, GA Pioneers, Albany, GA, 1980.

___GA COUNTY MARRIAGE RECORDS, Ingmire Publications, St. Louis, MO, 1982-. [Includes marriages for 88 GA counties, dated mostly in late 1700s and early 1800s.]

___LEGALLY RECORDED MARRIAGES IN GA, 1800-10, GA Genealogist, State Records 1-176.

___Liahona Research, GA MARRIAGE RECORDS, EARLY TO 1850, J and D, Orem, UT, 1992, 3 computer disks.

___MARRIAGE ANNOUNCEMENTS FOR OLD GA NEWSPAPERS, GA Genealogical Magazine, Numbers 1-33, 1961-9.

___N. R. Murray, HUNTING FOR BEARS COMPUTER INDEXES, GA COUNTY MARRIAGE RECORDS, Hunting for Bears, Hammond, LA, 1985.

___Precision Indexing, EARLY GA MARRIAGES, EARLY-1850, 2 Computer Disks, Precision Indexing, Bountiful, UT, 1991.

___M. Waddell, A REGISTER OF MARRIAGES BY M. WADDELL IN SC AND GA, 1795-1836, Heritage Papers, Danielsville, GA, 1967.

___M. B. Warren, GA MARRIAGES, 1811-20, Heritage Papers, Danielsville, GA, 1988.

___M. B. Warren and S. F. White, MARRIAGES AND DEATHS ABSTRACTED FROM EXTANT GA NEWSPAPERS, 1763-1830, Heritage Papers, Danielsville, GA, 1968-72, 2 volumes.

___M. E. Overby and J..M. Lancaster, MARRIAGES PUBLISHED IN THE [BAPTIST] CHRISTIAN INDEX, 1828-55, GA Baptist Historical Society, Washington, GA, 1971.

___B. H. Holcomb, MARRIAGE AND DEATH NOTICES FROM THE [METHODIST] SOUTHERN CHRISTIAN ADVOCATE, 1837-67, Southern Historical Press, Easley, SC, 1979, 2 volumes.

___B. H. Holcomb, MARRIAGE AND DEATH NOTICES FROM THE [PRESBYTERIAN] CHARLESTON OBSERVER, 1827-45, A Press, Greenville, SC, 1980.

___B. H. Holcomb, MARRIAGE AND DEATH NOTICES FROM THE LUTHERAN OBSERVER, 1831-61, AND THE SOUTHERN LUTHERAN, 1861-5, Southern Historical Press, Easley, SC, 1979.

___Daughters of the American Revolution, DAR RECORD TYPE-SCRIPTS, The Daughters, Atlanta, GA, transcripts located in GDAH, Atlanta, GA. [Many marriages included.]

___Automated Archives, CD3: AL, GA, AND SC MARRIAGE RECORDS, on CD-ROM, Automated Archives, Orem, UT, 1994. Also available on floppy disk.

___Automated Archives, CD226: GA MARRIAGE RECORDS, on CD-ROM, Automated Archives, Orem, UT, 1994. Also available on floppy disk.

Because of the incompleteness of official GA marriage records, especially in the early years, it is important that you make use of several non-official records. The most likely sources for such information (with the section in this chapter where they are discussed) are as follows: Bible(section 2), biography(section 3), cemetery(5), census(6), church(7), DAR(12), divorce(14), genealogical periodicals(19), manuscripts(23), military pensions(26-28), mortuary(29), newspaper(31), published genealogies(32), tax lists(34), and will-probate records(35). Numerous non-official sources of GA marriages, both at the state and county levels, are listed in:

___J. D. and E. D. Stemmons, THE VITAL RECORD COMPENDIUM, Everton Publishers, Logan, UT, 1979.

When you are seeking marriage date and place information in archives and libraries, be certain to explore all the above-mentioned sources, and don't fail to look under the county listings and the following subject headings in card catalogs: Marriage licenses, and Registers of births, etc.

25. Military records: colonial

Before going into detail on sources of military records (sections 25-28), you need to understand the types of records which are available and what they contain. There are five basic types which are of value to genealogists: (a) service, (b) pension, (c) bounty land, (d) claims, and (e) military unit history. Service records contain a number of the following: name, rank, military unit, personal description, plus dates and places of enlistment, mustering in, payrolls, wounding, capture, death, imprisonment, hospital stay, release, oath of allegiance, deserting, promotion, battles, heroic action, re-enlistment, leave of absence, mustering out, and discharge. <u>Pension</u> records (applications and payment documents) contain a number of the following: name, age, rank, military unit, personal description, name of wife, names and ages of children, residences during pension period, plus dates and places of enlistment, service, wartime experiences, birth, marriage, pension payments, and death. <u>Bounty land</u> records (applications and awards of land) contain a number of the following: name, age, rank, military unit, plus dates and places of enlistment, service, wartime experience, and birth. <u>Claims</u> of military participants for back pay and of civilians for supplies or service contain some of the following: name, details of the claim, date of the claim, witnesses to the claim, documents supporting the claim, action on the claim, amount awarded. <u>Military unit history</u> records trace the detailed events of the experiences of a given military unit throughout a war, often referring to officers, enlisted men, battles, campaigns, and deaths, plus dates and places of organization, mustering in, reorganization, mustering out, and other pertinent events. Now with this background, you are ready to learn where these records may be found.

As you will recall from the GA history in Chapter 1, one of the purposes of the colony was for it to act as a military buffer between Spanish FL and the English colonies. From the time of settlement in 1733, the colony established military towns at several crucial points. Fort Frederica was the largest of these, a regiment of British soldiers being garrisoned there. In 1739, Spain and England began the conflict known as the War of Jenkins' Ear. In 1742, Georgians repulsed a Spanish invasion force, ending the Spanish claim to the area. Then during 1754-63, the French and Indian War was fought out, chiefly on the frontiers of the thirteen colonies. GA took very little active part in this conflict because the Indians of the colony remained loyal to the English. Before the struggle was over, both French and Spanish raiders had plundered the GA coast.

The military records of this pre-Revolutionary period are not very voluminous. About all you can expect to find are lists of participants with little additional data. Three major sources of these records are:
___M. J. Clark, COLONIAL SOLDIERS OF THE SOUTH, 1732-74, Genealogical Publishing Co., Baltimore, MD, 1983.
___A. D. Candler and associates, THE COLONIAL RECORDS OF GA, State Printers, Atlanta, GA, and University of GA Press, Athens,

GA, 39 volumes, 28 published, others in typescript in GDAH, Atlanta, GA; with INDEXES at GDAH, Atlanta, GA, and UGL, Athens, GA, and GHS, Savannah, GA.

___ROSTERS OF GA RANGERS OF THE FRENCH AND INDIAN WAR, William L. Clements Library, University of MI, Ann Arbor, MI.

---

26. Military records: Revolutionary War

As mentioned in Chapter 1, GA was the scene of much warfare during the War for American Independence (1776-82), much of the area being held for long periods of time by Loyalist forces. Quite large volumes of records relating to this war are available for you to investigate: national service records, national pension records, national bounty land records, state service records, state bounty land records, and some county records. A total of about 2700 men fought in the GA contingent of the federal forces known as the Continental Army. Others fought in state or local troops or militia, never becoming a part of the Continental forces. You will usually find both national (federal, Continental) and state records on Continental personnel, but there are ordinarily mainly state and local records (only some national records) on those who did not join federal units. It is also well to recognize that many Patriots who were driven out of GA during the British occupation enlisted in other colonies, especially SC and NC. Further, and very important, since the GA population was so small, she was unable to raise enough troops for her defense. Therefore, the federal government permitted GA to recruit in NC and VA, which she did very successfully. Hence, many non-Georgians fought in GA military units.

The first step you should take in searching for your GA ancestor who may have served in this war or supported it is to employ the following large indexes and look for him in them:

___The National Archives, GENERAL INDEX TO COMPILED SERVICE RECORDS OF REVOLUTIONARY WAR SOLDIERS, SAILORS, ARMY STAFF, The Archives, Washington, DC, Microfilm Publication M860, 58 rolls. [Continental forces plus some others who fought along with them; copies in GDAH, NA, NAAB, FHL, FHC; can be borrowed through your LL or directly from AGLL, PO Box 244, Bountiful, UT 84010, or Census Microfilm Rental Program, PO Box 2940, Hyattsville, MD 20784.]

___The National Archives, INDEX TO COMPILED SERVICE RECORDS OF REVOLUTIONARY WAR SOLDIERS WHO

SERVED WITH THE AMERICAN ARMY IN GA MILITARY ORGANIZATIONS, The Archives, Washington, DC, Microfilm Publication M1051, 1 roll. [Sources same as above.]

___The National Genealogical Society, INDEX TO REVOLUTIONARY WAR PENSION [AND SOME BOUNTY LAND] APPLICATIONS IN THE NA, The Society, Washington, DC, 1976.

___F. Rider, AMERICAN GENEALOGICAL INDEX, Godfrey Memorial Library, MIddletown, CT, 1942-52, 48 volumes, and F. Rider, AMERICAN GENEALOGICAL-BIOGRAPHICAL INDEX, Godfrey Memorial Library, Middletown, CT, 1952-87, over 18- volumes, more to come. [Continental, state, and militia service.]

___US Pay Department, War Department, REGISTERS OF CERTIFICATES ISSUED BY JOHN PIERCE TO OFFICERS AND SOLDIERS OF THE CONTINENTAL ARMY, Genealogical Publishing Co., Baltimore, MD, 1983.

___National Society of the DAR, DAR PATRIOT INDEX, The Society, Washington, DC, 1966/79, 2 volumes. [Continental, state, militia, public service, military aid.]

If you discover from these sources that your ancestor served in the Continental forces or units which aided them, you may proceed to obtain his records from the NA or read them from these microfilms:

___The National Archives, COMPILED SERVICE RECORDS OF SOLDIERS WHO SERVED IN THE AMERICAN ARMY DURING THE REVOLUTIONARY WAR, The Archives, Washington, DC, Microfilm Publication M881, 1097 rolls.

___The National Archives, COMPILED SERVICE RECORDS OF AMERICAN NAVAL, QUARTERMASTER, AND COMMISSARY PERSONNEL WHO SERVED DURING THE REVOLUTIONARY WAR, The Archives, Washington, DC, Microfilm Publication M880, 4 rolls.

___The National Archives, REVOLUTIONARY WAR ROLLS, 1775-83, The Archives, Washington, DC, Microfilm Publication M246, 138 rolls.

___The National Archives, REVOLUTIONARY WAR PENSION AND BOUNTY LAND WARRANT APPLICATION FILES, The Archives, Washington, DC, Microfilm Publication M804, 2670 rolls.

The four microfilm sets are available at NA, some are at NAAB and GDAH, and some can be borrowed from AGLL, PO Box 244, Bountiful, UT 84010 or CMRF, PO Box 2940, Hyattsville, MD 20784. Alternately, you can write the NA (8th and PA Ave., Washington, DC 20408) for 3 copies of NATF-80 which you can use to request service, pension, and bounty land records by mail. A third alternative is to hire a searcher in Washington, DC to go to the NA for you. Lists of such searchers will be found in:

___J. N. Chambers, editor, THE GENEALOGICAL HELPER, Everton Publishers, Logan, UT, latest September-October issue.

The second step you should take, especially if you failed to find your progenitor in the first step, is to look into published state sources. Even if you did find your ancestor in the first step, you should not neglect this second possible source of data. Foremost among these state sources are some books:

___L. L. Knight, GA'S ROSTER OF THE REVOLUTION, Genealogical Publishing Co., Baltimore, MD, 1979. [5000 listed.]

___R. S. Davis, Jr., GA CITIZENS AND SOLDIERS OF THE AMERICAN REVOLUTION, Southern Historical Press, Easley, SC, 1979. [5000 persons.]

___E. T. McCall, ROSTER OF REVOLUTIONARY SOLDIERS IN GA, Genealogical Publishing Co., Baltimore, MD, 1968-9, 3 volumes.

___R. Blair, REVOLUTIONARY WAR SOLDIERS' RECEIPTS FOR GA BOUNTY GRANTS, Foote and Davis, Atlanta, GA, 1928.

___N. Brawner, MEMBERSHIP ROLL AND REGISTER OF ANCESTORS OF GA DAR, The Society, Atlanta, GA, 1946/76.

___GA Secretary of State, GA MILITARY RECORDS, 1775-1842, The Secretary, Atlanta, GA, 1940, 9 volumes.

___R. S. Davis, Jr., RESEARCHER'S LIBRARY OF GA, Southern Historical Press, Easley, SC, 1987. See pp. 209-28.

___R. S. Davis, Jr., GEORGIANS IN THE REVOLUTION, THE BATTLE OF KETTLE CREEK AND BURKE COUNTY, Southern Historical Press, Easley, SC, 1986.

___M. Carter, GA REVOLUTIONARY SOLDIERS, SAILORS, PATRIOTS, AND DESCENDANTS, GA Pioneers, Albany, GA, 1977, 2 volumes.

___A. M. Hitz, AUTHENTIC LIST OF ALL LAND LOTTERY GRANTS MADE TO VETERANS OF THE REVOLUTIONARY WAR BY GA, GA Surveyor General Department, Atlanta, GA, 1966.

___M. R. Hemperley, MILITARY BOUNTY LAND CERTIFICATES OF GA, Southern Historical Press, Easley, SC, 1983.

___M. L. Houston, REVOLUTIONARY SOLDIERS AND WIDOWS LIVING IN GA, 1827-8, Heritage Papers, Danielsville, Ga, 1965.

___L. K. McGhee, GA PENSION LIST OF ALL WARS FROM THE REVOLUTION DOWN TO 1883, The Author, Washington, DC, 1962.

___P. W. McMullin, GRASSROOTS OF AMERICA, A COMPUTER-IZED INDEX TO THE AMERICAN STATE PAPERS, LAND GRANTS AND CLAIMS, 1789-1837, Gendex Corp., Salt Lake City, UT, 1972. [Includes federal bounty land grants to Continental soldiers.]

___D. E. Payne, GA PENSIONERS [REVOLUTION, 1812, MEXICAN WARS], Sunbelt Publishing, McLean, VA, 1985.

___C. P. Wilson, ANNALS OF GA, Southern Historical Press, Easley, SC, 1969, volume 1. [GA Revolutionary pay rolls.]

___A. D. Candler, THE REVOLUTIONARY RECORDS OF THE STATE OF GA, 1769-84, Franklin-Turner Co., Atlanta, GA, 1908, 3 volumes, with TYPESCRIPT INDEX, GDAH, Atlanta, GA.

Most of these books will be found in GDAH, UGL, WML, and GHS. Some of them are in FHL(FHC), LGL, RL, and LL.

The _third_ step to be taken, both if you found your ancestor in the first two steps and if you didn't, is to look in numerous typescripts, microfilms, and manuscripts in GDAH. Among the better are:

___EARLY LEGISLATIVE MINUTES AND GOVERNORS' LETTER-BOOKS, WPA Indexed Typescripts, GDAH, Atlanta, GA. [Revolutionary War claims.]

___GA MILITARY AFFAIRS, RECORDS, AND ROSTERS, 1775-1842, WPA Indexed Typescripts, GDAH, Atlanta, GA, 9 volumes. [See earlier volumes.]

___GA MILITARY RECORD BOOK 1, 1779-1839, WPA Indexed Typescripts, GDAH, Atlanta, GA; also in Microfilm Library, GDAH, Atlanta, GA, Reels 40-16 through 40-18.

___GA State Society of the DAR, DAR RECORD TRANSCRIPTS, The Society, Atlanta, GA, transcripts in GDAH, Atlanta, GA. [Some contain military lists.]

___GA State Society of the DAR, HISTORIES OF REVOLUTIONARY SOLDIERS CONTRIBUTED BY GA DAR CHAPTERS, The Various Chapters, Various GA Locations, 26 volumes in GDAH, Atlanta, GA.

___GA State Society of the DAR, REVOLUTIONARY SOLDIERS BURIED IN GA, The Society, Atlanta, GA, in GDAH, Atlanta,

GA, also see GA Genealogical Society Quarterly, Volume 8, pages 211-222.
___GA TREASURY DEPARTMENT PAY RECORDS, 1782-1813, Microfilm Library, GDAH, Atlanta, GA.
___INDEX TO THE REVOLUTIONARY RECORDS OF GA, WPA Typescript, GDAH, Atlanta, GA.
___INDIAN DEPREDATIONS, PROPERTY LOSSES, 1775-later, WPA Indexed Transcripts, GDAH, Atlanta, GA, 5 volumes. [Claims of Georgians for losses.]
___MILITARY RECORD COLLECTION, 1776 to about 1861, unindexed, Research Area, GDAH, Atlanta, GA.

As indicated in Chapter 1, GA had many Loyalists, both permanent ones and temporary ones during the long British occupation (1779-82). Numerous records are available on them including:
___M. J. Clark, LOYALISTS IN THE SOUTHERN CAMPAIGN OF THE REVOLUTIONARY WAR, Genealogical Publishing Co., Baltimore, MD, 1981.
___P. W. Coldham, AMERICAN LOYALIST CLAIMS, National Genealogical Society, Washington, DC, 1980-, several volumes.
___CONFISCATIONS OF LOYALIST PROPERTY IN GA IN THE 1780s, Record Groups 1-6 and 37-8, Law Wing, GDAH, Atlanta, GA; see also A. D. Candler, REVOLUTIONARY RECORDS OF THE STATE OF GA, 1769-84, Franklin-Turner Co., Atlanta, GA, 1908, 3 volumes, with TYPESCRIPT INDEX, GDAH, Atlanta, GA.
___INDEX TO GA COLONIAL CONVEYANCES AND CONFIS-CATED LAND RECORDS, 1750-1804, Taylor Foundation, Atlanta, GA, 1981. [Includes Loyalist land confiscations.]
___EXCERPTS FROM GA LOYALIST CLAIMS, Microfilm Library, GDAH, Atlanta, GA. [Leads to more detailed records in Public Archives of Canada.]
___GA Genealogist 3:1-4, 4:5-8, 5:9-14, 7:15-22. [Loyalists who moved to East FL.] See also State Records 10-22 in Microfilm Library, GDAH, Atlanta, GA.
___GA Genealogical Magazine 39:49-76, 40:177-90, 41:315-26, 42:449-56. [Census records on Loyalists in FL in 1783.]
___GA Genealogical Society Quarterly 7:93-100. Index to some Loyalist claims.
___New England Historical and Genealogical Register 52:300-1, and GA Genealogical Society Quarterly 8:272-3. [Loyalists who moved to Jamaica and the Bahamas.]

___GA Pioneers 15(1):20-2.

Two extensive reference works to Loyalist source materials have been published. Many GA data are included:

___P. J. Bunnell, RESEARCH GUIDE TO LOYALIST ANCESTORS, Heritage Books, Bowie, MD, 1950.

___G. Palmer, editor, A BIBLIOGRAPHY OF LOYALIST SOURCE MATERIAL IN THE US, CANADA, AND GREAT BRITAIN, Meckler, Westport, CT, 1982.

Finally, do not fail to check various county records, both governmental (especially the land lottery lists) and non-governmental. Included among the latter are such things as Bible, biographical, cemetery, county histories, local genealogical periodicals, land, newspaper, and published genealogies. See other sections of this Chapter for details on these. For considerably more detail about genealogical data which can be obtained from Revolutionary War records, consult books especially dedicated to these sources:

___Geo. K. Schweitzer, REVOLUTIONARY WAR GENEALOGY, available from the author at the address given on this book's title page.

___J. C. and L. L. Neagles, LOCATING YOUR REVOLUTIONARY WAR ANCESTOR, Everton Publishers, Logan, UT, 1983.

---

27. Military records: War of 1812

During the period between the Revolutionary War and the Civil War (1784-1861), the US was involved in two major foreign wars: The War of 1812 (1812-5) and the Mexican War (1846-8). In addition, there were several minor conflicts in which GA soldiers were involved, including some Indian Wars. Since so few were engaged in these minor conflicts, we will only refer you to two main reference works where you will find the pertinent records discussed, and to three record compilations. However, we will treat the major wars in some detail because sizable numbers of Georgians were involved. The basic sources which will lead you to military service, pension, and bounty land records of Georgians who gave military service in minor conflicts during 1784-1861 (especially the Indian Wars 1815-58) are:

___The National Archives, GUIDE TO GENEALOGICAL RESEARCH IN THE NA, The Archives, Washington, DC, 1982, Chapters 4-9.

___The National Archives, MILITARY SERVICE RECORDS, The Archives, Washington, DC, 1985.

Particular attention needs to be paid to the NA microfilm indexes to volunteer service during 1784-1811 (Microfilm M694), in Indian Wars 1815-58 (M629), in the Cherokee disturbances and removal 1836-8 (M907), and to pensions for Indian War service (T318). The three compilations which are useful are:

___M. J. Clark, AMERICAN MILITIA IN THE FRONTIER WARS, 1790-96, Genealogical Publishing Co., Baltimore, MD, 1990.

___D. Stanton and C. J. Thaxton, GA INDIAN DEPREDATION CLAIMS, Thaxton Co., Americus, GA, 1988.

___V. D. White, INDEX TO VOLUNTEER SOLDIERS, 1784-1811, National Historical Publications, Waynesboro, TN, 1987.

A number of GA men were involved in the <u>War</u> <u>of</u> <u>1812</u>. They served both in national and state organizations, and therefore several types of national records (service, bounty land, pension), as well as state records need to be sought. Only a few national pensions were given before 1871, by which time not too many veterans were still living. To obtain <u>national</u> records (only for men who served in national units) you may write the NA and request copies of NATF-80, which may be used to order military service, bounty land, and pension information. Or you may choose to visit the NA or to employ a searcher in Washington to do the work for you. Alternately, some of the indexes and records are available on loan from AGLL, PO Box 244, Bountiful, UT 84010. Among the microfilm indexes and alphabetical files which you need to search or have searched for you are:

___The National Archives, INDEX TO COMPILED SERVICE RE- CORDS OF VOLUNTEER SOLDIERS WHO SERVED DURING THE WAR OF 1812, The Archives, Washington, DC, Microfilm Publication M602, 234 rolls. [Leads to service records, which are in the NA.]

___The National Archives, INDEX TO WAR OF 1812 PENSION (AND SOME BOUNTY LAND) APPLICATIONS, The Archives, Washington, DC, Microfilm Publication M313, 102 rolls. [Leads to applications, which are in the NA.]

___The National Archives, WAR OF 1812 MILITARY BOUNTY LAND WARRANTS, 1815-58, The Archives, Microfilm Publication M848, 14 rolls, 4 indexes in first roll. [Leads to bounty land warrant applications, which are alphabetically filed in NA.]

___The National Archives, POST-REVOLUTIONARY WAR BOUNTY LAND WARRANT APPLICATION FILE, The Archives, Washington, DC, arranged alphabetically.

Copies of the three microfilm publications mentioned above are available at NA, some NAFB, some LGL, and at FHL (and through FHC). Microfilm publications M602, M313, and M848 are available on interlibrary loan from AGLL (address above). Among published national sources for War of 1812 data are:

___F. I. Ordway, Jr., REGISTER OF THE GENERAL SOCIETY OF THE WAR OF 1812, The Society, Washington, DC, 1972.

___E. S. Galvin, 1812 ANCESTOR INDEX, National Society of the US Daughters of 1812, Washington, DC, 1970.

___C. S. Peterson, KNOWN MILITARY DEAD DURING THE WAR OF 1812, The Author, Baltimore, MD, 1955.

___V. D. White, INDEX TO WAR OF 1812 PENSION FILES, National Historical Publications, Waynesboro, TN, 1989.

Among the state source volumes, records, and microfilms which you should search for GA military service records are:

___A. Gregath, WAR OF 1812 AND OTHER PENSIONERS LIVING IN GA IN THE 1880s, University of GA Press, Athens, GA, 1983.

___J. S. Kratovil, INDEX TO THE WAR OF 1812 SERVICE RECORDS FOR VOLUNTEER SOLDIERS FROM GA, The Author, Atlanta, GA, 1986.

___D. E. Payne, GA PENSIONERS [Revolution, 1812, Mexican], Sunbelt Publishers, McLean, VA, 1985-6, 2 volumes.

___GA MILITARY AFFAIRS, RECORDS, AND ROSTERS, 1775-1842, WPA Indexed Transcripts, GDAH, Atlanta, GA, 9 volumes.

___GA MILITARY RECORD BOOKS, VOLUMES 1-4, 1779-1862, Microfilm Library, GDAH, Atlanta, GA, Reels 40-16 through 40-18.

___INDIAN DEPREDATIONS: PROPERTY LOSSES, 1775-1836, WPA Indexed Transcripts, GDAH, Atlanta, GA.

___J. Malone, SOLDIERS OF THE WAR OF 1812 WHOSE GRAVES HAVE BEEN LOCATED IN GA, Heritage Papers, Danielsville, GA, 1944.

___L. K. McGhee, GA PENSION LIST OF ALL WARS FROM THE REVOLUTION DOWN TO 1883, The Author, Washington, DC, 1962.

___GA OFFICIAL RECORDS, ADJUTANT GENERAL, Microfilm Library, GDAH, Atlanta, GA.

For considerable more detail about genealogical information which can be derived from the above War of 1812 records plus the many more that are available, you may consult a detailed book especially dedicated to this:

___Geo. K. Schweitzer, WAR OF 1812 GENEALOGY, available from the author at the address given on this book's title page.

The Mexican War was fought 1846-8. As before, NATF-80 should be obtained and used, or you should visit the NA, or you should hire a researcher as indicated in previously-given instructions (see section 26). Again, military service, pension, and bounty land records should all be asked for. The NA indexes which lead to the records and some alphabetical national records include:

___The National Archives, INDEX TO THE COMPILED SERVICE RECORDS OF VOLUNTEER SOLDIERS DURING THE MEXICAN WAR, The Archives, Washington, DC, Microfilm Publication M616, 41 rolls.

___The National Archives, INDEX TO MEXICAN WAR PENSION FILES, The Archives, Washington, DC, Microfilm Publication T317, 14 rolls.

___The National Archives, POST-REVOLUTIONARY WAR BOUNTY LAND APPLICATION FILE, The Archives, Washington, DC, arranged alphabetically.

Three useful publications, one a complete roster of troops in the Mexican War, another a list of the dead, a third an index to pension applications, are:

___W. H. Roberts, MEXICAN WAR VETERANS, 1846-8, Washington, DC, 1887.

___C. S. Peterson, KNOWN MILITARY DEAD DURING THE MEXICAN WAR, The Author, Baltimore, MD, 1957.

___B. S. Wolfe, INDEX TO MEXICAN WAR PENSION APPLICA-TIONS, Ye Olde Genealogie Shoppe, Indianapolis, IN, 1986.

Among state sources available for the Mexican War are the following:

___GA REGIMENTAL ROSTER, MEXICAN WAR, 1846-8, in G. White, HISTORICAL COLLECTIONS OF GA, Pudney and Russell, New York, NY, 1854.

___GA MILITARY RECORD BOOKS, VOLUMES 1-4, 1779-1862, Microfilm Library, GDAH, Atlanta, GA, Reels 40-16 through 40-18.

___D. E. Payne, GA PENSIONERS [Revolution, 1812, Mexican], Sunbelt Publishing, McLean, VA, 1985.

___L. K. McGhee, GA PENSION LIST OF ALL WARS FROM THE REVOLUTION DOWN TO 1883, The Author, Washington, DC, 1962.

___WAR OF 1812 ROSTERS, GA Genealogist, in several issues, consult
indexes.

28. Military records: Civil War

Records which are available for GA participants in the Civil War (1861-5) include ones for Confederates and ones for the small number who fought on the Union side. The Union records consist of national service records and national pension records. The service records are indexed in the following microfilm:

___The National Archives, INDEX TO COMPILED SERVICE RE-
CORDS OF VOLUNTEER UNION SOLDIERS WHO
SERVED IN ORGANIZATIONS FROM THE STATE OF GA,
The Archives, Washington, DC, Microfilm Publication M385, 1
roll.

And the service records themselves are reproduced in the following microfilm publication:

___The National Archives, COMPILED SERVICE RECORDS OF
VOLUNTEER UNION SOLDIERS WHO SERVED IN
ORGANIZATIONS FROM THE STATE OF GA, The Archives,
Washington, DC, Microfilm Publication M403, 1 roll.

The index to Union veteran pension applications is:

___The National Archives, GENERAL INDEX TO PENSION FILES,
1861-1934, The Archives, Washington, DC, Microfilm Publication
T288, 544 rolls.

This index points you to pension records which are filed in the NA. The first of the above microfilms (M385) is in NAAB, and all three are in NA and FHL(FHC). You may have them examined and the service and pension records may be obtained by using NATF-80 in a mail request to the NA. Or you may employ a searcher to do the work at the NA, or even go yourself. NATF-80 instructions were given in section 26. Microfilms M385 and T288 may also be borrowed from AGLL, either directly or through your local library (see section 26). A journal article of value to those who suspect they had a GA Union veteran is:

___VOLUNTEER UNION SOLDIERS FROM GA, GA Genealogical
Society Quarterly 15(2): 83-6.

The major Confederate records for GA consist of Confederate service records, GA state pension records, and GA state governor and adjutant general records. Confederate service records relate to GA participants who served in units under the supervision of the Confederate government. They do not include the many combatants who served in GA militia and home guard units, because these units remained under state and/or local supervision. The Confederate service records are indexed in:

___The National Archives, INDEX TO COMPILED SERVICE RE-CORDS OF CONFEDERATE SOLDIERS WHO SERVED IN ORGANIZATIONS FROM THE STATE OF GA, The Archives, Washington, DC, Microfilm Publication M226, 67 rolls.

___The National Archives, CONSOLIDATED INDEX TO COMPILED SERVICE RECORDS OF CONFEDERATE SOLDIERS, The Archives, Washington, DC, Microfilm Publication M253, 535 rolls.

___The National Archives, INDEX TO COMPILED SERVICE RE-CORDS OF CONFEDERATE SOLDIERS WHO SERVED IN ORGANIZATIONS RAISED DIRECTLY BY THE CONFED-ERATE GOVERNMENT AND OF CONFEDERATE GENERAL AND STAFF OFFICERS AND NON-REGIMEN-TAL ENLISTED MEN, The Archives, Washington, DC, Micro-film Publication M818, 26 rolls.

These indexes may be consulted in GDAH, FHL(FIIC), NA, and NAAR, or they may be borrowed from AGLL. They lead to the service records themselves which are in these microfilm sets:

___The National Archives, COMPILED SERVICE RECORDS OF CONFEDERATE SOLDIERS WHO SERVED IN ORGANIZA-TIONS FROM THE STATE OF GA, The Archives, Washington, DC, Microfilm Publication M266, 607 rolls.

___The National Archives, COMPILED SERVICE RECORDS OF CONFEDERATE SOLDIERS WHO SERVED IN ORGANIZA-TIONS RAISED DIRECTLY BY THE CONFEDERATE GOVERNMENT, The Archives, Washington, DC, Microfilm Publication M258, 123 rolls.

___The National Archives, COMPILED SERVICE RECORDS OF CONFEDERATE GENERAL AND STAFF OFFICERS AND NON-REGIMENTAL ENLISTED MEN, The Archives, Washington, DC, Microfilm Publication M331, 275 rolls.

These three service record compilations are available in GDAH, FHL(FHC), and NA, or they may be borrowed from AGLL. Requests for examination of the indexes and for copies of the service records may be made to the NA by using NATF-80. Or you may visit the NA or hire a searcher to do the work (see section 26, this Chapter). There is a published compilation of Confederate infantry soldiers of GA, but it is important to remember that data on cavalry, artillery, infantry battalions and legions, and state troops are not in the volume:

___L. Henderson, ROSTER OF CONFEDERATE SOLDIERS (INFANTRY) OF GA, 1861-5, The State of GA, Atlanta, GA, 1959-64, 6 volumes, with NAME INDEX, Reprint Co, Spartanburg, SC, 1982.

In 1879, GA began granting pensions to disabled Confederate soldiers. In 1891, the law was broadened to give pensions to poverty-stricken veterans and widows. All GA residents were eligible for pensions regardless of the state in which they had served. However, GA Confederates who left GA could not receive pensions. Through 1907, pension holders had to reapply every year. The pension applications and supporting documents are generally very valuable genealogically, often including birth, marriage, and/or death data. The GDAH has the GA pension records and indexes to them:

___GA CIVIL WAR PENSION RECORDS and SUPPLEMENTAL PAPERS, indexed and/or alphabetically arranged, GDAH, Atlanta, GA.

Microfilm copies of the pension records and the indexes are in the collections of the FHL, and therefore are available through FHC. The pension index has also been published:

___S. E. Lucas, Jr., GA STATE CIVIL WAR PENSION INDEX, Southern Historical Press, Easley, SC, 1981, 5 volumes.

In the GDAH, there is a valuable index to many other state-based Civil War participant records. Included in the indexed materials are records of the GA Governor, Adjutant General, and Inspector General, lists of men subject to military duty as of 04 March 1862, militia enrollment lists as of 01 January 1864, and muster rolls of the GA State Troops and Line. These records are of immense value; they identify a sizable number of the many GA men who were involved in the War but who never were affiliated with an official Confederate unit. The index which will lead you to the original records is:

___ALPHABETICAL CARD FILE OF THE GA SOLDIER ROSTER COMMISSION, GDAH, Atlanta, GA.

Other records of note in GDAH are:

___ROSTERS OF CONFEDERATE AND STATE TROOPS, arranged by unit and by county, GDAH, Atlanta, GA.

___CIVIL WAR PRIVATE MANUSCRIPT COLLECTIONS, GDAH, Atlanta, GA.

___UNITED DAUGHTERS OF THE CONFEDERACY TYPE-SCRIPTS OF CIVIL WAR PAPERS AND DIARIES, with CUMULATIVE INDEX, GDAH, Atlanta, GA.

___CIVIL WAR RECORDS, Card Catalog, Microfilm Library, GDAH, Atlanta, GA.

___U. S. Quartermaster General's Office, ROLL OF HONOR, Government Printing Office, Washington, DC, 1866, Volume 3. List of Union prisoners who died at Andersonville and are bvuried in the National Cemetery in Sumter County.

In addition to the above, there are also some county rosters and pension records, as well as some county tax lists which named Confederate pensioners and widows. These will be mentioned in Chapter 4 under the individual county listings.

For a detailed in-depth discussion of Civil War records as sources of genealogical information, consult:

___Geo. K. Schweitzer, CIVIL WAR GENEALOGY, order from the author at the address given on the title page of this book.

There is in the NA an index to service records of the Spanish-American War (1898-9), in which GA men fought:

___The National Archives, GENERAL INDEX TO COMPILED SERVICE RECORDS OF VOLUNTEER SOLDIERS WHO SERVED DURING THE WAR WITH SPAIN, The Archives, Washington, DC, Microfilm Publication M871, 126 rolls, leads to service records in the NA.

The pension records for this war are indexed in:

___The National Archives, GENERAL INDEX TO PENSION FILES, 1861-1934, The Archives, Washington, DC, Microfilm Publication T288, 544 rolls, leads to pension records in the NA.

Again properly submitted NATF-80s (see section 26 for instructions) will bring you both military service and pension records. Or you may choose to hire a searcher or go to the NA yourself. Microfilm T288 is available on loan from AGLL. A published volume of GA soldiers in this war is also available:

___C. J., D. B., and S. Thaxton, A ROSTER OF SPANISH-AMERICAN WAR SOLDIERS FROM GA, Thaxton Co., Americus, GA, 1984.

A state source of GA soldiers which you may find useful is:

___SPANISH-AMERICAN WAR RECORDS, 1898, Record Groups 22-3-12 and 22-3-18, arranged by regiment and company, GDAH, Atlanta, GA.

Some national records for World War I and subsequent wars may be obtained from the following address. However, many documents were destroyed by an extensive fire in 1972. Write for Form 160:

___National Personnel Records Center (MPR), 9700 Page Blvd., St.
Louis, MO 63132.

Draft records for World War I are in Record Group 163 (Records of the
Selective Service System of World War I) at:

___The National Archives, Atlanta Branch, 1557 St. Joseph Ave., East
Point, GA 30344.

A number of GA counties kept registers of World War I service and/or
discharge records. These counties will be indicated in Chapter 4. Records
of GA men who died in World War I are given in:

___B. E. Boss, THE GA STATE MEMORIAL BOOK, Atlanta, GA,
1921.

---

29. Mortuary records

Very few GA mortuary records have been transcribed or microfilmed, even though a few are to be found in manuscript form. This means that you must write directly to the mortuaries which you know or suspect were involved in burying your ancestor. Sometimes a death account will name the mortuary; sometimes it is the only one nearby; sometimes you will have to write several to ascertain which one might have done the funeral arrangements. And you need to realize that before there were mortuaries, the furniture or general merchandise store in some communities handled burials, especially in the supplying of coffins. You may discover that the mortuary that was involved is now out of business, and so you will have to try to discover which of the existing ones may have inherited the records. Mortuaries for GA with their addresses are listed in the following volumes:

___C. O. Kates, editor, THE AMERICAN BLUE BOOK OF FUNERAL
DIRECTORS, Kates-Boyleston Publications, New York, NY,
latest issue.

___NATIONAL DIRECTORY OF MORTICIANS, The Directory,
Youngstown, OH, latest issue.

One or both of these reference books will usually be found in the offices of most mortuaries. In general, the older mortuaries should be the more likely sources of records on your progenitor. In all correspondence with mortuaries be sure to enclose an SASE and make your letters very brief and to the point.

---

30. Naturalization records

In the colonial period, many of the immigrants to the territory that later became the US were from the British Isles and since the colonies were British, they were citizens. When immigrants of other nationalities began to arrive, they found that English traditions, customs, governmental structures, and language generally prevailed. The immigrant aliens were supposed to take oaths of allegiance and abjuration and/or to become naturalized by presenting themselves in court. In a few cases, naturalizations were by special acts of the colonial Assemblies. In 1740, shortly after the settlement of GA, the English Parliament passed a law setting requirements for naturalization: 7 years residence in one colony plus an oath of allegiance to the Crown.

In 1776-7, all those who supported the Revolution were automatically considered to be citizens. During the period 1777-91, immigrants were obligated to take an oath of allegiance. In the year 1778, the Articles of Confederation of the newly established US made all citizens of states citizens of the new nation. The US Congress in 1790 enacted a national naturalization act which required one year's state residence, two year's US residence, and a loyalty oath taken in court. In 1795, a five year's residence came to be required along with a declaration of intent three years before the oath. Then in 1798, these times became 14 and 5 years respectively. Revised statutes of 1802 reverted to the 5 and 3 years of 1795. The declaration and oath could be carried out in any court which kept records (US, GA, county, city). Wives and children of naturalized males became citizens automatically. And persons who gave military service to the US and received an honorable discharge also received citizenship.

In 1906, the Bureau of Immigration and Naturalization was set up, and this agency has kept records on all naturalizations since then. Thus, if you suspect your ancestor was naturalized after September 1906, write to the following address for a Form 6641 which you can use to request records:
____Immigration and Naturalization Service, 425 I Street, Washington, DC, 20536.
For naturalization records before October 1906, you need to realize that the process could have taken place in any of several courts. The most likely places for GA naturalization records are the Federal Courts in Savannah, Macon, Augusta, and Atlanta; the Savannah Civil, City and Superior Courts; the Returns of Qualified Voters for 1867; individual county court records, especially the Superior Court minutes and other records; and city court records. These may be located as follows:
____US FEDERAL COURT NATURALIZATION RECORDS, ATLANTA (1893-), AUGUSTA(1890-), MACON(1880-),

SAVANNAH (1790-), Petitions and Court Journals and Dockets, NAAB, East Point, GA.

___CHATHAM COUNTY NATURALIZATION RECORDS(1792-), Declarations, Certificates, and Court Records, Chatham County Records, GHS, Savannah, GA.

___SAVANNAH AND CHATHAM COUNTY NATURALIZATION RECORDS, SAVANNAH CIVIL COURT(1789-), SAVANNAH CITY COURT(1790-), CHATHAM COUNTY SUPERIOR COURT(1790-1879), Petitions, Certificates, and Court Records, GDAH, Atlanta, GA, and GHS, Savannah, GA. [Search both GDAH and GHS.]

___RETURNS OF QUALIFIED VOTERS FOR 1867, Record Group 1-1-108, GDAH, Atlanta, GA, naturalization data in some returns, arranged by county, but otherwise unindexed.

___COUNTY SUPERIOR COURT MINUTES AND ORDINARY RECORDS, Card Catalogs, Research Area and Microfilm Library, GDAH, Atlanta, Ga.

In addition to the above original records and microfilm copies of them, there are some published naturalization records for GA:

___Mrs. O. Otto, NATURALIZATION OATHS OF ALLEGIANCE GRANTED IN SUPERIOR COURT, SAVANNAH, GA, 1790-1879, The Compiler, Savannah, GA, no date.

___M. R. Hemperley, FEDERAL NATURALIZATION OATHS, SAVANNAH, GA, 1790-1860, GA Historical Quarterly 51(1967) 454-87.

___CHATHAM COUNTY NATURALIZATION PAPERS, 1828-1906, GA Genealogical Society Quarterly 9(1973) 205-17.

___LOOSE CHATHAM COUNTY NATURALIZATION PAPERS, 1828-1906, GA Genealogical Quarterly 15(1979) 69-82.

___EARLY NATURALIZATION RECORDS, GA Genealogical Society Quarterly 4(1968) 823-7.

31. Newspaper records

A sizable number of original and microfilmed newspapers are available for towns, cities, and counties of GA. These newspapers date from 1763 and carry valuable information including national news, local news, ads, legal notices, marriages, and deaths. The first GA newspaper was the GA Gazette which was started in Savannah in 1763, and with time out during the Revolution, continued until 1802. Some other short-lived papers cropped up before 1800, but all except the Augusta Chronicle expired quickly. The Augusta Chronicle came out in 1785 and continues today. Other important early newspapers were the Milledgeville Southern Recorder (1819), the Milledgeville Federal Union (1825), the Macon Telegraph (1826), the Columbus Enquirer (1828), and the Athens Banner-Herald (started 1828 as the Athenian). By 1850, GA had 51 newspapers, five of them being dailies. Of considerable importance to genealogists are several religious papers with GA coverage. In 1833, the Christian Index, a Baptist paper, began publication in Washington, GA. A Methodist journal, the Wesleyan Christian Advocate, was established at Charleston, SC, in 1836 as the Southern Christian Advocate, then transferred to Macon, GA in 1865. Two pioneer specialized newspapers in GA represented agricultural and medical interests: The Southern Cultivator (Augusta in 1842) and the Southern Medical and Surgical Journal (Augusta in 1845).

The largest collection of GA newspapers and microfilms of them is to be found in UGL at Athens, GA. Other collections with good regional and/or local holdings are to be found in GDAH in Atlanta, Atlanta Historical Society, Reese Library at Augusta College in Augusta, and GHS in Savannah. If no success is had in these, then other RL, LL, and college and university libraries in GA should be tried. The Emory University Libraries (in Emory) have general newspapers in their Special Collections and Methodist newspapers in the Theological Seminary holdings. Baptist newspapers are available in the Stetson Library of Mercer University in Macon. There are several important guides, finding aids, and indexes to GA newspapers which can lead you to pertinent materials:

___GA Library Association, GA LIBRARY RESOURCES: NEWSPAPERS, INDEXES, BIBLIOGRAPHIES, The Association, Atlanta, GA, 1973.

___GA Newspaper Project, COMPUTER PRINTOUT OF MICROFILMED GA NEWSPAPERS, The Project, UGL, Athens, GA, latest issue.

___L. Tilgham, NEWSPAPER INDEXES IN THE UGL, The Libraries, Athens, GA, 1981.

___GA Newspaper Project, NEWSPAPER PROJECT FILES AND LISTS, The Project, UGL, Athens, GA.

___INDEX TO SAVANNAH NEWSPAPERS, 1763-1845, UGL, Athens, GA, and GDAH, Atlanta, GA, and GHS, Savannah, GA.

___NEWSPAPER ENTRIES, Card Catalog, Microfilm Library, GDAH, Atlanta, GA.

___R. B. Flanders, NEWSPAPERS AND PERIODICALS IN THE
WASHINGTON MEMORIAL LIBRARY, MACON, GA, NC
Historical Review 7(193).

___INDEX TO SAVANNAH NEWSPAPERS, 1763-1930, GHS,
Savannah, GA.

___M. B. Colket, Jr., INDEXES TO SAVANNAH NEWSPAPERS,
National Genealogical Society Quarterly 79(Sep 1981) 181-3.

___INDEXES TO THE AUGUSTA CHRONICLE, 1861-73, National
Genealogical Society Quarterly 57(1969) 92.

___NEWSPAPER INDEX: ATLANTA CONSTITUTION, Microfilming
Corporation of America, Sanford, NC, 1980.

Three national listings which contain many GA newspapers along
with information on where the originals and/or microfilms of them can be
found are:

___C. S. Brigham, HISTORY AND BIBLIOGRAPHY OF AMERICAN
NEWSPAPERS, 1690-1820, American Antiquarian Society,
Worcester, MA, 1961, 2 volumes.

___W. Gregory, AMERICAN NEWSPAPERS, 1821-1936, H. W. Wilson,
New York, NY, 1937.

___Library of Congress, NEWSPAPERS IN MICROFORM, The Library,
Washington, DC, 1973, plus SUPPLEMENTS, to date.

Unfortunately, not too many newspapers have been indexed, so it is
usually necessary that you have some idea of the time span of your
ancestor, which will facilitate your page-by-page search. However, some
early newspapers have been indexed or genealogical data have been
abstracted from them and then indexed. Reference to some of these
indexes has been made in the previous paragraph, and abstracts will be
treated in the next paragraph. Some newspaper indexes are listed in the
following useful volumes:

___A. C. Milner, NEWSPAPER INDEXES, Metuchen, NJ, 1977-82, 3
volumes.

___N. M.and M. L. Lathrop, LATHROP REPORT ON NEWSPAPER
INDEXES, The Authors, Wooster, OH, 1979.

___B. M. Jarboe, OBITUARIES, A GUIDE TO SOURCES, Hall,
Boston, MA, 1982.

Do not fail to ask in various libraries, particularly in pertinent LL, about
newspaper indexes, since these often exist in card file or manuscript form
in these places.

A considerable amount of work has been done in abstracting, indexing, and publishing genealogical information from early GA newspapers. Included among these valuable works are:

___ANNALS OF SAVANNAH, 1850-1937, DIGEST AND INDEX TO THE SAVANNAH MORNING NEWS, Savannah, GA, 1961.

___GA State Society, DAR, DAR RECORD TYPESCRIPTS, The Daughters, Transcripts in GDAH, Atlanta, GA. [Several contain newspaper notices.]

___F. R. and E. K. Hartz, ABSTRACTS FROM THE GA JOURNAL (MILLEDGEVILLE) NEWSPAPER, 1809-40, The Authors, Vidalia, GA, 1990.

___B. H. Holcomb, MARRIAGE AND DEATH NOTICES FROM BAPTIST NEWSPAPERS OF SC, 1835-65, Reprint Co, Spartanburg, SC, 1981. [Includes Georgians.]

___B. H. Holcomb, MARRIAGE AND DEATH NOTICES FROM THE CHARLESTON OBSERVER, 1827-45, A Press, Greenville, SC, 1980. [Presbyterian, includes Georgians.]

___B. H. Holcomb, MARRIAGE AND DEATH NOTICES FROM THE LUTHERAN OBSERVER, 1831-61, AND THE SOUTHERN LUTHERAN, 1861-5, Southern Historical Press, Easley, SC, 1979.

___B. H. Holcomb, MARRIAGE AND DEATH NOTICES FROM THE SOUTHERN CHRISTIAN ADVOCATE, 1837-67, Southern Historical Press, Easley, SC, 1979, 2 volumes. [Methodist]

___R. A. Hodge, SOME GA REPORTED DEATHS (NEWSPAPERS), 1842-8, The Author, Fredericksburg, VA, 1977. [Three weekly newspapers.]

___F. Huxford, MARRIAGES AND OBITUARIES FROM EARLY GA NEWSPAPERS, Southern Historical Press, Easley, SC, 1989.

___F. Huxford, GENEALOGICAL MATERIAL FROM LEGAL NOTICES FROM EARLY GA NEWSPAPERS, Southern Historical Press, Easley, SC, 1989.

___E. T. LeMaster, ABSTRACTS OF GA DEATH NOTICES FROM THE SOUTHERN RECORDER, 1830-55, Orange County Genealogical Society, Orange, CA, 1968.

___E. T. LeMaster, ABSTRACTS OF MARRIAGE NOTICES FROM THE SOUTHERN RECORDER, 1830-55, Orange County Genealogical Society, Orange, CA, 1971.

___M. E. Overby, OBITUARIES PUBLISHED BY THE CHRISTIAN INDEX, 1822-99, GA Baptist Historical Society, Washington, GA, 1981, 2 volumes.

___M. E. Overby and J. M. Lancaster, MARRIAGES PUBLISHED IN THE CHRISTIAN INDEX, 1828-55, GA Baptist Historical Society, Washington, GA, 1971.

___W. Rocker, MARRIAGES AND OBITUARIES, MACON, GA, MESSENGER, 1818-65, Southern Historical Press, Easley, SC, 1985.

___A. O. Walker, PERSONAL INDEX TO THE AUGUSTA CHRONI-CLE, 1786-1910, Augusta Public Library, Augusta, GA, 1987-8, 2 volumes.

___M. B. Warren and S. F. White, MARRIAGES AND DEATHS ABSTRACTED FROM EXTANT GA NEWSPAPERS, 1763-1830, Heritage Papers, Danielsville, GA, 1968/72, 2 volumes.

___M. B. Warren, THE MACON, GA, TELEGRAPH, 1826-39, Heritage Papers, Athens, GA, 1991/2, 2 volumes.

___B. W. Wright, ABSTRACTS OF DEATHS REPORTED IN THE COLUMBUS ENQUIRER, 1832-52, The Author, Columbus, GA, 1980.

___B. W. Wright, ABSTRACTS OF MARRIAGES REPORTED IN THE COLUMBUS ENQUIRER, 1832-52, The Author, Columbus, GA, 1980.

___B. W. Wright, BURIALS AND DEATHS REPORTED IN THE COLUMBUS ENQUIRER, The Author, Columbus, GA, 1984.

___DEATH NOTICES, CITATIONS, LEGAL ADS, AND MARRIAGE ANNOUNCEMENTS FROM OLD GA NEWSPAPERS, GA Genealogical Magazine, Numbers 1-33, 1961-9.

32. Published indexes for the US

There are many published indexes, microfilm indexes, and card indexes which list exceptionally large numbers of published genealogies or lots of genealogical data at the national level. The most important indexes dealing exclusively with GA have been listed in section 18. This section sets out further indexes to genealogies all over the US (and overseas in some instances). These indexes contain many references to genealogies of GA people and therefore you must not fail to look into them. Among the larger ones are:

___INTERNATIONAL GENEALOGICAL INDEX, FHL and FHC, microfilm and computer disk.. [over 200 million entries]

___FAMILY GROUP RECORDS ARCHIVES, at FHL, available through FHC. [40 million entries]

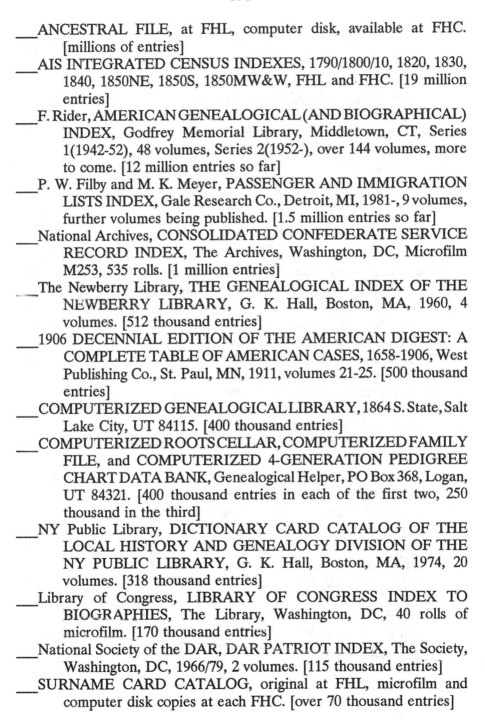

__ANCESTRAL FILE, at FHL, computer disk, available at FHC. [millions of entries]

__AIS INTEGRATED CENSUS INDEXES, 1790/1800/10, 1820, 1830, 1840, 1850NE, 1850S, 1850MW&W, FHL and FHC. [19 million entries]

__F. Rider, AMERICAN GENEALOGICAL (AND BIOGRAPHICAL) INDEX, Godfrey Memorial Library, Middletown, CT, Series 1(1942-52), 48 volumes, Series 2(1952-), over 144 volumes, more to come. [12 million entries so far]

__P. W. Filby and M. K. Meyer, PASSENGER AND IMMIGRATION LISTS INDEX, Gale Research Co., Detroit, MI, 1981-, 9 volumes, further volumes being published. [1.5 million entries so far]

__National Archives, CONSOLIDATED CONFEDERATE SERVICE RECORD INDEX, The Archives, Washington, DC, Microfilm M253, 535 rolls. [1 million entries]

__The Newberry Library, THE GENEALOGICAL INDEX OF THE NEWBERRY LIBRARY, G. K. Hall, Boston, MA, 1960, 4 volumes. [512 thousand entries]

__1906 DECENNIAL EDITION OF THE AMERICAN DIGEST: A COMPLETE TABLE OF AMERICAN CASES, 1658-1906, West Publishing Co., St. Paul, MN, 1911, volumes 21-25. [500 thousand entries]

__COMPUTERIZED GENEALOGICAL LIBRARY, 1864 S. State, Salt Lake City, UT 84115. [400 thousand entries]

__COMPUTERIZED ROOTS CELLAR, COMPUTERIZED FAMILY FILE, and COMPUTERIZED 4-GENERATION PEDIGREE CHART DATA BANK, Genealogical Helper, PO Box 368, Logan, UT 84321. [400 thousand entries in each of the first two, 250 thousand in the third]

__NY Public Library, DICTIONARY CARD CATALOG OF THE LOCAL HISTORY AND GENEALOGY DIVISION OF THE NY PUBLIC LIBRARY, G. K. Hall, Boston, MA, 1974, 20 volumes. [318 thousand entries]

__Library of Congress, LIBRARY OF CONGRESS INDEX TO BIOGRAPHIES, The Library, Washington, DC, 40 rolls of microfilm. [170 thousand entries]

__National Society of the DAR, DAR PATRIOT INDEX, The Society, Washington, DC, 1966/79, 2 volumes. [115 thousand entries]

__SURNAME CARD CATALOG, original at FHL, microfilm and computer disk copies at each FHC. [over 70 thousand entries]

___J. Munsell's Sons, INDEX TO AMERICAN GENEALOGIES, 1711-1908, Genealogical Publishing Co., Baltimore, MD, 1967. [60 thousand entries]

___M. J. Kaminkow, GENEALOGIES IN THE LIBRARY OF CONGRESS, Magna Carta, Baltimore, MD, 1981. [50 thousand entries]

The books listed above are generally available at GDAH, UGL, WML, and GHS, as well as most LGL, some RL, and a few LL. The FHL materials are at FHC or access to them can be had through FHC. The NA microfilms are available at NA and at some NAFB. And the computerized data materials may be accessed through the places named.

33. Regional publications

In addition to national, state, and local publications, there are also some regional publications which should not be overlooked by any GA researcher. For the most part, these are volumes which are basically historical in character, but carry much genealogical information. They vary greatly in accuracy and coverage, so it is well to treat the data cautiously. In general, they cover specific regions which are usually made up of a few or many GA counties. In deciding which ones of these books to search for your forebears, you will need to make good use of the geographic and county maps of Chapter 1. The following works are ones which should prove useful to you:

___J. H. Averitt, GA'S COASTAL PLAIN, Lewis Historical Publishing Co., New York, NY, 1964, volume 3.

___G. H. Cartledge, HISTORICAL SKETCHES, PRESBYTERIAN CHURCHES, AND EARLY SETTLERS IN NORTHEAST GA, Mize and Newton, Athens, GA, 1960.

___R. S. Davis, Jr., THE WILKES COUNTY PAPERS, 1773-1833, Southern Historical Press, Easley, SC, 1979. [Wilkes County at one time had over one-third of GA's population.]

___G. G. Davidson, EARLY RECORDS OF GA: WILKES COUNTY, Southern Historical Press, Easley, SC, 1932(1967).

___F. M. Garrett, ATLANTA AND ENVIRONS, A CHRONICLE OF ITS PEOPLE AND EVENTS, Lewis Publishing Co., New York, NY, 1954, volume 3.

___G. R. Gilmer, SKETCHES OF SOME OF THE FIRST SETTLERS OF UPPER GA, Americus Book Co., Americus, GA, 1855(1926).

___W. Harden, A HISTORY OF SAVANNAH AND SOUTH GA, Lewis Publishing Co., Chicago, IL, 1913, 2 volumes.

___F. Huxford, PIONEERS OF WIREGRASS, EARLY SETTLERS IN COUNTIES OF IRWIN, APPLING, WAYNE, CAMDEN, AND GLYNN, The Author, Homerville, GA, 1948-75, 7 volumes.

___F. Huxford, INDEXED FINDING LIST TO PIONEERS OF WIRE-GRASS GA, Huxford Genealogical Society, Homerville, GA.

___T. H. Martin, ATLANTA AND ITS BUILDERS, Century Memorial Publishing Co., Atlanta, GA, 1902, volume 2.

34. Tax, voter, and jury lists

Among the very useful records kept in GA counties are tax lists, voter lists, and jury lists. Some important lists of taxpayers and voters were also kept at the state and federal levels. Although many of these records have been lost, and some are at the time inaccessible, quite a few are available to GA researchers. First, we will consider tax lists. Prior to 1805, GA tax law varied from year to year, but beginning in 1805 the tax included a poll tax on males over 21 (and under 61, after 1825), a slave tax on each slave age 21-60, a tax on town lots and buildings, a tax on land (varied according to quality of the land), a tax on professionals (physicians, lawyers, for example), and a tax on carriages. In 1852, the tax system was altered to then include a poll tax, a slave tax, a land tax, a tax on money and accounts, and a tax on other property (after certain deductions and exemptions). Under both systems, the land being taxed was identified under the county, the militia district within the county, the watercourses on which it was located, and sometimes whose land it bordered. Tax lists were generally organized under militia districts of a county.

There is a valuable compilation of early GA tax lists which has been published. It contains data for the following counties and dates: Camden(1794, 1809), Chatham(1806), Glynn(1790/4), Hancock(1812), Lincoln(1818), Montgomery(1797/8, 1805/6), Pulaski(1818), Richmond-(1818), Warren(1794, 1805/18), and Wilkes(1792-4).

___R. Blair, SOME EARLY TAX LISTS OF GA, Southern Historical Press, Easley, SC, 1926(1971). [36000 names]

In addition, there have recently been printed five volumes of GA tax digest indexes which have an even broader coverage, both in time (1789-1817) and in geography (24 early counties):

___Taylor Foundation, AN INDEX TO GA TAX DIGESTS, 1789-1817, Reprint Co, Spartanburg, SC, 1986, 5 volumes.

Some tax default records have also been published:

___TAX LISTS: DEFAULTERS FOR VARIOUS GA COUNTIES, GA
     Genealogist, State Records 3-66.

A number of GA tax lists are in the county CH, but many of the surviving
ones are in the GDAH, either as original state copies or as microfilms.
These will be listed in Chapter 4 under the counties. Most of the lists
prior to 1873 are on microfilm, whereas those after that date are
manuscript state copies. There are also some available among the loose
records at GDAH.

___PRE-1873 GA COUNTY TAX DIGESTS(LISTS), Microfilm Library,
     GDAH, Atlanta, GA.

___POST-1872 GA COUNTY TAX DIGESTS(LISTS), Inventory in Law
     Wing, GDAH, Atlanta, GA.

___LOOSE RECORDS OF GA COUNTIES, Inventory in Law Wing,
     GDAH, Atlanta, GA. [Some tax lists included]

The tax digests for 1906-38 often contain lists of Civil War veterans. In
1865-71, the Internal Revenue Service compiled lists of assessments of GA
residents. These lists are available on microfilm at NA and NAAB and
as originals at NAAB.

___The National Archives, INTERNAL REVENUE ASSESSMENT
     LISTS FOR GA, 1865-6, The Archives, Washington, DC,
     Microfilm M762, 8 rolls. Originals for 1865-71 at NAAB.

These records reflect a federal tax which was placed on goods, services,
licenses, income over $600, and personal property during 1865-71.

There are two other types of records which are often related to tax
lists. These are records which were kept in the GA counties and were
known as homestead and pony homestead records. They must not be
confused with the federal homestead records which relate to the granting
of federal lands after 1862. The GA county homestead records consist of
petitions by land owners for property tax exemptions (on land, houses,
cattle) or release from obligations to creditors by reason of poverty. The
GA pony homestead records are similar, but they apply to taxes and debts
on personal property. The dates for which these records are available in
each of the GA counties are listed in Chapter 4 under the counties.

Now let us turn to the much less abundant voter lists and jury lists.
During the reconstruction period following the end of the Civil War, a
constitutional convention to bring GA back into the Union was held. In
order to vote for the delegates, a GA resident had to take an amnesty
oath and register. Over 118,000 persons qualified, slightly less than half
being black. Their names are listed in two sets of records which are arranged by county, but unfortunately not indexed. Many of the records list

only the names, but some of them give added personal data, including naturalization details. Both sets of records are in GDAH.

___REGISTRATION OF OATH BOOK, 1867, Record Group 1-1-107, GDAH, Atlanta, GA.

___RETURNS OF QUALIFIED VOTERS, 1867, Record Group 1-1-108, GDAH, Atlanta, GA.

There are also records of those who signed amnesty oaths which are among the GA county records which have been microfilmed and are in the Microfilm Library at GDAH. In addition, there are microfilms of some other county voter lists. All these will be indicated under the pertinent counties in Chapter 4. Among these same microfilms are to be found jury lists in various GA counties. In some counties, the lists were separated and recorded in books dedicated to this. In other counties, jury lists are in the Superior Court minutes, and therefore must be sought there. The county listings in Chapter 4 will tell you which counties have jury lists and/or Superior Court minutes on microfilm in GDAH.

35. Will and intestate records

When a person died leaving property (an estate), it was necessary for the governmental authorities to see that it was properly distributed according to GA law. If a will had been written (a testate situation), it had usually been filed in the proper governmental office. Upon the death of the person, the will was presented to the office for authentication. When this process, called probate, had been carried through, the executor(s) named in the will did the actual work of distributing the estate under the supervision of the authorities. If the will had not been previously filed and copied into the records, this was done. If no will had been written, this being called an intestate situation, the authorities appointed an administrator who carried out the distribution of the estate in accordance with the requirements of the law. During the colonial period, GA operated with primogeniture in intestate situations, but this was abandoned after the Revolution. In the various actions by which executors and administrators distributed the estate, many records were generated because complete accounting to the authorities was required. These records included annual returns, appraisements, general estate records, Inferior Court minutes and other records, inventories, Ordinary minutes and other records, twelve-month supports, and some others. As was pointed out in section 11, up until after the Revolution, GA had no counties, and practically all records, including estate records, were maintained at Savannah for all of GA. After the Revolution, counties were formed, and estate matters were transferred to the Inferior Courts in the counties until 1869, when the Ordinary or Probate Court took over the task.

Items of genealogical import which are often found in will and intestate records are date of death and/or probate, occupation, property owned, religion, citizenship, residence, wife's name, whether wife is living or not, parents' names, children's names, order of children's births, children which are minors, names of children's spouses, slaves, family friends, and associates. Among the colonial GA estate records are the following materials in GDAH:

___ GA COLONIAL RECORD BOOK G, APPRAISEMENTS 1777-8, Microfilm Library, GDAH, Atlanta, GA.

___ GA COLONIAL RECORD BOOKS F, FF, GG, INVENTORIES 1755-78, Microfilm Library, GDAH, Atlanta, GA.

___ GA COLONIAL RECORD BOOKS D, Z, G, LETTERS OF ADMINISTRATION AND ADMINISTRATIONS 1755-75, Microfilm Reels 40-31 and 81-5, Microfilm Library, GDAH, Atlanta, GA. [Books D and Z also in book by Dumont.]

___ GA COLONIAL RECORD BOOK N, LETTERS OF GUARDIAN-SHIP 1757-77, Microfilm Reel 40-31, Microfilm Library, GDAH, Atlanta, GA. [Also in book by Dumont.]

___ GA COLONIAL RECORD BOOKS A, AA, B, WILLS 1754-78, Microfilm Reels 40-29, 17-24, 40-34, Microfilm Library, GDAH, Atlanta, GA. [Also in books by Brooke, Bryan, and Dumont.]

___ GA LOOSE ESTATE PAPERS 1776-94, Microfilm Reels 230-2, 230-21, 230-22, 230-23, 230-24, 230-33, 230-34, Microfilm Library, GDAH, Atlanta, GA.

___ GA LOOSE WILLS 1733-77, Microfilm Reels 231-43, 231-44, Microfilm Library, GDAH, Atlanta, GA. [See books by Brooke and Bryan.]

As indicated in the notes following the above entries, several good publications listing or abstracting and indexing some of these early estate records have been compiled:

___ T. O. Brooke, IN THE NAME OF GOD, AMEN: GA WILLS, 1733-1860, Pilgrim Press, Atlanta, GA, 1976.

___ M. G. Bryan, ABSTRACTS OF THE COLONIAL WILLS OF GA, 1733-77, Reprint Co, Spartanburg, SC, 1962(1981).

___ INDEX TO PROBATE RECORDS OF COLONIAL GA, 1733-78, Taylor Foundation, Atlanta, GA, 1983.

___ W. H. Dumont, COLONIAL GA GENEALOGICAL DATA, 1748-83, National Genealogical Society, Washington, DC, 1971. [Not comprehensive.]

___J. H. McCall, INDEX TO GA WILLS, The Author, Jonesboro, GA, no date.

From the beginning of GA's counties just after the Revolution, estate record keeping was transferred to them. The various estate records available on microfilm in GDAH for each of GA's counties are listed in Chapter 4. Be sure to look under all types of records mentioned in the first paragraph of this section. In addition, there are also some published materials which you must not overlook:

___J. H. Austin, INDEX TO GA WILLS, 1777-1924, Genealogical Publishing Co., Baltimore, MD, 1976(1985).

___J. H. Austin, GA INTESTATE RECORDS, Genealogical Publishing Co., Baltimore, MD, 1986. [For the 57 counties formed before 1832.]

___S. Q. Smith, EARLY GA WILLS AND SETTLEMENTS OF ESTATES, WILKES COUNTY, Genealogical Publishing Co., Baltimore, MD, 1959(1976). [Wilkes County had well over one-third of GA's population at one time.]

36. WPA records

In 1935, the Works Progress Administration (WPA) was established to create jobs for the unemployed whose numbers were very high at this point in the Depression. Until 1941, many workers were engaged, including persons who transcribed, indexed and inventoried governmental and historical records. A great deal of work was done in GA, as is evidenced by the numerous references to the WPA materials in previous sections of this chapter. The purpose of this section is to alert you to the large amount of work that was done and to ask you to make sure you have looked into their materials in your ancestor quest. The WPA transcripts, indexes, and inventories are chiefly located in GDAH, UGL, and GHS, although you may find copies of some locally-pertinent materials in RL and LL. They may be located in card catalogs by looking under GA, the county, and US Government, Works Progress Administration. Among the things you will find are:

___WPA INDEX TO PUBLISHED COLONIAL RECORDS OF GA

___WPA INDEX TO REVOLUTIONARY RECORDS OF GA

___WPA INVENTORIES OF COUNTY ARCHIVES OF GA

___WPA INVENTORY OF CHURCH ARCHIVES OF GA

___WPA TYPESCRIPTS OF UNPUBLISHED COLONIAL RECORDS OF GA, indexed

___WPA TYPESCRIPTS, GA MILITARY AFFAIRS, 1775-1842, 9 volumes, indexed

___WPA TYPESCRIPTS, GA MILITARY RECORD BOOKS, 1779-,
    both typescripts and microfilms of typescripts, indexed
___WPA TYPESCRIPTS OF PASSPORTS ISSUED BY GA GOVER-
    NORS, 1785-1820, indexed
___WPA TYPESCRIPTS, INDIAN DEPREDATIONS, 8 books, indexed
___WPA TYPESCRIPT OF CHEROKEE AND CREEK INDIAN
    LETTERS, indexed
___WPA TYPESCRIPTS OF EARLY LEGISLATIVE MINUTES AND
    GOVERNOR'S LETTERBOOKS, indexed
___WPA TYPESCRIPTS OF GA COUNTY COURTHOUSE
    RECORDS, Manuscript Department, Special Collections, UGL,
    Athens, GA, indexed
___WPA TYPESCRIPTS OF GA CEMETERY, CHURCH, MAR-
    RIAGE, AND NEWSPAPER RECORDS, indexed

Chapter 3

RECORD LOCATIONS

Many original county and city records referred to in Chapter 2 and listed under the counties in Chapter 4 are stored in the CH (court houses) and the city buildings. However, many of these original county and city records have been transferred to GDAH (GA Department of Archives and History), particularly pre-1900 records for counties formed before 1900. In addition, the GDAH has microfilms of many of the original records. The CH of the GA counties are located in the county seats, which are listed along with their zip codes in Chapter 4. The original records usually consist of variously labelled books (ordinarily handwritten), files with file folders in them, and boxes with large envelopes, file folders, or loose records in them. The records are generally stored in the offices of county officials or in special storage vaults in the CH, or those that have been transferred to GDAH are stored in special controlled atmosphere rooms. The records which will be most likely to be found in the CH and the GDAH include civil records (road, merchant, license, school, voter, etc.), court records (Inferior, jury, Ordinary, Superior, etc.), land records (deed, mortgage, tax, etc.), probate records (administrator, appraisement, estate, inventory, twelve months support, will, etc.), and vital records (birth, marriage, death).

Once you have located the county in which your ancestor lived, it is generally not a good idea to go there first. It is better to explore the microfilmed, transcribed, and published copies of the records at central repositories, particularly GDAH, WML, and FHL (or FHC). This is because it is the business of these repositories to make the records available to you, whereas the primary task of the county officials and employees at the CH is to conduct the record keeping task as an aid to regulating the society and keeping the law. Therefore, it is best not to encroach upon their time and good graces until you have done as much work elsewhere as possible. Many of the most important county and city records have been microfilmed, transcribed, or published, so you can go through them at GDAH, WML, and FHL(FHC). Or you can hire a searcher to do the investigating for you if a trip is not workable or would be too expensive. Then, and only then, should you contact the LL and CH.

In practically all cases, you will find the overworked people in the local CH very helpful and cooperative, especially if you are courteous, brief in your requests, and do not bore them and consume their valuable time by going into any detail on your ancestral lines. Often they will photocopy materials for a small fee or they will make a copying machine available to you. Please exercise a great deal of caution with the old records that you use so that you in no way damage them. Your visit to a county seat should not begin at the CH; it should begin at the LL, then proceed to any other local repositories (cemeteries, mortuaries, newspapers, genealogical society libraries, historical society libraries). Then, as the last activity of your visit, go to the CH. Researchers who live near county seats (LL and CH), as well as ones near GDAH, UGL, WML, GHS, and NA may be located in:

_V. N. Chambers, editor, GENEALOGICAL HELPER, Everton Publishers, Logan, UT, latest September-October issue.

---

2. The major facilities

The best overall place in the world to do GA genealogical research is in Atlanta, GA. This city contains the most heavily stocked GA genealogical collection in existence, the GA Department of Archives and History (GDAH). Within 90 miles of Atlanta, there are two other important repositories, the University of GA Libraries (UGL) at Athens, and the Washington Memorial Library at Macon (WML), the latter also being the Middle GA Regional Library. In Savannah, 255 miles to the southeast of Atlanta, is the GA Historical Society Library (GHS), another quite notable repository for genealogical materials, particularly ones relating to early and eastern (or coastal) GA.

In the western United States is the largest genealogical library in the world, the Family History Library of the Genealogical Society of Utah (FHL), also known as the LDS Library or the Mormon Library. This facility has microfilm copies of many of the records in GDAH and has many of the publications to be found in GDAH, UGL, WML, and GHS. The FHL has about 400 branch Family History Centers (FHC) located all over the US, plus many more in other countries. Each of these branches has indexes to the holdings of FHL, and provides services allowing you to borrow the vast microfilm holdings of the FHL. You can then use the borrowed microfilms at the FHC through which you requested them.

In addition to the above facilities, there is in Atlanta a National Archives Field Branch (NAFB), the National Archives Atlanta Branch (NAAB), which holds some original southeastern US records and many microfilm copies of records in the National Archives (NA). There are also several regional libraries (RL) in GA which are larger than average and have sizable genealogical collections, usually devoted to their regions. Further, some of the GA colleges and universities, in addition to the University of GA, have manuscript and/or family history materials which are useful for genealogical research. All the above repositories will be treated in detail in this chapter.

---

3. The GA Department of Archives and History (GDAH)

The GA Department of Archives and History (hereafter abbreviated as GDAH) is located in the Ben W. Fortson, Jr. Archives and Records Building at 330 Capitol Avenue, SE, Atlanta, GA 30334. The telephone number is 1-404-656-2350 and the Fax number is 1-404-657-8427. The GDAH is situated two blocks south of the GA State Capitol in downtown Atlanta. Its hours of operation are 8:00 am to 4:15 pm on Monday through Friday, and 9:30 am to 3:15 pm on Saturday.. Exceptions to these hours are on state and federal holidays. Always be sure to check on these times since they are subject to change. The GDAH is readily accessible from the three major interstate routes which pass near it as they go through downtown Atlanta: I-20 and I-75/85. Parking is available in a lot behind the GDAH for a small fee. In the area 10 to 15 blocks north of the GDAH are numerous hotels (Area Code for all is 404): Best Western American (688-8600), Comfort Inn (524-5555), Days Inn (523-1144), Hilton (659-2000), Holiday Inn (659-2727), Hyatt (577-1234), Inn at Peachtree (577-6970), Marriott (521-0000), Quality Inn (577-1980), Radisson (659-6500), Ritz-Carlton (659-0400), Travelodge (659-4545), and Westin (659-1400). The convenient subway will take you from this area down to the GA State Station which is near the GDAH.

The GDAH is the best single place to start genealogical research for your GA ancestor. The primary function of the GDAH is to collect, preserve, and make available the records of the GA State Government. The Archives also serves as a repository for many other GA records which relate to GA history, particularly those of county and federal origin, plus many private materials. The Search Room contains over 15000 volumes of genealogical materials, state and county and city histories, legal publications, historical and genealogical periodicals, published censuses and indexes to them, and finding aids to numerous governmental and private records which are in storage. The Microfilm Library holds over 30000 reels of copies of county, state, federal, and private records including the following types: Bible, cemetery, census, church, court, immigration, land, manuscript, marriage, military, naturalization, newspaper, probate, tax, will. The GA General Surveyor Division of the GDAH holds over 1.5 million state land grants and plats, and about 10000 maps. More of the records discussed in Chapters 2 and 4 of this book are in GDAH than in any other single place.

When you enter GDAH, you will find yurself in a large lobby with a registration desk directly ahead, lockers and a snack area to the right, and rest rooms to the left. Go to the registration desk, complete an application for a research card, show some identification, sign in and obtain an admission badge, ask for a locker key, and request an information sheet, a copy of the rules, and a map of the Search Room. Put your coat, briefcase, bags, all plastic sheet protectors, and all personal belongings, except notebooks and pencils, in your assigned locker. Then, enter the Search Room using the door to the left of the registration desk. Check with the security officer there, take a seat, and read the rules. Chief among these regulations are: (1) only pencils, paper, and brief notes allowed, (2) no eating, drinking, smoking, or loud talk, (3) extreme care with all materials, (4) no reshelving of books and files, (4) properly refile all microfilm, and (5) a security check of all items upon leaving.

Now take your Search Room Map in hand, and glance around to see how the facilities are organized. From a position just inside the door, to your near left are bookshelves, then a door to the cash register, city directories, and periodicals, and to your far left more bookshelves. In front of the far-left bookshelves, notice the information desks with microfiche catalog card readers at the far end. Then straight ahead against the back wall you will see the card catalog, the general name file, family chart files, and to the right of them the vertical name file, and print and photograph indexes. On your near right, are several shelves with law books, beyond them DAR records, bookshelves, the family exchange file, and the door to the Microfilm Room (with microfilms and readers). On your far right are more bookshelves with an atlas stand in front of them. Microfiche catalog readers and copiers are at several places in the room. On Floor 2V just above you is the Original Documents Reading Area. Records to be examined there must be requested in the Search Room.

The key to the vast resources of the GDAH consists of its finding aids (indexes, card catalogs, microfiche catalog, files, alphabetical lists, inventories). These finding aids will tell you what records are available and exactly where you will find them. Practically all reference materials are listed in finding aids by name, location, subject, author, and/or title. You can remember these categores by recalling the word SLANT (Subject, Location, Author, Name, Title). When searching indexes, catalogs, files, and other finding aids, it is best to check to see if your forebear's NAME is listed, then to look under the LOCALITY where he lived (county, city, town, and also GA), then look under various SUBJECT headings that might apply (including the section headings in Chapter 2), then under the AUTHOR of any works that you want to see, and finally, under the TITLE of any volumes not previously covered. Please do not forget to look under GA when doing your locality search. Now, let us show you precisely what finding aids you need to use for your research, and what to look for in each of them. All the records mentioned in Chapters 2 and 4 which the GDAH holds can be found easily by this process.

In the Search Room, there will be found several microfiche catalog readers, each accompanied by:

___(R1) Book Catalog, on microfiche. Search by county, city, town, region, GA, subject, author, title, organization.

You will also see a set of large card catalog cabinets. They contain the following alphabetical (or chronological) card files:

___(R2) General Name File (148 drawers). Names abstracted from a vast number of GDAH records. Look under name.

___(R3) Manuscripts Subject File (5 drawers). Look under subject and name.

___(R4) Manuscripts Main File (2 drawers). Look under name, subject, location.

___(R5) Manuscripts Geographical File (2 drawers). Look under location: county, city, town.

___(R6) Manuscripts Chronological File (2 drawers). Look under date.

___(R7) Manuscripts Form File (1 drawer). Manuscripts listed by type of document: account books, legal documents, personal narratives, etc.

___(R8) Miscellaneous Church and Cemetery File (1 drawer). Look under GA, then under both denomination and county.

___(R9) DAR Compilations (1 drawer). Look under county.

___(R10) Vertical Subject File (1 drawer). Look under subject, name, location (county, city, town), organization.

___(R11) Serials (1 drawer). Names of periodicals, including historical and genealogical journals.

On top of the Card Catalogs Cabinets, you will find:

___(R12) Inventories of Manuscript Collections (4 boxes). Listings of contents of many manuscript groups.

And sitting by the Card Catalogs, there are the:

___(R13) Vertical File Cabinets, arranged by (A) 1 drawer of Loose Headright and Bounty Records, (B) 7 drawers of Genealogical Folders, (c) 2 drawers of Church and Cemetery Files, and (d) 2 drawers of GA Miscellany by Subject.

Also in or near the Search Room are to be found some further sets of finding aids:

___(R14) Family Exchange File. Cards submitted by persons searching various family names. Look under name.

___(R15) Knight GA Scrapbook Catalog. Located on a free-standing shelf just to the right as one enters the Search Room (above the law books). An extensive index to numerous GA events. Look under name, subject, locality (county, city, town).

___(R16) Indexes and Other Finding Aids to the Print and Photograph Collections in the GDAH. Look under name and locality.

___(R17) Finding Aids to US, GA, and GA County Records. Located to the left of the entrance with the periodicals.

___(R18) Finding Aids to GA Colonial Records. Located at F281.C71 on the bookshelves. Also on microfilm in the Microfilm Room, Drawer 40, Boxes 51-69.

___(R19) Microfiche Index to Vital Records (Deaths 1919-93, Marriages 1964-92, and Divorces 1965-92).

___(R20) Computer Disk Indexes to GA Marriage and Census Records.

When you find books that you wish to use, copy the reference numbers from the card or the entry, then go to the bookshelves and find the volume. If you cannot locate it, check at one of the information desks. When you find files or manuscripts that you want to see, request them at an information desk. The person in charge will locate the files or make arrangements for you to examine the manuscripts on Floor 2V.

In the Microfilm Room, you will be able to make use of finding aids located on some shelves and in two Card Catalogs located to the right of the entrance door. The first card catalog cabinet contains:

___(M1) GA County Records Catalog (11 drawers). Lists governmental records available on microfilm for GA counties. Look under county.

___(M2) GA Tax Digests (1 drawer). Refers to tax record lists available on microfilm for GA counties. Look under county.

___(M3) US Records Pertaining to GA (1 drawer). Includes Indian, Census (regular, agricultural, industrial, mortality, slaveholder), US Circuit Court, Freedmen's Bureau, Confederate Service Records, Cherokee Disturbance Military Records, Revolutionary War Records, US Military Post Returns.

___(M4) GA Official Records (1 drawer). Includes Adjutant General Military Records, Board of Corrections Penal Records, GA Colony Records (military, land, bond, claims, deed, estate, mortgage), Confederate Pensions, Secretary of State (biographies, county officials), Surveyor General Records (lotteries, headrights, maps, plats).

The second card catalog cabinet contains:

___(M5) GA Municipal Records Catalog (1 drawer). Lists governmental records available on microfilm for GA municipalities. Look under city or town.

___(M6) Books File (1 drawer). Microfilmed books. Look under subject, author, title.

___(M7) Bible Records (3 drawers). Look under name.

___(M8) Non-Governmental Records, Counties File (3 drawers). Includes cemetery, church, societies, business, school, newspapers, manuscripts. Look under county.

___(M9) Non-Governmental Recorrds, Cities File (1 drawer). Look under city or town.

___(M10) Cemeteries File (1 drawer). Look under county.

___(M11) Newspapers File (2 drawers). Look under city or town.

___(M12) Church and Synagogue Records File (2 drawers). Look under denomination, then under church name.

___(M13) Genealogical Information File (2 drawers). Look under name.

___(M14) Private Papers (2 drawers). Look under name.

___(M15) Subject File (3 drawers). Non-governmental records, including Civil War diaries and regimental histories. Look under subject and name.

___(M16) Private Collection Inventories (4 boxes on top of the cabinet). Look under name.

On the shelves will be found:

___(M17) GA Federal Census Indexes. Numerous published volumes. Look under name.

___(M18) GA Church Records on Microfilm at the GDAH.

When you locate microfilms that you want, copy from the reference card or list the drawer number and the film number. Then go to the proper film cabinet, remove the film, and take it to to a reader. Please do not forget to correctly replace the film after use.

On the law book shelves in the Search Room, you will find volumes relating to the laws, legislature, executive officers, and state courts of GA. The GDAH also has some very valuable preliminary looseleaf inventories of state and county records, including some original records which are not referenced elsewhere in the GDAH. These inventories are located on the right just inside the door to the city directories and periodicals. Among the most useful of these for family searchers are the following (RG stands for Record Group):

_(L1) RG-1-1-5 Incoming Correspondence to the Governor.
_(L2) RG-1-1-23 Governor' Proclamations on Murderers.
_(L3) RG-1-1-107/8 Qualified Voters of 1867. Also on microfilm.
_(L4) RG 1-2-32 County Officials and Militia Commissions.
_(L5) RG 1-4-42 Prison and Prisoner Records.
_(L6) RG 1-6 Loyalist Property Confiscations.
_(L7) RG 6-10-11 Medical Personnel Certifications.
_(L8) RG 21 Prison and Prisoner Records.
_(L9) RG 22-3-12/18 Spanish-American War Records. Also on microfilm.
_(L10) RG 31 Prison and Prisoner Records. Also on microfilm.
_(L11) RG 34-6 County Property Tax Digests (Lists). Also on microfilm.
_(L12) RG 37-8 Loyalist Property Confiscations.
_(L13) RG 49 GA Colonial Government. Also on microfilm.
_(L14) RG 56 GA Court of Appeals Records.
_(L15) RG 58 Confederate Pension Records. Also on microfilm.
_(L16) RG 92 GA Supreme Court Records.
_(L17) RG 101 through 259 Loose County and City Records.
Under no circumstance should you fail to check L11, L15, and L17. When you locate records which you want to see, copy down the exact numbers, names, and descriptions, then request them at an information desk.

In the GA Surveyor General Department, located on Floor 2V, are the records of the granting and surveying of GA land to its first owners by the colony and state. The major finding aids to this large collection of documents are a series of many published volumes of indexes which were listed in section 22 of Chapter 2. These may be consulted in the Research Room after you have found them through the use of the Microfiche Book Catalog. Once you have located an ancestor in these index volumes, you should consult the copies of the records in the Microfilm Room. The Surveyor General Department has several supplementary card indexes and manuscript finding aids which they can use to locate documents for you. Of interest are two card indexes to fractional land grants, these being lots which were too small to include in the lotteries, so they were sold at public auction. Other indexes relate to plats which were associated with the colonial and headright grants. The GA Surveyor General Department also has an extensive collection of maps for GA and its counties. These maps are listed in several finding aids including a computer database.

As you can see from the above, the GDAH is a literal treasure house of GA genealogical information. The finding aids are well organized and will lead you quickly to the records you need to examine. The most important of the finding aids should be used first: R1, R2, R9, R14, R17, R19, R20, M1, M2, M3, M4, M7, M8, M10, M12, M17, L10, L11, L15, L17. The R-- finding aids are in the Research Area, the M-- in the Microfilm Library, and the L-- in the room off to the left of the entrance. After examining these, you can proceed to the others in order to extend your research to every possible mention of your ancestor. The best way to use the vast resources of the GDAH is to go there yourself. The congenial, insightful, and knowledgeable experts who run the Department will give you guidance, but you must not expect them to do the searching for you. They will point you toward the documents, but you must do the detailed work. Second best, if you cannot go to GDAH, is to hire a researcher. Be very cautious and give a hired searcher a small amount to do at first to see if the work is well done and thoroughly documented. Limited amounts of information can be obtained from GDAH by mail, but no detailed research can be done for you by the professional personnel. If you send them an SASE, $15 if you are a GA resident and $25 if you are not, a brief letter describing your problem, they will conduct a preliminary search and will give you suggestions for further research. But they do not have the time to do any more than this by mail, because their principal tasks are serving the GA state government (accessing, maintaining, indexing, providing records) and the many patrons who come to them. Most of the records (of all sorts) mentioned in Chapter 2 and those to be listed in Chapter 4 can be found at GDAH.

---

4. The GA Historical Society (GHS)

The GA Historical Society (GHS) is located at 501 Whitaker St., Savannah, GA 31499. Its hours are 10 am-5 pm Tuesday through Friday, 9 am-3 pm on Saturdays, except for closings on and around holidays. Be sure and call them at 1-(912)-651-2128 to make certain they will be open on the day(s) you plan to visit. Even though there is no parking lot at the GHS, parking on the street can generally be found within a block or two. Since the GHS is in the old historical district of downtown Savannah, there are many accommodations available. Nearby historic inns include Magnolia Place [503 Whitaker St., 31499, 1-(912)-236-7674], Forsyth Park Inn [102 W. Hall St., 31401, 1-(912)-233-6800], The Gastonian [220 E. Gaston St., 31401, 1-(912)-232-2869], and Eliza Thompson House [5 W. Jones St., 31401, 1-(912)-236-3620]. Other inns within the historic district can be reserved by calling 1-(800)-262-4667. The nearest hotel is the DeSoto Hilton Hotel [15 E. Liberty St., 31401, 1-(912)-232-9000]. Many other hotels are located a bit farther away, including the less expensive Days Inn [201 W. Bay St., 31499, 1-(912)-236-4440].

When you arrive at the GHS, which is housed in Hodgson Hall, go up the exterior stairs, and enter the main door into a small foyer. (An elevator is available. Enter through the garden.) Then proceed through the doors straight ahead, and you will find yourself in a long narrow balconied room, with alcoves on the main floor. Sign the register and check your briefcase, bags, and packages at the reference desk on the right. Ask for copies of the regulations and guide sheets, find yourself a seat, and carefully read these materials. Pay special attention to the regulations: (1) all briefcases, bags, and packages must be checked, (2) no eating, drinking, smoking, loud talk, (3) careful, considerate use of all materials, (4) no reshelving of materials, (5) use of pencils only, (6) rare books, maps, manuscripts to be requested from the desk, (7) photocopying of approved materials done by the staff for a small fee. Staff members will be happy to provide you with an orientation to the room and guide you in your research. The entrance to the rest rooms is located in the second alcove to your left.

Now, take a look around in order to identify the major finding aids which will let you make rapid and comprehensive use of the many resources in this excellent repository. The GHS is especially rich in published state and county histories and records, has many useful indexes to them, has an unusually good manuscript collection (over 1500 cataloged items), has noteworthy map holdings, and has a good number of microfilm copies of newspapers and censuses. You will notice on the left of the room just across from the reference desk an alcove containing card catalog cabinets. They contain the major finding aids to the GHS holdings:

_Main Catalog, search under name, location (county and GA), subject, author, title (remember SLANT). This catalog also contains the index for the genealogy files.
_Manuscript Index, search under name, location, subject
_Biography Index, search under name
_Vertical File Index, search under name, location, subject
_Map Index, search under location
In this alcove you will see other important finding aids.

Please notice the census indexes and indexes to Savannah newspapers(1763-), and finding aids for other microfilms, such as GA colonial conveyances, index to GA Confederate pensions, the GA mortality census, and Chatham County and Savannah records (will, estate, tax). On the bookshelves in alcoves under the balcony will be found historical and genealogical periodicals, publications of heritage societies, Savannah city directories, published colonial records of GA with indexes, published GA Revolutionary War records with indexes, and publications of the GHS with indexes. You will also see a number of file cabinets in the room: the Genealogical File in the alcove beside the reference desk, and the many cabinets of the Vertical File on both sides of the entrance door. Staff members will pull the appropriate files for you. On the shelves of the balcony is the large collection of books which the GHS holds. They are arranged in order according to their Library of Congress reference numbers beginning in the upper left front corner of the balcony. Rare books and manuscripts are stored in the archival stacks, and must be asked for at the reference desk.

You are now ready to make use of the excellent finding aids mentioned above. The approach is relatively simple now that you know what is available. The five card catalog files mentioned in the second paragraph above should be used first. Employing the acronym SLANT (as described in the previous section), go through the main catalog looking for N(your ancestors' names), L(your ancestors' localities- examine all cards under GA and the counties), S(subjects), T(titles), and A(authors). When you find pertinent materials, go to the journals and books on the shelves, or use the microfilms, or request the rare books. Then use the other card indexes in a similar fashion (although some of the search categories may not apply), and request the manuscripts, genealogical files, vertical files, or maps, or use the referenced microfilms. Finally, look into the other resources as listed in the paragraph just above.

For a thorough investigation of the resources of the GHS, you need to visit them or hire a searcher to do the work. Because of their numerous duties, the excellent staff cannot do research for you, but they will guide you in the use of the materials. Small amounts of information can be obtained by mail, but you must ask them only one brief question. The question must be one which can be looked up in a readily-available index. There is a fee for this service; write them for details.

---

5. The University of GA and Washington Memorial Libraries

In addition to the GDAH and the GHS, there are two other very important record repositories in GA which you must not overlook. The are the University of GA Library (UGL) in Athens and the Washington Memorial Library (WML) in Macon. The UGL is located on the campus of the University of GA, Athens, GA 30602. The main reference telephone is 1-(404)-542-3251 and that for the Hargett Rare Book and Manuscript Library (including the GA Room) is 1-(404)-542-7123. There are three important areas for genealogists in the UGL: the Main Reference, the Microfilm Area (in the basement), and the Hargett Rare Book and Manuscript Library (on the third floor). The keys to most of the genealogical materials in the UGL are the three large card catalogs in the Main Reference area:

_The Main Card Catalog, Subject, search under name, location (county, city, and state), and subject
_The Main Card Catalog, Author-Title, search under author and title
_The On-line Computer Catalog, search under name, location (county, city, state), subject, author, title

All three of these must be used since they will lead you to all books, most microforms (including microfilms), and many of the manuscripts in the library.

The Microfilm Area has copies of all census records for GA plus many for surrounding states, the largest collection of microfilmed GA newspapers available anywhere, the Draper Collection microfilms (early frontier American records), and other useful genealogical records. Most of these are listed in the three main catalogs mentioned above, but there are some finding aids which can offer additional assistance:

_MAJOR MICROFILM HOLDINGS IN THE UGL, UGL, Athens, GA, latest edition.

_COMPUTER PRINTOUT OF THE GA NEWSPAPER PROJECT,
    The Project, UGL, Athens, GA, latest revision.
_Geographical Listing of Newspapers, Microform Area, UGL, Athens,
    GA.
The Hargett Library consists of the GA Room and the Rare Books and
Manuscripts Area. The GA Room has one of the largest collections of
GA Books available. These books are listed in the three main catalogs,
but they are also in:
_GA Room Card Catalog, Hargett Library, UGL, Athens, GA.
The GA Room also maintains a very large vertical file. This file is
arranged by subject, then alphabetically under each major subject topic.
Subject headings of special interest to genealogical researchers are Biogra-
phy (thousands of listings), County, City, and State. These materials
should not be overlooked. There are, in addition, useful Vertical File
Notebooks which will help you as you look in the records for various
subjects and locations of interest to you.

    The Rare Books and Manuscripts Area of the Hargett Library
holds rare books, maps, and manuscripts. The books for the most part are
cataloged in the main catalogs (see 1st paragraph) and the map and
manuscript finding aids are:
_Manuscript Card Index, Hargett Library, UGL, Athens, GA
_Manuscript Notebooks and Inventories, Hargett Library, UGL, Athens,
    GA
_Map Card Files, Hargett Library, UGL, Athens, GA
Two of the large manuscript collections are exceptionally important for
research in genealogy. Please do not fail to investigate both of them:
_The Telamon Cuyler Collection, over 50000 loose GA state and county
    records, arranged by governor, county, and subject
_The LeConte Genealogical Collection, thousands of files and cards on
    family genealogies

    The Washington Memorial Library (WML) is found at 1180
Washington Ave., Macon, GA 31201. The Genealogical and Historical
Room is where the majority of local and family history and genealogy
books are to be found. The telephone number is 1-(912)-744-0800. When
you go in by the main entrance, turn left, go down the hall, and enter the
Genealogical and Historical Room. In this room is one of the largest
collections of published genealogical material in the southeastern US,
including an astonishing amount on GA. The major keys to these
resources are four card catalogs located in the room:
_Main Card Catalog, search by name, location, subject, author, title

_Microfilm Card Catalog, search by the same categories
_Family Sketch Card Catalog, search by name
_County Card Catalog, search by county
There are several other smaller card catalogs and some other finding aids
which you should not fail to ask for.

---

6. Family History Library and its Branch Family History Centers (FHL/FHC)

The largest genealogical library in the world is the Family History Library of the Genealogical Society of UT (FHL). This library, which holds almost two million rolls of microfilm, almost 400,000 microfiche, plus a vast number of books, is located at 50 East North Temple St., Salt Lake City, UT 84150. The basic keys to the library are composed of six indexes. (1) The International Genealogical Index, (2) The Surname Index in the FHL Catalog, (3) Listings of the Indexes to the Family Group Records Collection, (4) The Ancestral File, (5) The Social Security Death Index, and (6) The Locality Index in the FHL Catalog. In addition to the main library, the Society maintains a large number of Branches called Family History Centers (FHC) all over the US. Each of these branches has microfiche and/or computer copies of the International Genealogical Index, the Surname Index, the Index to the Family Group Records Collection, the Ancestral File, the Social Security Death Index, and the Locality Index. In addition each FHC has a supply of forms for borrowing microfilm copies of the records from the main library. This means that the astonishingly large holdings of the FHL are available through each of its numerous FHC branches.

The FHC in or near GA are as follows:
___Atlanta Family History Center, 2100 Lake Jodeco Road, Jonesboro, GA
___Augusta Family History Center, 1704 Bunting Drive, North Augusta, SC
___Brunswick Family History Center, 2911 Community Road, Brunswick, GA
___Columbus Family History Center, 4400 Reese Road, Columbus, GA
___Douglas Family History Center, 200 Chester Avenue, Douglas, GA
___Gainesville Family History Center, 1234 Riverside Drive, Gainesville, GA

___Jonesboro Family History Center, 2100 Lake Jodeco Road, Jonesboro, GA

___Macon Family History Center, 1624 Williamson Road, Macon, GA

___Marietta Family History Center, 3195 Trickum Road, Marietta, GA

___Powder Springs Family History Center, 2595 New Macland Road, Powder Springs, GA

___Roswell Family History Center, 500 Norcross Street, Roswell, GA

___Savannah Family History Center, 1234 King George Boulevard, Savannah, GA

___Tucker Family History Center, 1947 Brocket Road, Tucker, GA

Other FHC are to be found in the cities listed below. They may be located by looking in the local telephone directory under the listing CHURCH OF JESUS CHRIST OF LATTER-DAY SAINTS-GENEALOGY LIBRARY or in the Yellow Pages under CHURCHES-LATTER-DAY SAINTS.

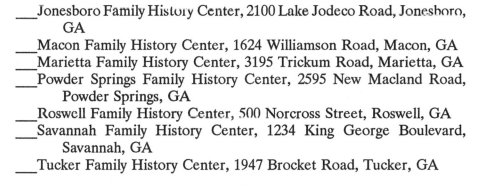

___In AL: Bessemer, Birmingham, Dothan, Huntsville, Mobile, Montgomery, Tuscaloosa, in AK: Anchorage, Fairbanks, Juneau, Ketchikan, Kotzebue, Sitka, Sodotna, Wasilla, in AZ: Benson, Buckeye, Camp Verde, Casa Grande, Cottonwood, Eagar, Flagstaff, Glendale, Globe, Holbrook, Kingman, Mesa, Nogales, Page, Payson, Peoria, Phoenix, Prescott, Safford, Scottsdale, Show Low, Sierra Vista, Snowflake, St. David, St. Johns, Tucson, Winslow, Yuma, in AR: Fort Smith, Jacksonville, Little Rock, Rogers,

___In CA (Bay Area): Antioch, Concord, Fairfield, Los Altos, Menlo Park, Napa, Oakland, San Bruno, San Jose, Santa Clara, Santa Cruz, Santa Rosa, In CA (Central): Auburn, Clovis, Davis (Woodland), El Dorado (Placerville), Fresno, Hanford, Merced, Modesto, Monterey (Seaside), Placerville, Sacramento, Seaside, Stockton, Turlock, Visalia, Woodland, In CA (Los Angeles County): Burbank, Canoga Park, Carson, Cerritos, Chatsworth (North Ridge), Covina, Glendale, Granada Hills, Hacienda Heights, Huntington Park, La Crescenta, Lancaster, Long Beach (Los Alamitos), Los Angeles, Monterey Park, Northridge, Norwalk, Palmdale, Palos Verdes (Rancho Palos Verdes), Pasadena, Torrance (Carson), Valencia, Van Nuys, Whittier, In CA (Northern): Anderson, Chico, Eureka, Grass Valley, Gridley, Mt. Shasta, Quincy, Redding, Susanville, Ukiah, Yuba City, In CA (Southern, except Los Angeles): Alpine, Anaheim, Bakersfield, Barstow, Blythe, Buena Park, Camarillo, Carlsbad, Corona, Cypress (Buena Park), El Cajon (Alpine), Escondido, Fontana, Garden Grove (Westminster), Hemet, Huntington Beach, Jurupa

(Riverside), Los Alamitos, Mission Viejo, Moorpark, Moreno Valley, Needles, Newbury Park, Orange, Palm Desert, Palm Springs (Palm Desert), Poway (San Diego), Redlands, Ridgecrest, Riverside, San Bernardino, San Diego, San Luis Obispo, Santa Barbara, Santa Maria, Simi Valley, Thousand Oaks (Moorpark), Upland, Ventura, Victorville, Vista, Westminster,

___ In CO: Alamosa, Arvada, Aurora, Boulder, Colorado Springs, Columbine, Cortez, Craig, Denver, Durango, Fort Collins, Frisco, Grand Junction, Greeley, La Jara, Littleton, Louisville, Manassa, Meeker, Montrose, Longmont, Northglenn, Paonia, Pueblo, in CT: Bloomfield, Hartford, Madison, New Canaan, New Haven, Waterford, Woodbridge, in DC: Kensington, MD, in DE: Newark, Wilmington, in FL: Boca Raton, Cocoa, Ft. Lauderdale, Ft. Myers, Gainesville, Hialeah, Homestead, Jacksonville, Lake City, Lake Mary, Lakeland, Miami, Orange Park, Orlando, Palm City, Panama City, Pensacola, Plantation, Rockledge, St. Petersburg, Tallahassee, Tampa, West Palm Beach, Winterhaven, in GA: Atlanta, Augusta, Brunswick, Columbus, Douglas, Gainesville, Jonesboro, Macon, Marietta, Powder Springs, Roswell, Savannah, Tucker, in HI: Hilo, Honolulu, Kaneohe, Kauai, Kona, Laie, Lihue, Miliani, Waipahu,

___ In ID: Basalt, Blackfoot, Boise, Burley, Caldwell, Carey, Coeur D'Alene, Driggs, Emmett, Firth, Hailey, Idaho Falls, Iona, Lewiston, McCammon, Malad, Meridian, Montpelier, Moore, Mountain Home, Nampa, Pocatello, Paris, Preston, Rexburg, Rigby, Salmon, Sandpoint, Shelley, Soda Springs, Twin Falls, Weiser, in IL: Champaign, Chicago Heights, Fairview Heights, Nauvoo, Peoria, Rockford, Schaumburg, Wilmette, in IN: Bloomington, Evansville, Fort Wayne, Indianapolis, New Albany, Noblesville, South Bend, Terre Haute, West Lafayette, in IA: Ames, Cedar Rapids, Davenport, Sioux City, West Des Moines, in KS: Dodge City, Olathe, Salina, Topeka, Wichita, in KY: Hopkinsville, Lexington, Louisville, Martin, Paducah, in LA: Alexandria, Baton Rouge, Denham Springs, Monroe, Metairie, New Orleans, Shreveport, Slidell,

___ In ME: Augusta, Bangor, Cape Elizabeth, Caribou, Farmingdale, Portland, in MD: Annapolis, Baltimore, Ellicott City, Frederick, Kensington, Lutherville, in MA: Boston, Foxboro, Tyngsboro, Weston, Worcester, in MI: Ann Arbor, Bloomfield Hills, East Lansing, Escanaba, Grand Blanc, Grand Rapids, Hastings, Kalamazoo, Lansing, Ludington, Marquette, Midland, Muskegon, Traverse City, Westland, in MN: Anoka, Duluth, Minneapolis,

Rochester, St. Paul, in MS: Clinton, Columbus, Gulfport, Hattiesburg, in MO: Cape Girardeau, Columbia, Farmington, Frontenac, Hazelwood, Independence, Joplin, Kansas City, Liberty, Springfield, St. Joseph, St. Louis, in MT: Billings, Bozeman, Butte, Glasgow, Glendive, Great Falls, Havre, Helena, Kalispell, Missoula, Stevensville, in NE: Grand Island, Lincoln, Omaha, Papillion,

___In NV: Elko, Ely, Henderson, LaHonton Valley, Las Vegas, Logandale, Mesquite, Reno, Tonapah, Winnemucca, in NH: Concord, Exeter, Nashua, Portsmouth, in NJ: Caldwell, Dherry Hill, East Brunswick, Morristown, North Caldwell, in NM: Albuquerque, Carlsbad, Farmington, Gallup, Grants, Las Cruces, Santa Fe, Silver City, in NY: Albany, Buffalo, Ithaca, Jamestown, Lake Placid, Liverpool, Loudonville, New York City, Pittsford, Plainview, Queens, Rochester, Scarsdale, Syracuse, Vestal, Williamsville, Yorktown, in NC: Asheville, Charlotte, Durham, Fayetteville, Goldsboro, Greensboro, Hickory, Kinston, Raleigh, Skyland, Wilmington, Winston-Salem, in ND: Bismarck, Fargo, Minot, in OH: Akron, Cincinnati, Cleveland, Columbus, Dayton, Dublin, Fairborn, Kirtland, Perrysburg, Reynoldsburg, Tallmadge, Toledo, Westlake, Winterville,

___In OK: Lawton, Muskogee, Norman, Oklahoma City, Stillwater, Tulsa, in OR: Beaverton, Bend, Brookings, Central Point, Coos Bay, Corvallis, Eugene, Grants Pass, Gresham, Hermiston, Hillsboro, Keizer, Klamath Falls, LaGrande, Lake Oswego, Lebanon, Minnville, Medford, Newport, Nyssa, Ontario, Oregon City, Portland, Prineville, Roseburg, Salem, Sandy, The Dallas, in PA: Altoona, Broomall, Clarks Summit, Erie, Kane, Philadelphia(Broomall), Pittsburgh, Reading, Scranton(Clarks Summit), State College(Altoona), York, in RI: Providence, Warwick, in SC: Charleston, Columbia, Florence, Greenville, North Augusts, in SD: Gettysburg, Rapid City, Rosebud, Sioux Falls, in TN: Chattanooga, Franklin, Kingsport, Knoxville, Madison, Memphis, Nashville, in TX: Abilene, Amarillo, Austin, Bay City, Beaumont, Bryan, Conroe, Corpus Christi, Dallas, Denton, Duncanville, El Paso, Ft. Worth, Friendswood, Harlingen, Houston, Hurst, Katy, Kileen, Kingwood, Longview, Lubbock, McAllen, Odessa, Orange, Pasadena, Plano, Port Arthur, Richland Hills, San Antonio, Sugarland,

___In UT: American Fork, Altamont, Beaver, Blanding, Bloomington, Bluffdale, Bountiful, Brigham City, Canyon Rim, Castle Dale, Cedar City, Delta, Duchesne, Escalante, Farmington, Ferron,

Fillmore, Granger, Heber, Helper, Highland, Holladay, Hunter, Huntington, Hurricane, Hyrum, Kanab, Kaysville, Kearns, Laketown, Layton, Lehi, Loa, Logan, Magna, Manti, Mapleton, Midway, Moab, Monticello, Moroni, Mt. Pleasant, Murray, Nephi, Ogden, Orem, Panguitch, Parowan, Pleasant Grove, Price, Provo, Richfield, Riverton, Roosevelt, Rose Park, Salt Lake City, Sandy, Santaquin, South Jordan, Springville, St. George, Syracuse, Tooele, Trementon, Tropic, Vernal, Wellington, Wendover, West Jordan, West Valley City, in <u>VA</u>: Annandale, Bassett, Charlottesville, Chesapeake, Dale City, Falls Church, Fredericksburg, Hamilton, Martinsville, McLean, Newport News, Norfolk, Oakton, Pembroke, Richmond, Roanoke, Salem, Virginia Beach, Waynesboro, Winchester, in <u>VT</u>: Berlin, Montpelier,

In <u>WA</u>: Auburn, Bellevue, Bellingham, Bremerton, Centralia, Colville, Edmonds, Ellensburg, Elma, Ephrata, Everett, Federal Way, Ferndale, Lake Stevens, Longview, Lynnwood, Marysville, Moses Lake, Mt. Vernon, North Bend, Olympia, Othello, Port Angeles, Pullman, Puyallup, Quincy, Renton, Richland, Seattle, Silverdale, Spokane, Sumner, Tacoma, Vancouver, Walla Walla, Wenatchee, Yakima, in <u>WV</u>: Charleston, Fairmont, Huntington, in <u>WI</u>: Appleton, Eau Clair, Hales Corner, Madison, Milwaukee, Shawano, Wausau, in <u>WY</u>: Afton, Casper, Cheyenne, Cody, Gillette, Green River, Jackson Hole, Kemmerer, Laramie, Lovell, Lyman, Rawlins, Riverton, Rock Springs, Sheridan, Urie, Worland.
The FHL is constantly adding new branches so this list will probably be out-of-date by the time you read it. An SASE and a $2 fee to the FHL (address in first paragraph above) will bring you an up-to-date listing of FHC.

When you go to FHL or FHC, <u>first</u> ask for the microfiche GA International Genealogical Index and examine it for the name of your ancestor, then if you are at FHL, request the record. If you are at FHC, ask them to borrow the microfilm containing the record from FHL. The cost is only a few dollars, and when your microfilm arrives (usually 4 to 6 weeks), you will be notified so that you can return and examine it. Then, repeat the process using the computer International Genealogical Index. <u>Second</u>, ask for the microfiche or computer Surname Catalog. Examine it for the surname of your ancestor. If you think any of the references relate to your ancestral line, and if you are at FHL, request the record. If you are at FHC, ask them to borrow the record for you. <u>Third</u>, ask for the Listings of Indexes to the Family Group Records Collection which will be found in the Author/Title Section of the microfiche FHL Catalog.

There are several listings, so be sure you see them all. Locate the micro-film number which applies to the index of the surname you are seeking. If you are at FHL, request the microfilm. If you are at FHC, ask them to borrow the microfilm for you. When it comes, examine the microfilm to see if any records of your surname are indicated. If so, obtain them and see if they are pertinent.

Fourth, ask for the computer Ancestral File and look up the name you are seeking. If it is there, you will be led to sources of information, either people who are working on the line, or records pertaining to the line. Be careful with the material in this file, because in some of the cases, there appears to be no documentation. Fifth, if you are seeking a person who died after 1937, request the computer Social Security Death Index and look her/him up in it. Sixth, ask for the computer or microfiche GA Locality Catalog. Examine all listings under the main heading of GEORGIA. Then examine all listings under the subheading of the county you are interested in. These county listings will follow the listings for the state of GA. Toward the end of the county listings, there are listed materials relating to cities and towns in the county. Be sure not to over-look them. If you are at FHL, you can request the materials which are of interest to you. If you are at FHC, you may have the librarian borrow them for you. A large number of the records referred to in Chapter 2 and those listed under the counties in Chapter 4 will be found in the GA locality catalog.

The FHL and each FHC also have a set of Combined Census Indexes. These indexes are overall collections of censuses and other records for various time periods. Set 1 covers all colonies and states 1607-1819, Set 2 covers all states 1820-9, Set 3 covers all states 1830-9, Set 4 covers all states 1840-9, Set 5 covers the southern states 1850-9, Set 6 covers the northern states 1850-9, Set 7 covers the midwestern and western states 1850-9, Set 7A covers all the states 1850-9, and further sets cover various groups of states 1860 and after. Additional details concerning the records in FHL and FHC along with instructions for finding and using them will be found in:

    __ J. Cerny and W. Elliott, THE LIBRARY, A GUIDE TO THE LDS
        FAMILY HISTORY LIBRARY, Ancestry Publishing, Salt Lake
        City, UT, 1988.
    __J. C. Parker, GOING TO SALT LAKE CITY TO DO FAMILY
        HISTORY RESEARCH, Marietta Publishing Co., Turlock, CA,
        1993, or latest edition. Not just useful if you are going to Salt

Lake City, but also very useful if you are going to one of the branch FHCs.

---

7. The National Archives (NA) and Its Branches (NAFB)

The National Archives and Records Service (NA), located at Pennsylvania Ave. and 8th St., Washington, DC 20408, is the national repository for _federal_ records, many being of importance to genealogical research. The NA does not concern itself with colonial records (pre-1776) or with state records or with records of smaller local regions, such as counties. Among the most important NA records which pertain to GA are the following (with the section in Chapter 2 where they were discussed): census 1820-1910 (section 6), emigration and immigration (section 15), military (sections 26-28), and naturalization (section 30). Please recall that there are many types of records under the military category (military service, bounty land, pension, claims, civilian). Extensive detail on these records is provided in:

_NA Staff, GENEALOGICAL RESEARCH IN THE NATIONAL AR-CHIVES, National Archives and Records Service, Washington, 1984.

The numerous records of the NA may be examined in Washington in person or by a hired researcher. Microfilm copies of many of the major records and/or their indexes may also be seen in Field Branches of the National Archives (NAFB) which are located in or near _Atlanta_ (NAAB-National Archives Atlanta Branch), Boston, Chicago, Denver, Fort Worth, Kansas City, Los Angeles, New York, Philadelphia, San Francisco, and Seattle. They may be located by looking in the telephone directories of these cities under FEDERAL ARCHIVES AND RECORDS CENTER. The National Archives Atlanta Branch (NAAB) is particularly rich in microfilm copies or originals of _federal_ records applying to GA. Included are the GA census records (1820-80, 1900-10), census indexes (1880, 1900-10), Revolutionary War records, War of 1812 records, Civil War records, Internal Revenue Assessment Lists for GA (1865-6), passenger lists (1820-68, 1890-1924), Indian records, Federal Courts in GA (1789-1928), and customs records (1754-1920). The address of the NAAB is 1557 St. Joseph Avenue, East Point, GA 30344, and the telephone number is (404)-763-7477.

Many of the NA records pertaining to GA are also available at GDAH as microfilm copies, especially the census, military, and passenger list records. In addition, practically any local library in the US can borrow NA microfilms for you from AGLL (American Genealogical Lending Library, PO Box 244, Bountiful, UT 84010). Included among the available items are census records (1820-1910), census indexes (1880, 1900-10), military records (Revolutionary, War of 1812, Civil War), ship passenger lists (Savannah 1820-68, 1890-1924), mortality census records (1850-80), and Indian censuses. Many NA microfilms are also available from FHL through FHC.

---

8. Regional libraries (RL)

In the state of GA there are a number of regional libraries (RL) and larger city and county libraries which have good genealogical collections. Their holdings are larger than those of most local libraries (LL), but are smaller than the holdings of UGL, WML, and GHS. As might be expected, the materials in each RL are best for the immediate and the surrounding counties. Among the better of these RL for genealogical research are the following (listed in order of the cities where they are found):

_Lake Brashear Regional Library, 307 E. Lamar St., Americus 31709.
_Athens Regional Library, 120 W. Dougherty St., Athens 30601.
_Atlanta Public Library, One Margaret Mitchell Square, Atlanta 30303.
_Southwest GA Regional Library, Shotwell and Monroe Sts., Bainbridge 31717.
_Brunswick Regional Library, 208 Gloucester St., Brunswick 31523.
_Chattahoochee Valley Regional Library, 1120 Bradley Dr., Columbus 31995.
_DeKalb Library, 3560 Kensington Rd., DeKalb 30032.
_Satilla Regional Library, 701 E. Ward St., Douglas 31533.
_Ocmulgee Regional Library, 505 Second Ave., Eastman 31023.
_Chestatee Regional Library, 127 N. Main St., Gainesville 30505.
_Cherokee Regional Library, 305 S. Duke St., LaFayette 30728.
_Lake Lanier Regional Library, 275 Perry St., Lawrenceville 30245.
_Cobb County Public Library, 30 Atlanta St., SE, Marietta 30060.
_Colquitt-Thomas Regional Library, 204 Fifth St., SE, Moultrie 31768.
_Sara Hightower Regional Library, 606 W. First St., Rome 30161.
_Statesboro Regional Library, Main Street South and Grady, Statesboro 30458.
_Ohoopee Regional Library, 606 Jackson St., Vidalia 30474.
_South GA Regional Library, 300 Woodrow Wilson Dr., Valdosta 31601.
_Okefenokee Regional Library, 401 Lee Ave., Waycross 31502.
_Piedmont Regional Library, 301 Midland Ave., Winder 30680.

When a visit is made to any of these libraries, your <u>first</u> endeavor is to search the card and/or computer catalogs. You can remember what to look for with the acronym SLANT. This procedure should give you very good coverage of the library holdings which are indexed in the catalog(s).

The <u>second</u> endeavor at any of these libraries is to ask about any special indexes, catalogs, collections, finding aids, or materials which might be pertinent to your search. You should make it your aim particularly to inquire about Bible, cemetery, church, map, manuscript, military, mortuary, and newspaper materials. In some cases, microform (microfilm, microfiche, microcard) records are not included in the regular card catalog but are separately indexed. It is important that you be alert to this possibility.

In addition to the RL mentioned above, there are several college and university libraries in GA (in addition to UGL) which have notable specialized genealogical collections:
_Emory University Libraries, especially the Woodruff Library and the
    Pitts Theology Library, Emory University, Atlanta 30322.
_Reese Library, Augusta College, 2500 Walton Way, Augusta 30910.
_Roberts Library, Middle GA College, Cochran 31014.
_Pitts Library, Andrew College, College St., Cuthbert 31740.
_Stetson Library, Mercer University, 1330 Edgewood Ave., Macon 31207.
_Valdosta State College Library, 1500 N. Patterson St., Valdosta 31698.

---

9. Large genealogical libraries (LGL)

Spread around the US there are a number of large genealogical libraries (LGL) which have at least some GA genealogical source materials. In general, those libraries nearest GA (AL, FL, NC, SC, TN) are the ones that have the better GA collections, but there are exceptions. The thirteen libraries of this type which have the largest overall collections are:
_Genealogical Society of UT Family History Library (FHL), 35 North
    West Temple St., Salt Lake City, UT 84150.
_Public Library of Fort Wayne and Allen County, 301 West Wayne St.,
    Fort Wayne, IN 46802.
_New England Historic Genealogical Society Library, 101 Newbury St.,
    Boston, MA 02116.
_NY Public Library, 5th Avenue and 42nd St., New York, NY 10016.

_Library of Congress, First and Second Sts. at East Capitol St. and Independence Ave., Washington, DC 20540.
_NY Genealogical and Biographical Society Library, 122-126 East 58th St., New York, NY 10022.
_Library of the National Society of the Daughters of the American Revolution, 1776 D St., Washington, DC 20006.
_Western Reserve Historical Society Library, 10825 East Blvd., Cleveland, OH 44106.
_Detroit Public Library, 5201 Woodward Ave., Detroit, MI 48202.
_Newberry Library, 60 West Walton St., Chicago, IL 60610.
_State Historical Society of WI Library, 816 State St., Madison, WI 53703.
_Dallas Public Library, 1515 Young St., Dallas, TX 75201.
_Los Angeles Public Library, 630 West 5th St., Los Angeles, CA 90071.

Among other large libraries which have good genealogical collections are the following:
_In AL: Birmingham Public Library, Davis Library at Samford University in Birmingham, AL Department of Archives and History in Montgomery, in AZ: Tucson Public Library, in AR: AR State Library in Little Rock, Central AR Library in Little Rock, in CA: see above, Sutro Branch of the CA State Library in San Francisco, San Diego Public Library, San Francisco Public Library,
_In CO: Denver Public Library, in CT: CT Historical Society Library in Hartford, CT State Library in Hartford, Godfrey Memorial Library in Middletown, in DE: Dover Public Library, Historical Society of DE in Wilmington, in DC: see above, in FL: Miami-Dade Public Library, State Library of FL in Tallahassee, Tampa Public Library, in ID: ID State Historical Society Library in Boise, in IL: see above, in IN: see above, IN State Library in Indianapolis, in IA: IA State Historical Department Library in Des Moines, IA State Historical Department Library in Iowa City, in KS: KS State Historical Society Library in Topeka,
_In KY: KY Department for Libraries and Archives in Frankfort, KY Historical Society Library in Frankfort, Filson Club Library in Louisville, in LA: LA State Library in Baton Rouge, in ME: ME State Library in Augusta, ME Historical Society Library in Portland, in MD: MD State Archives Library in Annapolis, MD Historical Society Library in Baltimore, in MA: see above, Boston Public Library, in MI: see above, Library of MI in Lansing, in MN: Minneapolis Public Library, MN Historical Society Library in St. Paul, in MS: MS Department of Archives and History in Jackson,

in <u>MO</u>: Kansas City Public Library, St. Louis Public Library, in <u>MT</u>: MT Historical Society Library and Archives in Helena,

_In <u>NE</u>: NE State Historical Society Library in Lincoln, Omaha Public Library, in <u>NV</u>: Las Vegas Branch of the FHL, NV Historical Society Library in Reno, in <u>NH</u>: NH Historical Society Library in Concord, in <u>NJ</u>: NJ Historical Society Library in Newark, NJ State Library in Trenton, in <u>NM</u>: Albuquerque Public Library, University of NM Library in Albuquerque, in <u>NY</u>: see two listings above, NY State Library in Albany, in <u>NC</u>: NC State Library in Raleigh, in <u>ND</u>: ND State Library in Bismarck, in <u>OH</u>: see above, State Library of OH in Columbus, Public Library of Cincinnati, OH Historical Society in Columbus, in <u>OK</u>: OK Historical Society in Oklahoma City, in <u>OR</u>: Genealogical Forum of Portland Library, Library Association of Portland, in <u>PA</u>: State Library of PA in Harrisburg, Historical Society of PA Library in Philadelphia, Historical Society of Western PA Library in Pittsburgh,

_In <u>RI</u>: RI Historical Society Library in Providence, in <u>SC</u>: South Caroliniana Library in Columbia, in <u>SD</u>: SD Department of Cultural Affairs Historical Center and SD State Library in Pierre, in <u>TN</u>: Knox County Library in Knoxville, Memphis Public Library, TN State Library in Nashville, in <u>TX</u>: see above, TX State Library in Austin, Fort Worth Public Library, Clayton Library for Genealogical Research in Houston, in <u>UT</u>: see above, Brigham Young University Library in Provo, in <u>VT</u>: VT Historical Society Library in Montpelier, in <u>VA</u>: VA State Library in Richmond, VA Historical Society Library in Richmond, in <u>WA</u>: Seattle Public Library, Spokane Public Library, in <u>WV</u>: WV Archives and History Library in Charleston, in <u>WI</u>: see above, Milwaukee Public Library, in <u>WY</u>: WY State Library in Cheyenne.

10. Local libraries (LL)

Listed under the GA counties in Chapter 4 are most of the important local libraries (LL) in the state. These libraries are of a very wide variety, some having sizeable genealogical materials, some having practically none. Many of the LL are branches or affiliates of a nearby larger library (sometimes called regional libraries), which have much greater holdings. Many of the regional libraries have very good genealogical collections, especially those listed in section 8 of this chapter. You should never overlook a LL in a county or city of your interest since quite often they have local records or collections available nowhere else. In addition, local librarians are frequently very knowledgeable concerning genealogical sources in their areas. Further, they are also usually acquainted with the people in the county(city) who are experts in the county's(city's) history and genealogy. Thus, both local libraries and local librarians can be of exceptional value to you.

When you visit a LL, the general procedure described previously should be followed. First, search the card and/or computer catalog(s). Look under the headings summarized by SLANT: subject, location, author, name, title, doing them in the order N-L-S-A-T. Then, second, inquire about special indexes, catalogs, collections, materials, and microforms. Also ask about any other local sources of data such as cemetery records, church records, maps and atlases, genealogical and historical societies, mortuary records, and old newspapers, plus indexes to all of these. Also do not forget to visit appropriate offices related to these types of records: offices of cemeteries, churches, societies, mortuaries, and newspapers.

If you choose to write to a LL, please remember that the librarians are very busy people. Always send them an SASE and confine your questioning to one straight-forward brief item. Librarians are usually glad to help you if they can employ indexes to answer your question, but you must not expect them to do research for you. In case research is required, they can often supply you with a list of researchers which you may hire.

LIST OF ABBREVIATIONS

A	=	Agricultural census
CH	=	Court house(s)
FHC	=	Family History Center(s)
FHL	=	Family History Library
G	=	GA State census records
GA	=	Georgia
GDAH	=	GA Department of Archives and History
GHS	=	GA Historical Society (Savannah)
GSU	=	Genealogical Society of UT (Utah)
I	=	Industrial census records
LGL	=	Large genealogical library
LL	=	Local library(-ies)
M	=	Mortality census records
NA	=	National Archives
NAAB	=	National Archives, Atlanta Branch
NAFB	=	National Archives, Field Branch
P	=	Pensioner census, Revolutionary War
R	=	Regular census records
RL	=	Regional library(-ies)
S	=	Slaveowner census records
Su	=	Substitute census records
UGL	=	University of GA Libraries (Athens)
WML	=	Washington Memorial Library (Macon)

Chapter 4

RESEARCH PROCEDURE & COUNTY LISTINGS

1. Finding the county

Now that you have read Chapters 1-3, you should have a good idea of GA history, its genealogical records, and the locations and availabilities of these records. Your situation is now that you can begin to use these resources. Locating and tracing your progenitor(s) in GA during the colonial period (1733-76) is usually not a problem because all records were kept at the colony level (at Savannah), the population of GA was relatively small (9600 in 1760, 40000 in 1775), and most of the people lived in the coastal area or along the lower Savannah River. There are abundant indexed records during this time (before 1777), particularly those listed in section 10 of Chapter 2 [colonial records], but also some listed in sections 6 [census substitutes], 7 [early religious groups], 15 [immigration records], 18 [genealogical indexes], 22 [colonial trustee land leases and grants, royal headright land grants, colonial conveyance books], 24 [colonial marriages], 25-26 [colonial and Revolutionary military records], 31 [GA's colonial newspaper], 32 [published indexes for the US], and 35 [early GA estate records].

In the post-Revolutionary period (1782-), however, knowledge that your ancestor was simply from the state of GA is not sufficient to permit you to proceed with the research. You first need to know the county because most genealogically-applicable records after 1782 were kept by the county. If you happen to know your forebear's county, you may skip the remainder of this section. If not, your first priority must be a search for the county. The most efficient method for discovering the county depends on the time period in which your progenitor lived in GA. We will discuss county finding techniques for three basic periods in GA state history: (1) after 1920, (2) 1820-1920, (3) 1782-1819. If your ancestor lived in GA <u>after 1920</u>, information as to the county of his residence is probably available to you from older members of your family. There are also the state-wide birth and death records after 1919 [sections 4 and 13, Chapter 2].

Should your ancestor's time period be <u>1820-1920</u>, the major resources for locating the county are the 1820/30/40/50/80, 1900/10/ 20 census indexes [section 6, Chapter 2]. If these fail to locate your forebear, then you need to look carefully into a number of other state-wide (or wider) indexes which could list her or him. Among the most useful of these are:

___Large name indexes for the US, sections 18 and 32, Chapter 2

___Large name indexes for GA, section 18, Chapter 2

___Indexes to GA land grants and plats, section 22, Chapter 2

___Surname listings in card catalogs, GDAH, UGL, WML, GHS, and microfilm indexes at FHC(FHL)

___Will and intestate record indexes in books by Austin and Brooke, section 35, Chapter 2

___Indexes to Mexican, Civil, and Spanish-American War service and pension records, also bounty land for Mexican War, sections 27-28, Chapter 2

___Indexes in land lottery books, 1820/21/27/32, section 22, Chapter 2

If your ancestor's time period was 1782-1819, the major resources for locating the county are the indexes to the land lotteries of 1805/07/20 [section 22, Chapter 2] and the substitute census indexes of 1756-1815, 1790, 1790-1818, and 1802 [section 6, Chapter 2]. If these should not tell you what you seek, then try:

___Large name indexes for the US, sections 18 and 32, Chapter 2

___Large name indexes for GA, section 18, Chapter 2

___Indexes to GA land grants and plats, section 22, Chapter 2

___Surname listings in card catalogs, GDAH, UGL, WML, GHS, and in microfilm indexes at FHC(FHL)

___Will and intestate record indexes in books by Austin and Brooke, section 35, Chapter 2

___Indexes to Revolutionary War and War of 1812 service, bounty land, and pension records, sections 26-27, Chapter 2

As you can see from the above considerations, the key item for the period after 1920 is family information. The key items for the period 1820-1920 are the census indexes. These indexes are available in GDAH, UGL, WML, GHS, FHL, FHC, NA, NAFB, NAAB, and in many LGL, RL, and LL. The key items for the period 1782-1819 are the land lottery indexes and the substitute census indexes. They may be located in GDAH, UGL, WML, GHS, FHL, FHC, and in many LGL, RL, and LL. The key resources for the colonial period 1733-77 are the many indexed colonial records. If these key items do not turn up your ancestor, the subsidiary finding aids mentioned above need to be gone through. It is also well to remember that in the colonial period there were no counties, thus all records and indexes apply to the whole colony. Also please recall that by 1800 there were only 24 counties, so if it is necessary, a county-by-county search about this time is not too forbidding.

This work of locating your GA ancestor can generally be done from where you live or nearby. This is because the key finding items are either indexes or indexed records which means that they may be rapidly scanned. Also many of them are in published form which means that they are in numerous LGL outside of GA as well as being available through FHC. Therefore, you should not have to travel too far to find many of the indexes that you need. If, however, it is more convenient, you may hire a searcher in Atlanta to delve into the records at GDAH to locate your progenitor. This should not cost too much because you can instruct your searcher to look into the records which are noted above in this section.

2. Recommended approaches

Having identified the county of your forebear's residence or having definitely located your ancestor in colonial GA, you are in position to begin to ferret out the details. This means that you need to identify what non-governmental, federal, state(colonial), and county records are available, then to locate them, and finally to examine them in detail. The most useful non-governmental records have been discussed in Chapter 2 (sections 2-3, 5, 7-9, 12, 15-16, 18-19, 23-24, 29, 31-33, 36). The federal records which are most important for your consideration also have been treated in Chapter 2 (sections 6, 15-16, 26-28, 30). State records of the greatest utility for genealogical research are examined in certain sections of Chapter 2 (4, 10-11, 14-16, 22, 24-28, 30, 35). Colonial governmental records were listed principally in section 10 of Chapter 2, but other sections also deal with them (6, 11, 14, 22, 25, 35). The types of records which were generated by GA counties are listed in Chapter 2 (last paragraph, section 11), and they are discussed in various sections of Chapter 2 (4, 11, 13-14, 22, 24, 28, 30, 34-35). County records which have been collected, microfilmed, and/or published, and are available chiefly in GDAH and somewhat in FHL(FHC) are listed in detail in later sections of this chapter. You should make a thorough examination of all the records which apply to your progenitor's dates, since this will give you the best chance of finding the maximum amount of information.

The general approach for doing an utterly thorough job of researching a GA ancestor is to follow this pattern:

___1st: family sources (oral, records, mementos, Bible)

___2nd: locating your forebear (see section 1, this chapter)

___3rd: nearest LGL (publications, indexes, maybe microfilms)

___4th: nearest FHC or FHL (surname & locality indexes, International Genealogical Index, integrated census indexes)

___5th: GDAH (original & microfilmed federal, state, colony, county, & non-governmental records)

___6th: GA Surveyor General Department (colonial & state land records)

___7th: UGL (surname files, publications, newspapers)

___8th: WML & GHS (manuscripts, publications)

___9th: LL (manuscript materials, indexes, typescripts)

___10th: CH (original records not seen elsewhere, court packets and files)

___11th: NAFB or NAAB (military service, pension, bounty land, land grant, immigration records)

___12th: NA (military service, pension, bounty land, land grant immigration records not seen previously)

The precise way in which you use this scheme is chiefly determined by how far you are from Atlanta, GA, where the GDAH is located. It is there (in the GDAH) that the best collection of GA genealogical materials in the whole world exists. Therefore, the major idea that you must recognize as you look at the above research plan is that you _must_ either visit GDAH or hire a researcher to go for you. In short, research in GDAH is an absolute necessity, because there are many records there that are found no where else.

If you live _very far_ from GDAH (Atlanta), you should follow the 12-step procedure essentially as it is. In the 3rd and 4th steps (LGL, FHC, FHL), just as many materials as possible should be examined, since that will reduce what remains to be done in GDAH. It is preferable to visit FHL rather than FHC, so you should elect that option if you are near enough to Salt Lake City, UT (where FHL is). You then need to hire a researcher to go to GDAH and the GA Surveyor General Department (5th and 6th steps, both in Atlanta), or you can go yourself. Be sure and explain carefully to your hired researcher exactly what records you have seen so that your money will not be wasted on duplicated work. Once the 5th and 6th steps (GDAH, GA Surveyor General Department) have been completed, a hired researcher or a personal visit will be involved for the 7th through the 10th steps. The 11th step can be done at the NAFB in your region, and the 12th step can be conducted by a hired researcher, a personal visit, or mail.

If you live <u>within</u> <u>range</u> of GA, the 12-step pattern can be modified substantially. By "within range" is meant that you deem a visit to GA workable within the near future. In such a case, you may skip the 3rd and 4th steps, then do the 5th through 11th steps by personal visit. Your trip should be preceded by careful planning of what you should search for in each place and telephone calls to ensure that the facilities will be open.

In selecting a research approach, whether it be one of the above or one at which you arrive by consideration of Chapter 3, you need to think about three items. The <u>first</u> is expense. In visiting Atlanta (for GDAH and GA Surveyor General Department), 3 or 4 full working days should be planned for if sizable county listings in Chapter 4 indicate many records to be available. If few microfilmed records are available, 1 or 2 days should suffice. To visit Salt Lake City (for FHL), 2 or 3 full working days should be planned for if sizable records are listed as being available there in FHC or
___FHL CATALOG, LOCALITY SECTION, FHL, Salt Lake City,
UT, available on microfilm and computer at FHL and all FHCs. If few records are available, one day should suffice. In using the facilities of a FHC, your initial visit for index checking and microfilm ordering will require about half a day, but your return visits will take more time depending on how many microfilms you order and whether they come together or piecemeal (more likely the latter). To visit UGL, WML, and GHS after having visited GDAH will require no more than a day each. Your visit to a county seat (LL and CH) will require 1 to 3 days depending on how many records you have been able to explore in microfilm or published form at GDAH, UGL, WML, GHS, FHL, and/or FHC. For all the above visits, travel, meal, and lodging costs will be involved, and in addition, costs for borrowing microfilm from FHC must be included. The total of all these expenses must be weighed over against the cost of hiring researchers to go to GDAH, UGL, WML, GHS, LL, and CH. Of course, your desire to look at the records for yourself may be an important consideration.

The <u>second</u> item is a reminder about interlibrary loans. With the exception of the microfilms of FHL (available through FHC), the microfilms of AGLL, and some census and military microfilms (available through your LL), very few libraries and even fewer archives will lend out their genealogical holdings on interlibrary loan. This is practically always the case for original records and manuscripts. Therefore, the amount of information that you may obtain through interlibrary loan is severely limited.

The third item is also a reminder, this being a restatement of what was said several times in Chapter 3. You will have noticed that correspondence with librarians and archivists of GDAH, UGL, WML, GHS, FHL, FHC, LGL, RL, LL, and county employees in CH has not been mentioned in the above paragraphs. The reason is that these helpful and hard-working state, local, and private employees do not have time to do detailed work for you because of the demanding duties of their offices. In some cases, these people have time to look up one specific item for you (a land grant date, a deed record, a will, a plat book entry, a military pension) if an overall index is available. But please don't ask them for detailed data, and please don't write them a long letter. If you do write them, enclose a long SASE, a check for $5 with the payee line left blank, and a brief request (no more than one-third page) for one specific item. Ask them to use the check if there is a charge for their services or for copying, and if they do not have the time to look themselves, that they hand the check and your letter to a researcher who can do the work. All of this, as you can see, will allow you to do the locating of your ancestor by mail, but little if any of the subsequent research can be done in this fashion.

3. The format of the listings

In the numerous sections to follow, summaries of basic origin information on GA counties along with lists of original, microfilmed, and published records outside the counties are given. There are four major sources of GA county governmental records: (1) original records in the CH, (2) original records and microfilms of them in the GDAH, (3) microfilm copies of some original records in FHL which are available through FHC, and (4) published copies of some original records in GDAH, UGL, WML, GHS, FHL(available through FHC), LGL, RL, and LL. There are five major sources of county non-governmental records: (1) originals, microfilms of originals, and published records in GDAH, (2) originals, microfilms of originals, and published records in UGL and GHS, (3) microfilm copies of some published records in FHL which are available through FHC, (4) published records in WML, FHL, LGL, RL, and LL, and (5) many church and specialized manuscript archives.

The major source of both governmental and non-governmental records for the period before 1900 (the most important period for most genealogists) is the GDAH. Second to it is the collection at FHL, even though it has considerably less material. For the period after 1900, the major source of governmental county records is the CH, and the major source of non-governmental records is GDAH, with FHL, UGL, WML, GHS, and LL also having materials. In the county sections which follow, you will find for counties organized before 1900 a listing of CH record microfilms in GDAH (some of which are also in FHL) and a listing of important published records, most of which will be found in GDAH, UGL, WML, and GHS, and some of which will be found in FHL(FHC), LGL, RL, and LL. For counties organized after 1900, county governmental records are not available in GDAH, so they must be sought in the counties at the CH. Non-governmental records for these post-1900 counties are usually available in GDAH and at FHL(FHC). They are listed.

Take a look at the Appling County materials (the next section), which we will use to illustrate the format for the county record summaries. In the first paragraph the name of the county is given, then the date the county was formed along with the county, counties, or area from which it came. Next the county seat and the zip code are given, and finally any disasters in which records may have been lost are listed.

The next paragraph lists county records which are available in various forms outside the county. First look under the heading GDAH CH microfilms. Here you will find listed originals and microfilm copies of original county CH (governmental) records which are available at GDAH. Some of the records are also available in FHL in microfilm form, and they may be borrowed through FHC. (Those available in FHL are listed in detail in the locality indexes in every FHC.) Record types which you will find listed here will include many of the following: amnesty, apprentice, annual returns, bastardy, birth, Confederate, death, deed & mortgage, estate, free persons of color, homestead, Inferior Court minutes, inventories & appraisements, jury, Land Court minutes, land lottery, liquor/tavern, lunacy, marriage, naturalization, pauper, physicians register, pony homestead, school, slave importer, Superior Court minutes, tax, twelve months support, voter, will. Some of these are obvious or have been explained in Chapter 2. However, explanations are in order for several. Amnesty records are for people who pledged allegiance to US law in 1867 in order to qualify to vote in the GA Constitutional Convention election. Annual returns were yearly reports on unsettled estates filed by the administrator or executor. Free persons of color records listed blacks and mulattos who were free (not slaves). Homestead records refer chiefly to people who are applying for exemption from taxes or debt obligations on houses and land because of poverty. Inventories were lists of items in an estate, and appraisements were assignments of value to them. Liquor/tavern records were mainly the issuing of licenses. Pauper records dealt with the poor who were applying for relief. Pony homestead records are also poor records; they are requests for exemptions from taxes or debts on personal property. Slave importer records refer to persons who brought slaves into GA. Twelve months support records deal with a year's support given to a widow while the estate is being settled. Notice that the years for which each type of record is available are listed in parentheses. A listing such as (1857-1957) following Inferior Court minutes indicates that the records cover these years continuously or almost continuously (only a few years left out). An asterisk * attached to dates tells you that the materials are indexed or partially indexed.

The second heading in the paragraph reads <u>Published</u> records in GDAH. Here are listed published materials (books, typescripts, microfilms, journal articles) and a few manuscripts. Most of them can be located in GDAH, UGL, WML, and GHS, and some of them will be found in FHL(FHC), RL, and LL. The locality index at FHC will identify those held by FHL. A detailed listing of most of these published materials will be found in the volume:

____J. E. Dorsey, GA GENEALOGY AND LOCAL HISTORY, A BIBLIOGRAPHY, Reprint Co., Spartanburg, SC, 1983.

The types of published materials, some of which are available for most counties, are: Baptist, Bible, biography, bonds, Catholic, cemetery, census (R=regular, I=industrial, P=pensioners, A=agricultural, M=mortality, S=slave), census substitute (Su), Christian Church, church, city directory, city history, Confederate, county history, DAR, death, deed, early settler, Episcopal, estate, estray, family history, genealogical collection, genealogical periodical, Inferior Court minutes, Jewish, jury, land grant, land lottery, Lutheran, manuscript, marks & brands, marriage, Masonic, Methodist, militia, Moravian, mortuary, naturalization, newspaper, petition, physician, Presbyterian, Quaker, Salzburgers, state census, Superior Court minutes, tax, town history, voter, will, WPA. Most of these are self-explanatory, but comments on a couple of them might help. Estray records refer to animals which have strayed from their owners. Marks & brands records list symbols which people put on their animals for identification. In some cases, dates for the records are given; in other cases, especially when the dates are somewhat diverse, they are omitted.

In the third paragraph of each county listing, as the Appling County example shows, are given libraries, particularly ones which can be of assistance genealogically. Then, genealogical and/or historical societies are listed. Addresses for all these institutions are provided so that you may correspond with them. But, please remember: brief letters, only one or two questions which can be answered from an index, and an SASE. And, also be aware that addresses of local societies are highly subject to change.

---

4. APPLING COUNTY

Appling County, formed 1818 from Indian land ceded 1814/8, county seat Baxley (31513), fire 1850.

GDAH CH microfilms (FHL): annual returns(1873-1935*), Confederate(1861-5), deed & mortgage(1828-1915*), estate(1856-1956), free persons of color(1843-56), Inferior Court minutes(1857-1957), inventories & appraisements(1897-1945*), jury(1904-7), lunacy(1911-20), marriage(1869-1952*), Ordinary minutes(1879-1951*), physicians register(1856-1934*), Superior Court minutes(1868-1922*), tax(1851), twelve months support(1893-1953*), will(1877-1937*). Published records in GDAH (etc): biography, cemetery, census(1820RI, 1830R, 1840RP, 1850RAIMS, 1860RAIMS, 1870RAIM, 1880RAIM, 1900R, 1910R, 1920R), county history, deed, early settlers, family history, genealogical collection, manuscript, Methodist, militia.

Libraries: Appling County Public Library, 301 City Hall Drive, Baxley 31513; Okefenokee Regional Library, 401 Lee Avenue, Waycross 31502.

---

5. ATKINSON COUNTY

Atkinson County, formed 1918 from Coffee and Clinch Counties, county seat Pearson (31642). Seek records at CH. Published records in GDAH (etc): cemetery, census (1920R), county history, DAR.

Libraries: Pearson Public Library, Pearson 31642; Satilla Regional Library, 701 E. Ward St., Douglas 31533.

---

6. BACON COUNTY

Bacon County, formed 1914 from Appling, Pierce, and Ware Counties, county seat Alma (31510). Seek records at CH. Published records in GDAH (etc): census (1920R), county history, town history.

Libraries: Bacon County Public Library, Alma 31510; Okefenokee Regional Library 401 Lee Avenue, Waycross 31502. Society: Historical Society of Alma-Bacon County, PO Box 2026, Alma 31510.

7. BAKER COUNTY

Baker County, formed 1825 from Early County, county seat Newton (31770), fire 1872, floods 1925/9.

GDAH CH microfilms (FHL): annual returns(1872-1920*), deed & mortgage(1850-1908*), homestead(1883-1944*), inventories & appraisements(1875-1918*), marriage-(1874-1953*), Ordinary minutes(1874-1924*), Superior Court minutes(1879-1914*), tax(1845), twelve months support(1882-1924*), will(1868-1962*). Published records in GDAH (etc): census(1840RP, 1850RAIMS, 1860RAIMS, 1870RAIM, 1880RAIM, 1900R, 1910R, 1920R), Confederate, jury, marriage, newspaper.

Library: DeSoto Trail Regional Library, 145 E. Broad St., Camilla 31730.

8. BALDWIN COUNTY

Baldwin County, formed 1803 from Indian land ceded 1802/5, county seat Milledgeville (31061), fire 1861, deed and Superior Court records lost.

GDAH CH microfilms (FHL): apprentice(1866-72), annual returns(1813-1901*), deed & mortgage(1861-1902*), estate(1807-1939*), free persons of color(1832-64), homestead(1868-1905*), Inferior Court minutes(1806-68*), inventories & appraisements(1807-1900*), Land Court minutes(1854-69*), land lottery(1820-1), liquor/tavern license(1831-90), marriage(1806-1925*), Ordinary minutes(1807-1900*), physicians register(1875-1963), school(1852-67), Superior Court minutes(1861-1903*), tax(1807-79), twelve months support(1830-1900*), will(1806-1936). Published records in GDAH (etc): Baptist, Bible, cemetery, census(1802Su, 1820RI, 1830R, 1840RP, 1850RAIMS, 1860RAIMS, 1870RAIM, 1880RAIM, 1900R, 1910R, 1920R), Church of Christ, city history, county history, DAR, death(1860-90), family history, land lottery(1820-1/7), marriage(1806-52), Methodist, newspaper, Presbyterian, tax(1810/3/9), will(1806-64), WPA.

Libraries: Vinson Memorial Library, 200 W. Hancock St., Milledgeville 31061; Middle GA Regional Library, 1180 Washington

Ave., Macon 31201. <u>Society</u>: Old Capital Historical Society, PO Box 4, Milledgeville 31061.

9. BANKS COUNTY

Banks County, formed 1858 from Habersham and Franklin Counties, county seat Homer (30547).

<u>GDAH</u> <u>CH</u> <u>microfilms</u> <u>(FHL)</u>: annual returns(1859-1910, 1917-37*), Confederate(1890-1924), deed & mortgage(1859-1936*), homestead(1867-1962), inventories & appraisements(1859-1910*), jury(1896-1904*), Land Court minutes(1873-1927*), marriage(1859-1907*), Ordinary minutes(1859-1911*), Superior Court minutes(1859-1902), tax(1874), twelve months support(1886-1930*), voter(1898), will(1859-1911). <u>Published</u> <u>records</u> <u>in</u> <u>GDAH</u> <u>(etc)</u>: Baptist, cemetery, census(1860RAIMS, 1870RAIM, 1880RAIM, 1900R, 1910R, 1920R), county history, DAR, genealogical collection, manuscript, marriage(1853-74), mortality census(1860).

<u>Libraries</u>: Banks County Public Library, Homer 30547; Piedmont Regional Library, 301 Midland Ave., Winder 30680.

10. BARROW COUNTY

Barrow County, formed 1914 from Gwinnett, Walton, and Jackson Counties, county seat Winder (30680). Seek records in CH.

<u>Published</u> <u>records</u> <u>in</u> <u>GDAH</u> <u>(etc)</u>: Bible, cemetery, census (1920R), Christian Church, county history, DAR, family history, Methodist, town history.

<u>Library</u>: Piedmont Regional Library, 301 Midland Ave., Winder 30680.

11. BARTOW COUNTY

Bartow County, formed in 1832 from Cherokee County, county seat Cartersville (30120), fire 1864, known as Cass County until 1861.

<u>GDAH</u> <u>CH</u> <u>microfilms</u> <u>(FHL)</u>: annual returns(1853-1901*), Confederate(1861-5), deed & mortgage(1837-1962*), homestead(1868-1951*), Inferior Court minutes(1865-8), inventories & appraisements(1853-1908*), marriage(1836-1907*), Ordinary minutes(1853-1904), Superior Court minutes(1865-1903), tax(1871), will(1836-1922). <u>Published</u> <u>records</u> <u>in</u> <u>GDAH</u> <u>(etc)</u>: Baptist, cemetery, census(1840RP, 1850RAIMS, 1860RAIMS, 1870RAIM, 1880RAIM, 1900R, 1910R, 1920R), city history, county history, DAR, early settlers,

Episcopal, marriage(early, 1872), Methodist, militia(1837/45), Presbyterian, state census(1834), town history.

Library: Bartow County Library, 429 W. Main St., Cartersville 30120. Society: Etowah Valley Historical Society, Kingston 30145.

12. BEN HILL COUNTY

Ben Hill County, formed 1906 from Irwin and Wilcox Counties, county seat Fitzgerald (31750). Seek records in the CH.

Published records in GDAH (etc): cemetery, census(1910R, 1920R), city history, county history.

Library: Ben Hill County Library, 123 N. Main St., Fitzgerald 31750.

13. BERRIEN COUNTY

Berrien County, formed 1856 from Lowndes, Irwin, and Coffee Counties, county seat Nashville (31639).

GDAH CH microfilms (FHL): annual returns(1858-1911*), Confederate(1891-1922), deed & mortgage(1850-1928*), homestead(1873-99*), inventories & appraisements-(1862-1910*), marriage(1856-1967*), Ordinary minutes(1856-1906), pony homestead(1899-1930*), school(1858-63*), Superior Court minutes(1856-1905), tax(1867, 1872-), twelve months support(1897-1925*), will(1855-1956*). Published records in GDAH (etc): Baptist, cemetery, census(1860RAIMS, 1870RAIM, 1880RAIM, 1900R, 1910R, 1920R), county history, family history, marriage.

Libraries: Berrien County Library, 102 N. McKinley St., Nashville 31639; Coastal Plain Regional Library, Griffin Rural Life Building, ABAC Station, Tifton 31794.

14. BIBB COUNTY

Bibb County, formed 1822 from James, Monroe, and Twiggs Counties, county seat Macon (31202).

GDAH CH microfilms (FHL): apprentice(1866-99), annual returns(1823-1900, 1906-7*), Confederate(1890-1926*), deed & mortgage(1822-1919*), estate(1821-1964*), homestead(1868-1902*), Inferior Court minutes(1824-64*), inventories & appraisements(1881-1914*), marriage(1823-1963*), Ordinary minutes(1827-1900*), school(1860), Superior Court minutes(1823-1909*), tax(1835-6, 1845, 1871, 1874-), will(1823-1929*). Published records in GDAH (etc): Baptist, cemetery, census(1830R, 1840RP, 1850RAIMS, 1860RAIMS, 1870RAIM, 1880RAIM, 1900R, 1910R, 1920R), city history, county history, DAR, Episcopal, Jewish, jury(1823), land, marriage, Methodist, newspaper, physician, Presbyterian, will.

Libraries: Middle GA Regional Library, 1180 Washington Ave., Macon 31201; Stetson Library, Mercer University, Macon 31207. Societies: Middle GA Historical Society, 935 High St., Macon 31201; GA Baptist Historical Society, Stetson Library, Mercer University, Macon 31207.

15. BLECKLEY COUNTY

Bleckley County, formed 1912 from Pulaski County, county seat Cochran (31014). Seek records in CH.

Published records in GDAH (etc): Baptist, Bible, cemetery, census (1920R), city history, county history, DAR, family history, marriage(1913-55).

Libraries: Bleckley Public Library, Second St., Cochran 31014; Ocmulgee Regional Library, 505 Second Ave., Eastman 31023; Roberts Library, Middle GA College, Cochran 31014.

16. BRANTLEY COUNTY

Brantley County, formed 1920 from Charlton, Pierce, and Wayne Counties, county seat Nahunta (31553). Seek records in CH.

Published records in GDAH (etc): cemetery, county history.

Libraries: Brantley County Library, Nahunta 31553; Glynn County Regional Library, 208 Gloucester St., Brunswick 31523.

17. BROOKS COUNTY

Brooks county, formed 1858 from Lowndes and Thomas Counties, county seat Quitman (31643).

GDAH CH microfilms (FHL): annual returns(1859-1905*), Confederate(1890-1908), homestead(1877-1940*), inventories & appraisements(1859-1922*), marriage(1859-1966*), Ordinary minutes(1859-1909*), physicians register(1856-1953), Superior Court minutes(1859-1908*), tax(1866-), twelve months support(1860-1926*), voter (1898-1900), will(1860-1964*). Published records in GDAH (etc): cemetery, census(1860RAIMS, 1870RAIM, 1880RAIM, 1900R, 1910R, 1920R), Confederate, county history, DAR, Inferior Court minutes(1859-80), marriage, newspaper, will(1860-99), WPA.

Library: Brooks County Library, Culpepper St., Quitman 31643.

18. BRYAN COUNTY Bryan County, formed 1793 from Chatham County, county seat Pembroke (31321), fire 1866, Ordinary records lost, land from Effingham County added 1794.

GDAH CH microfilms (FHL): annual returns(1882-1943), deed & mortgage(1793-1937*), estate(1870-1939*), homestead(1873-1919), Inferior Court minutes(1794-1811, 1833-53), inventories & appraisements(1865-1952), jury(1924-43), liquor/tavern license(1850-67, 1871-1917), lunacy(1910-24), marriage(1865-1948*), Ordinary minutes-(1865-96), physicians register(1880-1946), pony homestead(1897-1951), Superior Court minutes(1794-1923), tax(1861, 1871, 1874-), twelve months support(1876-1903), voter(1914), will(1870-1933). Published records in GDAH (etc): cemetery, census(1802Su, 1820RI, 1830R, 1840RP, 1850RAIMS, 1860RAIMS, 1870RAIM, 1880RAIM, 1900R, 1910R, 1920R), county history, court(1793-1827), DAR, deed(1793-1850), jury(1794-7), land lottery(1805), manuscript, militia(1800-10).

Libraries: Pembroke Public Library, Pembroke 31321; Statesboro Regional Library, Main St. South and Grady, Statesboro 30458.

19. BULLOCH COUNTY Bulloch County, formed 1796 from Bryan and Screven Counties, county seat Statesboro (30458), fire 1864.

GDAH CH microfilms (FHL): annual returns(1817-1968*), Confederate, deed & mortgage(1796-1967*), estate(1795-1900*), homestead(1868-1966*), Inferior Court minutes(1812-36), inventories & appraisements(1874-1946*), liquor/tavern license(1854), lunacy(1899-1966*), marriage(1795-1969*), Ordinary minutes(1795-1967*), physicians register(1881-1958), pony homestead(1899-1919), school(1846-64, 1878-90), Superior Court minutes(1806-1969), tax(1854/66/68, 1874-), twelve months support-(1893-1953*), voter(1865-98), will(1795-1969). Published records in GDAH (etc): Baptist, cemetery, census(1802Su, 1820RI, 1830R, 1840RP, 1850RAIMS, 1860RAIMS, 1870RAIM, 1880RAIM, 1900R, 1910R, 1920R), city history, county history, DAR, deed, estate, family history, genealogical collection, Inferior Court docket & minutes, land lottery(1805/32), marks & brands, Methodist, militia(1800-10), Superior Court docket, will.

Library: Statesboro Regional Library, Main St. South and Grady, Statesboro 30458.

20. BURKE COUNTY	Burke County, formed 1777 from colonial GA, county seat Waynesboro (30830), fires 1825, 1843, 1856, 1870,

GDAH CH microfilms (FHL): apprentice(1867-1919), annual returns(1856-1900), Confederate(1880-1916), deed & mortgage(1843-1900*), Inferior Court docket(1830-63), inventories & appraisements(1856-1926*), marriage(1855-1940*), Ordinary minutes(1849-1907*), Superior Court minutes(1845-1902), tax(1798, 1855-60/63, 1874-), twelve months support(1868-1903*), voter(1890, 1902/4), will(1853-1930). Published records in GDAH (etc): Baptist, Bible, biography, cemetery, census(1756-1815Su, 1790Su, 1802Su, 1820RI, 1830R, 1840RP, 1850RAIMS, 1860RAIMS, 1870RAIM, 1880RAIM, 1900R, 1910R, 1920R), Confederate(1862), county history, DAR, death, deed, early settlers, family history, genealogical collection, land lottery(1805/7), manuscript, marriage(1843-5, 1855-69), Methodist, militia(1781-2), newspaper, Presbyterian, tax(1790/8), town history, will(1853-70), WPA.
Library: Burke County Library, Fourth St., Waynesboro 30830.
Society: Burke County Historical Association, Waynesboro 30830.

21. BUTTS COUNTY	Butts County, formed 1825 from Henry and Monroe Counties, county seat Jackson (30233).

GDAH CH microfilms (FHL): annual returns(1826-87*), Confederate, deed & mortgage(1825-1916*), homestead(1867-1954*), Inferior Court minutes(1826-81*), inventories & appraisements(1826-1918*), liquor/tavern license(1873-81), lunacy(1898-1908), marriage(1826-1948*), Ordinary minutes(1844-1903*), physicians register(1873-1942), Superior Court minutes(1834-81), twelve months support(1881-1927*), will(1826-1948*). Published records in GDAH (etc): Baptist, Bible, cemetery, census(1830R, 1840RP, 1850RAIMS, 1860RAIMS, 1870RAIM, 1880RAIM, 1900R, 1910R, 1920R), county history, DAR, deed, estate, family history, genealogical collection, manuscript, marriage, Methodist, town history, will.
Libraries: Hawkes Library, 431 College St., Jackson 30233; Flint River Regional Library, 800 Memorial Drive, Griffin 30223.

22. CALHOUN COUNTY	Calhoun County, formed 1854 from Baker and Early Counties, county seat Morgan (31766), fires 1888, 1920.

GDAH CH microfilms (FHL): annual returns(1869-1924), Confederate, deed & mortgage(1854-1920*), homestead(1867-1927), Inferior Court minutes(1854-75), liquor/tavern license(1873-88), marriage(1880-1908), Ordinary minutes(1854-96), physicians register(1881-1908), Superior Court minutes(1852, 1859-1906), will(1855-90). Published records in GDAH (etc): cemetery, census(1860RAIMS, 1870RAIM, 1880RAIM, 1900R, 1910R, 1920R), newspaper, WPA.

Libraries: Calhoun County Libraries, Arlington 31713 and Edison 31746; Kinchafoonee Regional Library, 334 N. Main St., Dawson 31742.

23. CAMDEN COUNTY

Camden county, formed 1777 from colonial GA, county seat Woodbine (31569). GDAH CH microfilms (FHL): annual returns(1809-1918), deed & mortgage(1786-1958*), free persons of color(1819-43), homestead(1869-80), Inferior Court minutes(1794-1914), inventories & appraisements(1794-1908), Land Court minutes(1787-1849), liquor/tavern license(1841-60), marriage(1819-1966*), naturalization(1793-1860, 1903-20), Ordinary minutes(1802-1948), physicians register(1856-1954), slave importer(1818-47), Superior Court minutes(1797-1957*), will(1795-1829, 1868-1945*). Published records in GDAH (etc): Baptist, biography, cemetery, census(1756-1815Su, 1790Su, 1802Su, 1820RI, 1830R, 1840RP, 1850RAIMS, 1860RAIMS, 1870RAIM, 1880RAIM, 1900R, 1910R, 1920R), county history, deed, estate, Inferior Court minutes, jury, land grant, land lottery(1805), marriage, militia(1800-10), Presbyterian, Quaker, Superior Court minutes, tax(1794, 1803), town history, voter(1792, 1803), will.

Library: Glynn County Regional Library, 208 Gloucester St, Brunswick 31523. Society: Guale Historical Society, PO Box 398, St. Marys 31558.

24. CAMPBELL COUNTY

Campbell County, formed 1828 from Coweta, Carroll, DeKalb, and Fayette Counties, county seat Campbellton, absorbed by Fulton County 1932. Be sure also to check Fulton County CH and Atlanta Historical Society for records.

GDAH CH microfilms (FHL): apprentice(1868-90), annual returns(1829-1931*), Confederate(1890-1928), deed & mortgage(1828-1931*), estate(1828-1931*), homestead(1868-98*), Inferior Court minutes(1829-73*), inventories & appraisements(1829-1931*), marriage(1827-1931*), Ordinary minutes(1868-1931*), physicians register(1881-1925*), pony homestead(1897-1931*), tax(1855-69), twelve months support(1852), will(1833-1948*). Published records in GDAH (etc): Baptist, cemetery, census(1830R, 1840RP, 1850RAIMS, 1860RAIMS, 1870RAIM, 1880RAIM, 1900R, 1910R, 1920R), Confederate, DAR, early settlers, jury, land, marriage, tax(1855), will.

Libraries: See Fulton County. Societies: See Fulton County.

---

25. CANDLER COUNTY

Candler County, formed 1914 from Bulloch, Emanuel, and Tattnall Counties, county seat Metter (30439). Seek records in CH.

Published records in GDAH (etc): Baptist, cemetery, city history, DAR, newspaper.

Libraries: Candler County Library, Metter 30439; Statesboro Regional Library, Main St. South and Grady, Statesboro 30458.

---

26. CARROLL COUNTY

Carroll county, formed 1825 from Indian land ceded 1826/7, county seat Carrollton (30117), fire 1927.

GDAH CH microfilms (FHL): apprentice(1890-1935*), annual returns(1829-1901*), birth(1875), Confederate(1890-1912), death(1875), deed & mortgage(1827-1934*), estate(1826-1919*), homestead(1869-94*), Inferior Court minutes (1827-62), Inferior Court records(1829-45), inventories & appraisements(1829-1902), marriage(1827-1904*), Ordinary minutes(1852-1910), physicians register(1881-1962), pony homestead(1883-1913*), Superior Court minutes(1857-1903*), tax(1832/41-7, 1852), twelve months support(1881-1902*), will(1829-1922). Published records in GDAH (etc): Baptist, biography, cemetery, census(1830R, 1840RP, 1850RAIMS, 1860RAIMS, 1870RAIM, 1880RAIM, 1900R, 1910R, 1920R), Christian Church, church, Confederate, county history, DAR, early settlers, genealogical collection, genealogical periodical, jury, land, land lots, land lottery(1827), manuscript, marriage, Masonic, Methodist, militia, Presbyterian, tax(1842), town history, voter.

Library: West GA Regional Library, 710 Rome St., Carrollton 30117. Society: Carroll County Historical Society, 710 Rome St., Carrollton 30117; Carroll County Genealogical Society, PO Box 576, Carrollton 30117.

---

27. CASS COUNTY

Cass county, formed 1832 from Cherokee County, name changed to Bartow County in 1861. See Bartow County for record listing.

28. CATOOSA COUNTY

Catoosa County, formed 1853 from Walker and Whitfield Counties, county seat Ringgold (30736).

GDAH CH microfilms (FHL): annual returns(1860-1902), deed & mortgage(1854-1902*), estate(1874-1975), Inferior Court minutes(1854-61), inventories & appraisements(1874-1928), jury(1874-1920), marriage(1858-1910*), Ordinary minutes(1854-1920), physicians register(1881-1933), school(1875-96), Superior Court minutes(1854-1903*), will(1874-1961*). Published records in GDAH (etc): Baptist, census(1860RAIMS, 1870RAIM, 1880RAIM, 1900R, 1910R, 1920R), Confederate, county history, marriage.

Libraries: Catoosa County Library, Gym St., Ringgold 30736; Dalton Public Library, 310 Cappes St., Dalton 30720.

29. CHARLTON COUNTY

Charlton County, formed 1854 from Camden County, county seat Folkston (31537), fires 1877, 1928.

GDAH CH microfilms (FHL): annual returns(1854-1912), deed & mortgage(1852-1915*), estate(1882-1954*), homestead(1873-1908*), inventories & appraisements(1854-1912), marriage(1854-1961*), Ordinary minutes(1854-1911*), physicians register(1894-1958), Superior Court minutes(1879-1920*), tax(1855/71), will(1868-1966*). Published records in GDAH (etc): census(1860RAIMS, 1870RAIM, 1880RAIM, 1900R, 1910R, 1920R), county history, DAR, early settlers, family history, marriage, Methodist.

Libraries: Charlton County Library, Folkston 31537; Glynn County Regional Library, 208 Gloucester St., Brunswick 31523. Society: Charlton County Historical Society, Rt. 3, Box 142C, Folkston 31537.

30. CHATHAM COUNTY

Chatham County, formed 1777 from colonial GA, county seat Savannah (31402).

GDAH CH microfilms (FHL): annual returns(1780-1900), birth(1803-47*), Confederate(1890-1925), death(1803-47*), deed & mortgage(1785-1903*), estate(1777-1852*), free persons of color(1780-1865), homestead(1868-1922), Inferior Court minutes(1790-1845), inventories & appraisements(1783-1925), land lottery(1819-21, 1832), lunacy(1854-1949), marriage(1805-1924*), naturalization(1789-1910*), Ordinary minutes(1800-1901), physicians register(1881-1919), pony homestead(1876-1922), state census(1845/52),

Superior Court minutes(1782-1905*), tax(1793/8-9, 1806/21-7/31-5/42-8/55/66-9/75-8/81-4/93-7), twelve months support(1890-1920), will(1775-1936). Published records in GDAH (etc): Baptist, Catholic, cemetery, census(1756-1815Su, 1790Su, 1802Su, 1820RI, 1830R, 1840RP, 1850RAIMS, 1860RAIMS, 1870RAIM, 1880RAIM, 1900R, 1910R, 1920R), city census, city directory, city history, Confederate, county history, DAR, death(1854), deed, Episcopal, estate, family history, genealogical periodical, Jewish, land grant, land lottery(1805), Lutheran, manuscript, marriage, Methodist, military(1812-21), militia, Moravian, mortuary, naturalization, newspaper, Presbyterian, Salzburgers, tax(1898), voter, will, WPA.

Libraries: Chatham-Effingham-Liberty Regional Library, 2002 Bull St., Savannah 31499; GA Historical Society Library, 501 Whitaker St., Savannah 31499. Societies: GA Historical Society, 501 Whitaker St., Savannah 31499; GA Salzburger Society, 9375 Whitfield Ave., Savannah 31406; Savannah Area Genealogical Society, PO Box 15385, Savannah 31416.

31. CHATTAHOOCHEE COUNTY

Chattahoochee County, formed 1854 from Muscogee and Marion Counties, county seat Cusseta (31805).

GDAH CH microfilms (FHL): annual returns(1854-1910*), Confederate(1890-1920), deed & mortgage(1854-1918*), homestead(1863-1914*), Inferior Court minutes(1854-68*), inventories & appraisements(1854-1940*), jury(1879-1902), marriage(1854-1947*), Ordinary minutes(1854-1920*), school(1857-84*), Superior Court minutes(1854-1902*), tax(1854-72), voter(1896-1900, 1907-9), will(1854-1935*). Published records in GDAH (etc): cemetery, census(1860RAIMS, 1870RAIM, 1880RAIM, 1900R, 1910R, 1920R), county history, marriage.

Libraries: Chattahoochee County Library, Cusseta 31805; Chattahoochee Valley Regional Library, 1120 Bradley Dr., Columbus 31995.

32. CHATTOOGA COUNTY

Chattooga County, formed 1838 from Floyd and Walker Counties, county seat Summerville (30747).

GDAH CH microfilms (FHL): apprentice(1866-1907), annual returns(1851-1910*), bastardy(1897-1912*), birth(1874-6*), Confederate(1861-5), death(1875-6*), deed & mortgage(1839-1937*), estate(1839-1939*), homestead(1871-

1922*), Inferior Court minutes(1839-64), inventories & appraisements(1851-1904*), marriage(1839-1939*), Ordinary minutes(1862-1912*), physicians register(1882-1927*), Superior Court minutes(1867-1903), tax(1871), twelve months support(1899-1929*), will(1856-1924*). Published records in GDAH (etc): Baptist, cemetery, census(1840RP, 1850RAIMS, 1860RAIMS, 1870RAIM, 1880RAIM, 1900R, 1910R, 1920R), county history, early settlers, family history, marriage.

Library: Chattooga County Library, 200 S. Commerce St., Summerville 30747.

33. CHEROKEE COUNTY

Cherokee County, formed 1830 from Indian land ceded 1835, county seat Canton (30114), fires 1865, 1928.

GDAH CH microfilms (FHL): apprentice(1866-1904), annual returns(1848-1911*), Confederate(1861-71, 1914-9), deed & mortgage(1832-1920*), homestead(1868-1915*), Inferior Court minutes(1832-88), inventories & appraisements(1848-1924*), marriage(1841-1910*), Ordinary minutes(1848-1901), pauper(1859-71), Superior Court minutes(1832-1903), tax(1849-71), will(1866-1921). Published records in GDAH (etc): Baptist, cemetery, census(1840RP, 1850RAIMS, 1860RAIMS, 1870RAIM, 1880RAIM, 1900R, 1910R, 1920R), Confederate, county history, early settlers, justices of the peace, land, land lottery, marriage, Methodist, state census(1834).

Library: Sequoyah Regional Library, 400 E. Main St., Canton 30114.

34. CLARKE COUNTY

Clarke County, formed 1801 from Jackson County, county seat Athens (30601).

GDAH CH microfilms (FHL): apprentice(1802-22, 1837-1911), annual returns(1802-1959), birth(1808-52, 1875-6), Confederate(1861-9, 1884-1934), death(1875-6), deed & mortgage(1801-1960*), estate index, free persons of color(1847-62), homestead(1846-1943), Inferior Court minutes(1802-56, 1866), inventories & appraisements(1811-28, 1850-71), jury(1879-1911), Land Court minutes(1834-75), lunacy(1895-1909), marriage(1805-1956*), Ordinary minutes(1851-1960*), pauper(1883-6), physicians register(1895-1910), pony homestead(1884-1926), power of attorney(1807-14, 1835-68), school(1852-79), Superior Court minutes(1801-1958*), tax(1802-), twelve months support(1881-1952), voter(1890-8, 1908*), will(1802-1955). Published records in GDAH (etc): Baptist, Bible, cemetery, census(1802Su, 1820RI, 1830R, 1840RP, 1850RAIMS, 1860RAIMS, 1870RAIM, 1880RAIM, 1900R, 1910R, 1920R), city records, city history, Confederate, county history, DAR, death(1834-77), Episcopal, estate, family history, genealogical periodical, jury(1808), land lottery(1805), marriage, Methodist, militia(1863), newspaper, Presbyterian, tax(1806/10/57), will.

Libraries: Athens Regional Library, 120 W. Dougherty St., Athens 30601; University of GA Libraries, Athens 30602. Society: Athens-Clarke Heritage Foundation, 489 Prince Ave., Athens 30601.

35. CLAY COUNTY

Clay County, formed 1854 from Early and Randolph Counties, county seat Ft. Gaines (31751).

GDAH CH microfilms (FHL): apprentice(1866-7*), Confederate(1889-1958), deed & mortgage(1854-1922*), homestead(1876-1918*), inventories & appraisements(1854-1947*), marriage(1854-1933*), Ordinary minutes(1854-97*), physicians register(1881-1955*), Superior Court minutes(1854-1905*), tax(1855/64), will(1852-1966*). Published records in GDAH (etc): census(1860RAIMS, 1870RAIM, 1880RAIM, 1900R, 1910R, 1920R), city history, county history.

Libraries: Clay County Library, Ft. Gaines 31751; Kinchafoonee Regional Library, 334 N. Main St., Dawson 31742. Society: Ft. Gaines Historical Society, 308 E. Jefferson St., Ft. Gaines 31751.

36. CLAYTON COUNTY

Clayton County, formed 1858 from Fayette and Henry Counties, county seat Jonesboro (30236), fire 1864.

GDAH CH microfilms (FHL): annual returns(1860-3, 1874-1919), birth(1875), Confederate(1890-1927), deed & mortgage(1859-1952*), estate(1859-1938*), homestead-(1859-1940), Inferior Court minutes(1859-78), inventories & appraisements(1859-1957), jury(1882-1918), liquor/tavern license(1859-73), marriage(1859-1961*), physicians register(1882-1917), school(1860-75), Superior Court minutes(1859-1914), tax(1861-9), twelve months support(1882-1928), voter(1898-1920), will(1859-1921). Published records in GDAH (etc): Baptist, cemetery, census(1860RAIMS, 1870RAIM, 1880RAIM, 1900R, 1910R, 1920R), city history, Confederate, county history, family history, genealogical periodical, land lottery, marriage, Methodist, Presbyterian, Superior Court minutes.

Library: Clayton County Library, 124 Smith St., Jonesboro 30236. Society: Ancestors Unlimited, PO Box 1507, Jonesboro, GA 30236.

37. CLINCH COUNTY

Clinch County, formed 1850 from Ware and Lowndes Counties, county seat Homerville (31634), fires 1856, 1867, most records destroyed.

GDAH CH microfilms (FHL): apprentice(1866-96*), annual returns(1867-1945*), Confederate(1862, 1896-1930), deed & mortgage(1850-1966*), homestead(1866-1957*), Inferior Court minutes(1868-1901), inventories & appraisements(1869-1960*), marriage(1867-1965*), Ordinary minutes(1867-1921*), physicians register(1893-1963), Superior Court minutes(1867-1906*), tax(1868-), twelve months support(1892-1923*), voter(1889-1904, 1914-41), will(1868-1966*). Published records in GDAH (etc): cemetery, census-(1850RAIMS, 1860RAIMS, 1870RAIM, 1880RAIM, 1900R, 1910R, 1920R), county history, DAR, early settlers, genealogical periodical, Lutheran, marriage, town history, WPA.

Libraries: Clinch County Library, Homerville 31634; Okefenokee Regional Library, 401 Lee Ave., Waycross 31502. Society: Huxford Genealogical Society, 102 Courtland Ave., Homerville 31634.

38. COBB COUNTY

Cobb County, formed 1832 from Cherokee County, county seat Marietta (30060), fire 1864, most records destroyed. Cobb County records in GDAH, but county will not permit researchers to use them.

GDAH CH microfilms (FHL): tax(1848-9, 1851). Published records in GDAH (etc): cemetery, census(1840RP, 1850RAIMS, 1860RAIMS, 1870RAIM, 1880RAIM, 1900R, 1910R, 1920R), church, city history, Confederate, county history, DAR, genealogical periodical, Inferior Court minutes, marriage, Methodist, Presbyterian, state census(1834), town history.

Library: Cobb County Public Library, 30 Atlanta St., SE, Marietta 30060. Society: Cobb County Genealogical Society, PO Box 1413, Marietta 30061.

39. COFFEE COUNTY

Coffee County, formed 1854 from Clinch, Ware, Telfair, and Irwin Counties, county seat Douglas (31533), fires

1898, 1938, many records lost. GDAH does not have microfilms of the surviving records.

GDAH CH microfilms (FHL): tax(1869-72). Published records in GDAH (etc): Baptist, cemetery, census(1860RAIMS, 1870RAIM, 1880RAIM, 1900R, 1910R, 1920R), county history, deed, jury(1854), marriage.

Library: Satilla Regional Library, 701 E. Ward St., Douglas 31533.

---

40. COLQUITT COUNTY

Colquitt County, formed 1856 from Thomas and Lowndes Counties, county seat Moultrie (31768), fire 1881, most records lost.

GDAH CH microfilms (FHL): annual returns(1905-22*), birth(1875*), death (1875*), deed & mortgage(1881-1911*), homestead(1883-1933*), inventories & appraisements(1903-30), marriage(1891-1967*), Ordinary minutes(1902-22*), physicians register(1886-1966*), pony homestead(1903-13*), Superior Court minutes(1881-1907*), tax(1857/69), twelve months support(1903-18*), will(1900-67*). Published records in GDAH (etc): Baptist, cemetery, census(1860RAIMS, 1870RAIM, 1880RAIM, 1900R, 1910R, 1920R), Confederate, county history, marriage, town history, WPA.

Library: Colquitt-Thomas Regional Library, 204 Fifth St., SE, Moultrie 31768. Society: Colquitt County Historical Society, Moultrie 31768.

---

41. COLUMBIA COUNTY

Columbia County, formed 1790 from Richmond County, county seat Appling (30802).

GDAH CH microfilms (FHL): annual returns(1809-1919*), Confederate(1890-1913, 1920-6, 1931-3), deed & mortgage(1791-1911*), estate(1833-56*), free persons of color(1819-36), homestead(1876-1948*), Inferior Court minutes(1791-1868*), inventories & appraisements(1790-1959*), jury(1794-1802, 1840-6, 1879-1910*), land lottery(1805/7/21), liquor/tavern license(1852-71), marriage(1787-1967*), Ordinary minutes-(1799-1828, 1834-1913*), physicians register(1881-1901*), school(1828-49), Superior Court minutes(1790-1908), tax(1805-8, 1812-67, 1872, 1876-), twelve months support(1858-1940*), voter(1895-7, 1909-12), will(1789-1963*). Published records in GDAH (etc): Baptist, cemetery, census(1790Su, 1802Su, 1820RI-partial, 1830R, 1840RP, 1850RAIMS, 1860RAIMS, 1870RAIM, 1880RAIM, 1900R, 1910R, 1920R), court records, DAR, deed, estate, Inferior Court minutes, jury(1794-1802), land lottery(1805), marriage, militia(1793), military(1793, 1812-21), tax(1805/8), will.

Library: Augusta Regional Library, 902 Greene St., Augusta 30901.

42. COOK COUNTY

Cook County, formed 1918 from Berrien County, county seat Adel (31620). Seek records in CH.

Published records in GDAH (etc): cemetery, census(1920R), county history, DAR, WPA.

Libraries: Cook County Library, Adel 31620; Coastal Plain Regional Library, Griffin Rural Life Building, Tifton 31793.

43. COWETA COUNTY

Coweta County, formed 1825 from Indian land ceded 1826/7, county seat Newnan (30263).

GDAH CH microfilms (FHL): apprentice(1866-1911*), annual returns(1829-1911*), Confederate(1890-1941), death(1927-66*), deed & mortgage(1827-1904*), estate(1827-1966*), homestead(1874-1915*), Inferior Court minutes(1829-73*), inventories & appraisements(1828-1910*), marriage(1827-1966*), Ordinary minutes(1857-1916*), physicians register(1880-1961), school(1853-8), Superior Court minutes(1828-1908*), tax(1845-8, 1854-7, 1860-7, 1872-9), twelve months support(1857-1922*), voter(1905/8), will(1828-1966*). Published records in GDAH (etc): Baptist, cemetery, census(1830R, 1840RP, 1850RAIMS, 1860RAIMS, 1870RAIM, 1880RAIM, 1900R, 1910R, 1920R), Christian Church, Confederate, county history, DAR, Episcopal, genealogical periodical, jury, land lottery(1827), marriage, Methodist, pension(1812), Presbyterian, town history, voter(1832).

Libraries: Coweta Carnegie Branch Library, 1 La Grange St., Newnan 30263; Troup Harris Coweta Regional Library, 500 Broome St., La Grange 30240. Society: Coweta Historical Society, 30 Temple Ave., Newnan 30263; Coweta County Genealogical Society, PO Box 1014, Newnan 30264.

44. CRAWFORD COUNTY

Crawford County, formed 1822 from Houston County, county seat Knoxville (31050), fire 1829, many records lost.

GDAH CH microfilms (FHL): annual returns(1836-1928*), Confederate(1914-62*), deed & mortgage(1830-1940*), estate(1868-1905), homestead(1866-1946*), Inferior Court minutes(1830-63), inventories & appraisements(1833-1913*), marriage(1823-45, 1873-1943*), Ordinary minutes(1880-1918*), Superior Court minutes(1830-1900), tax(1840-5, 1851/6/8, 1868, 1871), twelve months support(1871-93*), will(1835-1948*). Published records in GDAH (etc): cemetery, census(1830R, 1840RP, 1850RAIMS, 1860RAIMS, 1870RAIM, 1880RAIM, 1900R, 1910R, 1920R), county history, DAR, jury(1846), marriage, Methodist, will.

Libraries: Crawford County Library, Rt. 1, Roberta 31066; Middle GA Regional Library, 1180 Washington Ave., Macon 31201.

---

45. CRISP COUNTY

Crisp County, formed 1905 from Dooly County, county seat Cordele. See records in the CH.

Published records in GDAH (etc): cemetery, census(1910R, 1920R), county history, DAR, town history.

Library: Cordele Carnegie Library, 115 E. 11th Ave., Cordele 31015; Lake Blackshear Regional Library, 307 E. Lamar St., Americus 31709.

---

46. DADE COUNTY

Dade County, formed 1837 from Walker County, county seat Trenton (30752), fires 1865, 1895.

GDAH CH microfilms (FHL): annual returns(1853-1914*), Confederate(1908-52), deed & mortgage(1849-1928*), inventories & appraisements(1853-1914*), marriage(1866-1962*), Ordinary minutes(1853-1919*), pauper(1885-1902), Superior Court minutes(1854-1906*), voter(1909-16, 1920-8), will(1884-1948*). Published records in GDAH (etc): census(1840RP, 1850RAIMS, 1860RAIMS, 1870RAIM, 1880RAIM, 1900R, 1910R, 1920R), church, Confederate, county history, marriage.

Libraries: Dade County Library, Railway Lane, Trenton 30752; Cherokee Regional Library, 305 S. Duke St., Lafayette, 30728.

---

47. DAWSON COUNTY

Dawson County, formed 1857 from Lumpkin and Gilmer Counties, county seat Dawsonville (30534).

GDAH CH microfilms (FHL): annual returns(1858-1962), Confederate(1890-1920), deed & mortgage(1858-1934*), divorce(1857-80), homestead(1868-98), inventories &

appraisements(1858-1962), marriage(1858-1961*), Ordinary minutes(1858-1922), physicians register(1881-1907), pony homestead(1898-1950), Superior Court minutes(1858-1905), twelve months support(1896-1962), will(1857-1959*). Published records in GDAH (etc): cemetery, census(1860RAIMS, 1870RAIM, 1880RAIM, 1900R, 1910R, 1920R), church, county history, DAR, homestead.

Libraries: Dawson County Library, Dawsonville 30534; Lake Lanier Regional Library, 275 Perry St., Lawrenceville 30245.

48. DECATUR COUNTY Decatur County, formed 1823 from Early County, county seat Bainbridge (31717).

GDAH CH microfilms (FHL): annual returns(1835-1901), Confederate(1865-9, 1890-1926), deed & mortgage(1823-1960*), homestead(1868-1927), Inferior Court minutes(1829-64), jury(1869-77), land lottery(1832), marriage(1824-1942*), Ordinary minutes(1824-1900), physicians register(1881-1911), Superior Court minutes(1825-1901), tax(1824-62), voter(1886/8/92/4, 1902), will(1824-1913). Published records in GDAH (etc): Baptist, Bible, cemetery, census(1830R, 1840RP, 1850RAIMS, 1860RAIMS, 1870RAIM, 1880RAIM, 1900R, 1910R, 1920R), Confederate, county history, family history, jury(1826), marriage, Methodist, military(1812), tax(1824), WPA.

Library: Southwest GA Regional Library, Shotwell and Monroe Sts., Bainbridge 31717.

49. DEKALB COUNTY Dekalb County, formed 1822 from Fayette, Gwinnett, and Henry Counties, county seat Decatur (30030), fires 1842, 1898, 1916, most records lost in 1842.

GDAH CH microfilms (FHL): annual returns(1842-1902), Confederate(1890-1938), deed & mortgage(1840-1910*), estate(1840-1929*), Inferior Court minutes(1823-70*), inventories & appraisements(1842-1904*), marriage(1840-1928*), naturalization(1918), Ordinary minutes(1840-1929*), physicians register(1881-1933), Superior Court minutes(1836-1905*), tax(1846-50/5), twelve months support(1874-1908*), will(1841-1919*). Published records in GDAH (etc): atlas, Baptist, biography, cemetery, census(1830R, 1840RP, 1850RAIMS, 1860RAIMS, 1870RAIM, 1880RAIM, 1900R, 1910R, 1920R), city history, Confederate, county history, DAR, genealogical collection, Inferior Court minutes, manuscript, marriage, Methodist, physician, Superior Court, tax(1855), town history.

Library: DeKalb Library, 3560 Kensington Rd., DeKalb 30032.
Society: DeKalb Historical Society, Old Courthouse, Decatur 30030.

50. DODGE COUNTY Dodge County, formed 1870 from Pulaski, Telfair, and Montgomery Counties, county seat Eastman (31023).

GDAH CH microfilms (FHL): apprentice(1880-1926*), annual returns(1871-1905*), Confederate(1920-39*), deed & mortgage(1871-1934*), estate(1871-1966*), homestead-(1872-1921*), inventories & appraisements(1871-1955*), marriage(1871-1966*), naturalization(1904-11), Ordinary minutes(1871-1900*), pauper(1892-1904), physicians register(1881-1962), Superior Court minutes(1871-1911*), tax(1871-7, 1880), twelve months support(1873-1965), voter(1888-1914, 1919-20, 1926*), will(1875-1966*). Published records in GDAH (etc): Bible, cemetery, census(1880RAIM, 1900R, 1910R, 1920R), county history, DAR, family history, marriage.

Library: Dodge County Library, 505 Second Ave., Eastman 31023.

51. DOOLY COUNTY Dooly County, formed 1821 from Indian land ceded 1821, county seat Vienna (31092), fire 1847, most records lost.

GDAH CH microfilms (FHL): apprentice(1873-1919*), annual returns(1847-1909*), Confederate(1880-1925), deed & mortgage(1847-1900*), homestead(1868-1916*), Inferior Court minutes(1847-96*), inventories & appraisements(1837-1912*), marriage(1856-1908*), Ordinary minutes(1847-1902*), physicians register(1880-1964*), state census(1845), Superior Court minutes(1847-1901*), tax(1881), twelve months support(1886-1910*), will(1847-1901*). Published records in GDAH (etc): cemetery, census(1830R, 1840RP, 1850RAIMS, 1860RAIMS, 1870RAIM, 1880RAIM, 1900R, 1910R, 1920R), city history, county history, genealogical collection, land lottery(1827), military(1818-35), physician, state census(1845), WPA.

Libraries: Dooly County Public Library, Vienna 31092; Lake Blackshear Regional Library, 307 E. Lamar St., Americus 31709.

52. DOUGHERTY COUNTY Dougherty County, formed 1853 from Baker County, county seat Albany (31701).

GDAH CH microfilms (FHL): annual returns(1849-1917), deed & mortgage(1854-1902*), homestead(1881-1912), Inferior Court minutes(1854-69), inventories &

appraisements(1854-1919), liquor/tavern license(1880-92), marriage(1854-1901), physicians register(1868-1951), Superior Court minutes(1856-99), twelve months support(1884-1958), will(1854-1925). Published records in GDAH (etc): Baptist, cemetery, census(1860RAIMS, 1870RAIM, 1880RAIM, 1900R, 1910R, 1920R), church, city history, Confederate, county history, DAR, family history, genealogical periodical, marriage, Methodist, WPA.

Library: Dougherty County Public Library, 300 Pine Ave., Albany 31701. Society: Southwest GA Genealogical Society, PO Box 4672. Albany 31706.

---

53. DOUGLAS COUNTY

Douglas County, formed 1870 from Campbell and Carroll Counties, county seat Douglasville (30134), fires 1896, 1957.

GDAH CH microfilms (FHL): annual returns(1871-1912*), Confederate(1920-34), deed & mortgage(1871-1917*), homestead(1889-1919), inventories & appraisements(1871-1933*), marriage(1871-1941*), Ordinary minutes(1871-3, 1882-1912*), physicians register(1881-1963*), Superior Court minutes(1871-1904*), twelve months support(1883-1959*), will(1870-1932*). Published records in GDAH (etc): Baptist, biography, cemetery, census(1880RAIM, 1900R, 1910R, 1920R), Confederate, family history, genealogical periodical, manuscript, physician.

Libraries: Douglas County Library, 8501 Bowdon St., Douglasville 30134; West GA Regional Library, 710 Rome St., Carrollton 30117.

---

54. EARLY COUNTY

Early County, formed 1818 from Indian land ceded 1814, county seat Blakely (31723), fire 1896.

GDAH CH microfilms (FHL): annual returns(1850-1906), birth(1875-7*), Confederate(1861-5), death(1875), deed & mortgage(1821-1900), homestead(1868-1930), Inferior Court minutes(1820-82), inventories & appraisements(1822-1914), marriage(1820-1915*), Ordinary minutes(1866-1902), Superior Court minutes(1820-1902*), tax(1820, 1840/2, 1850), voter(1896/8, 1900), will(1822-1941*). Published records in GDAH (etc): Baptist, cemetery, census(1820RI, 1830R, 1840RP, 1850RAIMS, 1860RAIMS, 1870RAIM, 1880RAIM, 1900R, 1910R, 1920R), county history, DAR, early settlers, Episcopal, family history, genealogical collection, marriage, newspaper, will.

Libraries: Early County Library, Blakely 31723; DeSoto Trail Regional Library, 145 East Broad St., Camilla 31730. Society: Early County Historical Society, 255 N. Main St., Blakely 31723.

55. ECHOLS COUNTY Echols County, formed 1858 from Lowndes and Clinch Counties, county seat Statenville (31648), fire 1897, most records lost.

GDAH CH microfilms (FHL): annual returns(1898-1967*), deed & mortgage(1867-1910*), inventories & appraisements(1898-1960*), marriage(1898-1967*), Ordinary minutes(1880-1917*), physicians register(1907-40), Superior Court minutes(1898-1914*), tax(1867), twelve months support(1899-1964*), voter(1895-8, 1900-2, 1910-2), will(1875-1952*). Published records in GDAH (etc): cemetery, census(1860RAIMS, 1870RAIM, 1880RAIM, 1900R, 1910R, 1920R), church, county history, marriage, will, WPA.

Libraries: Statenville Branch Library, Statenville 31648; South GA Regional Library, 300 Woodrow Wilson Dr., Valdosta 31601.

56. EFFINGHAM COUNTY Effingham County, formed 1777 from colonial GA, county seat Springfield (31329), some records lost in Civil War, fire 1890.

GDAH CH microfilms (FHL): annual returns(1817-1919), coroner(1916-50), deed & mortgage(1786-1918*), estate(1791-1934*), homestead(1860-1934), Inferior Court minutes(1832-72), inventories & appraisements(1827-1949), jury(1910-32), Land Court minutes(1829-1907), lunacy, militia(1990-4), miscellaneous(1791-1834*), Ordinary minutes(1827-1922*), physicians register(1881-1953), pony homestead(1873-1901*), Superior Court minutes(1821-1901), tax(1855-8, 1860-79), twelve months support(1866-1940), voter(1911-32), will(1829-1950). Published records in GDAH (etc): Baptist, cemetery, census(1756-1815Su, 1790Su, 1802Su, 1820RI, 1830R, 1840RP, 1850RAIMS, 1860RAIMS, 1870RAIM, 1880RAIM, 1900R, 1910R, 1920R), county history, DAR, deed, early records, early settlers, family history, land grant, land lottery(1805), Lutheran, manuscript, marks & brands, marriage, militia(1794), miscellaneous records, Moravian, Ordinary records, Salzburgers, will.

Libraries: Effingham County Library, Springfield 31329; Chatham-Effingham-Liberty Regional Library, 11935 Abercorn St., Savannah 31499.

57. ELBERT COUNTY

Elbert County, formed 1790 from Wilkes County, county seat Elberton (30635).

GDAH CH microfilms (FHL): amnesty(1865), apprentice(1809-16, 1830-1903*), annual returns(1791-1907*), birth(1875-8), Confederate(1861, 1890-1932), death(1875-8), deed & mortgage(1791-1912*), estate(1828-35*), free persons of color(1819-58), homestead(1867-72), Land Court(1822-59), land lottery(1807/21/7/32), liquor/tavern license(1839-58), lunacy(1897-1909), marriage(1804-1913*), militia(1809-18), Ordinary minutes(1791-1910), pony homestead(1897-1933), slave importer(1822-47), Superior Court minutes(1790-1904), tax(1848-51, 1860), twelve months support(1856-1924*), will(1791-1919*). Published records in GDAH (etc): Baptist, cemetery, census(1790Su, 1802Su, 1820RI, 1830R, 1840RP, 1850RAIMS, 1860RAIMS, 1870RAIM, 1880RAIM, 1900R, 1910R, 1920R), city history, Confederate, county history, DAR, early records, family history, jury, land grant, land lottery(1805/7), marriage, Methodist, militia(1793/6), newspaper, physician, Revolutionary pension, Superior Court minutes, tax(1815), town history, War of 1812, will.

Library: Elbert County Library, 345 Heard St., Elberton 30635.

58. EMANUEL COUNTY

Emanuel County, formed 1812 from Bulloch and Montgomery Counties, county seat Swainsboro (30401), fires 1841, 1855, 1857, 1919, 1938.

GDAH CH microfilms (FHL): annual returns(1836-50, 1866-1960*), birth(1822-63), deed & mortgage(1830-1961*), free persons of color(1855), homestead(1869-1916), Inferior Court minutes(1841-59), inventories & appraisements(1812-1956*), jury(1896-1902), Land Court minutes(1858-67), liquor/tavern license(1856-75), marriage(1817-1916*), Ordinary minutes(1841-1961), physicians register(1888-1959), school (1823-80), Superior Court minutes(1810-1961), tax(1841/51), twelve months support(1857-1961*), will(1815-1961*). Published records in GDAH (etc): Baptist, cemetery, census(1820RI, 1830R, 1840RP, 1850RAIMS, 1860RAIMS, 1870RAIM, 1880RAIM, 1900R, 1910R, 1920R), county history, DAR, early settlers, estate, estray, family history, genealogical collection, marks & brands, marriage, Methodist, militia, newspaper, tax, town history, voter, will, WPA.

Libraries: Franklin Memorial Library, Swainsboro 30401; Statesboro Regional Library, Main Street South and Grady, Statesboro 30458. Society: Emanuel Historic Preservation Society, PO Box 1101, Swainsboro 30401.

59. EVANS COUNTY

Evans County, formed 1914 from Bulloch and Tattnall Counties, county seat Claxton (30417). Seek records in CH.

Published records in GDAH (etc): Baptist, census (1920R), county history, Methodist, newspaper.

Libraries: Evans County Library, Claxton 30417; Statesboro Regional Library, Main Street South and Grady, Statesboro 30458.

60. FANNIN COUNTY

Fannin County, formed 1854 from Gilmer and Union Counties, county seat Blue Ridge (30513), fire 1936.

GDAH CH microfilms (FHL): annual returns(1866-1916*), Confederate(1914-28), deed & mortgage (1854-1936*), homestead(1869-1917*), inventories & appraisements(1865-1903*), marriage(1854-1901*), Ordinary minutes(1865-1908*), Superior Court Minutes(1854-1904*), tax(1863/6), twelve months support(1866-1900*), will (1854-1929*). Published records in GDAH (etc): birth, cemetery, census(1860RAIMS, 1870RAIM, 1880RAIM, 1900R, 1910R, 1920R), county history, death, marriage, town history.

Libraries: Fannin County Library, Blue Ridge 30513; Mountain Regional Library, College St., Young Harris 30582.

61. FAYETTE COUNTY

Fayette County, formed 1821 from Indian land ceded 1821, county seat Fayetteville (30214).

GDAH CH microfilms (FHL): annual returns(1824-1911), Confederate(1861-1949), deed & mortgage(1821-1903), homestead(1869-1922), Inferior Court minutes(1823-62), inventories & appraisements(1824-1911), liquor/tavern license(1883-5), marriage(1823-1913*), Ordinary minutes(1823-1903), physicians register(1892-1952), pony homestead(1883-1919), school(1928/33/8), Superior Court minutes(1827-1914), tax(1823-69), twelve months support(1879-1941), will(1823-1953). Published records in GDAH (etc): administrator, Baptist, cemetery, census(1830R, 1840RP, 1850RAIMS, 1860RAIMS, 1870RAIM, 1880RAIM, 1900R, 1910R, 1920R), city history, county history, DAR, guardian, manuscript, marriage, Methodist, newspaper, Ordinary records, tax, will.

Libraries: Margaret Mitchell Library, 195 Lee St., Fayetteville 30214; Flint River Regional Library, 800 Memorial Dr., Griffin 30223.

Society: Fayette County Historical Society, PO Box 421, Fayetteville 30214.

62. FLOYD COUNTY

Floyd County, formed 1832 from Cherokee County, county seat Rome 30161.

GDAH CH microfilms (FHL): annual returns(1842-1902), Confederate (1861-5, 1890-1940), deed & mortgage(1833-1934*), homestead(1868-1933), Inferior Court minutes(1837-75), inventories & appraisements(1842-1901),liquor/tavernlicense(1898-1928),lunacy(1898-1909),marriage(1834-1904*), Ordinary minutes(1837-46, 1852-9, 1866-1904), pauper(1850-69), school(1830-80), Superior Court minutes(1840-1901), tax(1852), twelve months support(1883-1912), voter(1896), will(1852-1918). Published records in GDAH (etc): Baptist, biography, cemetery, census(1840RP, 1850RAIMS, 1860RAIMS, 1870RAIM, 1880RAIM, 1900R, 1910R, 1920R), city directory, city history, county history, DAR, early settlers, family history, genealogical collection, genealogical periodical, marriage, Methodist, military, mortuary, newspaper, physician, Presbyterian, Superior Court, town history.

Library: Sara Hightower Regional Library, 606 W. First St., Rome 30161. Society: Northwest GA Historical and Genealogical Society, PO Box 2484, Rome 30161.

63. FORSYTH COUNTY

Forsyth County, formed 1832 from Cherokee County, county seat Cumming (30130), fire 1973.

GDAH CH microfilms (FHL): apprentice(1865-74), annual returns(1858-1901*), deed & mortgage(1832-1904*), homestead(1868-1903*), Inferior Court minutes(1843-65), inventories & appraisements(1848-1905*), marriage(1834-1910*), Ordinary minutes(1852-1901*), physicians register(1881-1959*), school(1848-75*), state census(1845), Superior Court minutes(1832-1903), tax(1853), twelve months support(1883-1916*), will(1833-1939*). Published records in GDAH (etc): Baptist, cemetery, census(1840RP, 1850RAIMS, 1860 RAIMS, 1870RAIM, 1880RAIM, 1900R, 1910R, 1920R), county history, early settlers, genealogical periodical, manuscript, marriage, Methodist, state census(1834/45), will.

Libraries: Forsyth County Library, 201 E. Maple St., Cumming 30130; Lake Lanier Regional Library, 275 Perry St., Lawrenceville 30245. Society: Forsyth County Historical and Genealogical Society, PO Box 762, Cumming 30130.

64. FRANKLIN COUNTY

Franklin County, formed 1784 from Indian land ceded 1783, county seat Carnesville (30521). Also see many pre-1850 typescripts at GDAH and the loose records at UGL and Perkins Library at Duke University, Durham, NC.

GDAH CH microfilms (FHL): annual returns(1801-1903), Confederate(1862-5, 1921), deed & mortgage(1785-1902*), homestead(1868-1904*), Inferior Court minutes(1790-1812, 1826-75*), inventories & appraisements(1786-1903*), loose papers(1790-1881), marriage(1805-1938*), naturalization(1914), Ordinary minutes(1786-1905*), physicians register(1881-1961), pony homestead(1898-1938*), school(1823-7, 1844-50), slave importer(1818-31), Superior Court minutes(1814-1901*), tax(1798-1811, 1818-61), twelve months support(1800-1929*), will(1786-1911*). Published records in GDAH (etc): cemetery, census(1756-1815Su, 1790Su, 1802Su, 1830R, 1840RP, 1850RAIMS, 1860RAIMS, 1870RAIM, 1880RAIM, 1900R, 1910R, 1920R), Confederate, county history, DAR, deed, early settlers, Episcopal, estate, family history, Inferior Court, jury, land grant, land lottery(1827), manuscript, marriage, Methodist, military(1795), Ordinary minutes, tax, town history, will, WPA.

Libraries: Carnesville Public Library, Carnesville 30521; Athens Regional Library, 120 W. Dougherty St., Athens 30601.

65. FULTON COUNTY

Fulton County, formed 1853 from DeKalb County, county seat Atlanta 30303, absorbed Campbell and Milton Counties in 1932. Some records in the Atlanta Historical Society.

GDAH CH microfilms (FHL): apprentice(1899-1913*), annual returns(1854-1901*), deed & mortgage(1854-1910*), estate(1854-1921*), homestead(1873-1960*), Inferior Court minutes(1854-62), inventories & appraisements(1854-1906*), marriage(1854-1921*), naturalization(1878-1906*), Ordinary minutes(1854-1902*), physicians register(1853-1962*), Superior Court minutes(1854-1901*), tax(1854-7, 1862-9, 1873-), will(1854-1948*). Published records in GDAH (etc): Baptist, biography, Catholic, cemetery, (1860RAIMS, 1870RAIM, 1880RAIM, 1900R, 1910R, 1920R), city directory(1859-), city history, Confederate, county history, DAR, early settlers, Episcopal, family history, genealogical periodical, Jewish, land lots, manuscript, marriage, Methodist, physician, Presbyterian, tax(1854), town history, voter, WPA.

Libraries: Atlanta Public Library, One Margaret Mitchell Square, Atlanta 30303; Atlanta Historical Society, 3099 Andrews Dr., Atlanta 30305; Emory University Libraries, Atlanta 30322; Genealogical Center Library, PO Box 88100, Atlanta 30356; GA Department of Archives and History (GDAH), 330 Capitol Ave. SE, Atlanta 30334. Societies: Atlanta Historical Society, 3101 Andrews Dr., Atlanta 30305; GA Genealogical

Society, PO Box 38066, Atlanta 30334; Alpharetta Old Milton County Historical and Genealogical Society, 10 S. Main St., Alpharetta 30201; African-American Family Historical Association, PO Box 115268, Atlanta 30310; National Society of Computer Genealogists, 2815 Clearview Place, Atlanta 30340.

---

66. GILMER COUNTY

Gilmer County, formed 1832 from Cherokee County, county seat Ellijay (30540).

GDAH CH microfilms (FHL): annual returns(1849-1904), Confederate (1885-1911), deed & mortgage(1833-1960*), homestead(1833-1959), Inferior Court minutes(1835-68), inventories & appraisements(1836, 1853-1909), jury(1857-60, 1880-96), marriage(1835-1960*), Ordinary minutes (1856-1908), pauper(1842-73), physicians register(1881-1956), pony homestead(1877-1923), school(1835-40, 1852-63), Superior Court minutes (1833-1905), tax(1855, 1864-9), twelve months support(1868-1959*), voter(1895-8), will(1836-1960*). Published records in GDAH (etc): cemetery, census(1840RP, 1850RAIMS, 1860RAIMS, 1870RAIM, 1880 RAIM, 1900R, 1910R, 1920R), church, county history, family history, marriage, Methodist, military(Revolution).

Libraries: Gilmer County Public Library, 15 Dalton St., Ellijay 30540; Sequoyah Regional Library, 400 E. Main St., Canton 30114.

---

67. GLASCOCK COUNTY

Glascock County, formed 1857 from Warren County, county seat Gibson (30810).

GDAH CH microfilms (FHL): apprentice(1857-88*), annual returns(1857-1925*), Confederate(1890-1933), deed & mortgage(1858-1924*), homestead(1868-1910*), Inferior Court minutes(1858-88), inventories & appraisements(1858-1924*), marriage(1858-1966*), Ordinary minutes(1858-1917), physicians register(1898-1933), Superior Court minutes(1858-1921*), tax(1858, 1860-4, 1866-80), twelve months support(1858-1916), voter(1909), will(1859-1966*). Published records in GDAH (etc): cemetery, census(1860RAIMS, 1870RAIM, 1880RAIM, 1900R, 1910R, 1920R), county history.

Library: Jefferson County Library, 306 W. Broad St., Louisville 30434.

68. GLYNN COUNTY

Glynn county, formed 1777 from colonial GA, county seat Brunswick (31520), fire late 1820s, some records lost, storm damage 1896.

GDAH CH microfilms (FHL): annual returns(1866-1921*), Confederate(1914-24), deed & mortgage (1765-1926), homestead(1870-1920), Inferior Court minutes(1813-70), inventories & appraisements (1792-1921), jury(1901-15), marriage(1818-1933*), Ordinary minutes (1870-1923*), physicians register(1881-1959), Superior Court minutes (1787-92, 1877-1916), tax(1790-4), twelve months support(1907-47), will(1810-1916). Published records in GDAH (etc): biography, cemetery, census(1756-1815Su, 1790-Su, 1802Su, 1820RI, 1830R, 1840RP, 1850 RAIMS, 1860RAIMS, 1870RAIM, 1880RAIM, 1900R, 1910R, 1920R), city history, DAR, deed, Episcopal, estate, Inferior Court, Jewish, jury, land grant & lot, land lottery(1805), manuscript, marriage, Methodist, militia, military, tax, town history, will, WPA.

Library: Brunswick Regional Library, 208 Gloucester St., Brunswick 31523. Society:Coastal GA Historical Society, 600 Beach View, St. Simons Island 31522; Historical Society of the South GA Conference United Methodist Church, PO Box 407, St. Simons Island 31522.

69. GORDON COUNTY

Gordon County, formed 1850 from Floyd and Cass(Bartow) Counties, county seat Calhoun (30701), fire 1864, storm damage 1888.

GDAH CH microfilms (FHL): annual returns(1866-1902*), Confederate(1861-5,1880-1906,1911-36*), deed & mortgage(1850-1922*), homestead(1870-1921*), Inferior Court minutes(1850-72), inventories & appraisements(1856-1908*), marriage(1864-1966*), Ordinary minutes (1855-1904*), physicians register(1881-1924*), Superior Court minutes(1850-1906*), tax(1851-63), twelve months support(1865-1917*), will (1856-1964*). Published records in GDAH (etc): Baptist, cemetery, census(1850RAIMS,1860RAIMS,1870RAIM,1880RAIM,1900R,1910R, 1920R), city history, Confederate, county history, deed, early settlers, marriage, town history.

Libraries: Calhoun Public Library, Park Ave., Calhoun 30701; Dalton Regional Library, 310 Cappes St., Dalton 30720. Society: Gordon County Historical Society, 102 Court St., Calhoun 30701.

70. GRADY COUNTY

Grady County, formed 1905 from Decatur and Thomas Counties, county seat Cairo (31728). Seek records in the CH.

Published records in GDAH (etc): Baptist, cemetery, census(1910R, 1920R), city history, Confederate, county history, family history, land lot, manuscript, Methodist.

Library: Roddenbery Memorial Library, N. Broad St., Cairo 31728.

71. GREENE COUNTY

Greene County, formed 1786 from Washington County, county seat Greensboro (30642), Indians demolished CH 1787.

GDAH CH microfilms (FHL): annual returns(1792-1850*), Confederate, death(1811-33), deed & mortgage(1785-1889*), homestead(1868-1935), Inferior Court minutes(1787-1860*), inventories & appraisements(1786-1890*), Land Court minutes(1794-8), land lottery(1806/25/32), liquor/tavern license(1820-1935), marriage(1786-1908*), Ordinary minutes(1852-93), Superior Court minutes(1792-1905*), tax(1788-1815, 1822-37, 1853-4, 1859), twelve months support(1856-96), will(1786-1921*). Published records in GDAH (etc): Baptist, cemetery, census(1790Su, 1802Su, 1820RI, 1830R, 1840RP, 1850RAIMS, 1860RAIMS, 1870RAIM, 1880RAIM, 1900R, 1910R, 1920R), Confederate, county history, DAR, death, deed, estate, land lottery(1805/22/32), marriage, Methodist, military, militia, Ordinary records, Revolutionary veterans, Superior Court records, tax, War of 1812, will, WPA.

Libraries: Greene County Library, 201 Greene St., Greensboro 30642; Bartram Trail Regional Library, 204 E. Liberty St., Washington 30673.

72. GWINNETT COUNTY

Gwinnett County, formed 1818 from Indian land ceded 1817-8, county seat Lawrenceville (30245), fire 1871, many records lost.

GDAH CH microfilms (FHL): annual returns(1856-1902), Confederate(1861-5, 1890-1935*), deed & mortgage(1871-1917*), estate (1856-1920*), homestead(1858-1914), Inferior Court minutes(1819-74), inventories & appraisements(1856-1912), marriage(1818-1965*), Ordinary minutes(1858-1906*), physicians register(1881-1962), school (1884), Superior Court minutes(1871-1902), tax(1866/72), voter(1898), will(1847-1917*). Published records in GDAH (etc): Baptist, cemetery, census(1820RI, 1830R, 1840RP, 1850RAIMS, 1860RAIMS, 1870RAIM, 1880RAIM, 1900R, 1910R, 1920R), church, Confederate, Congregational, county history, early settlers, family history, genealogical collection, genealogical periodical, land lottery(1820), manuscript, marriage, militia, Presbyterian, town history.

Library: Lake Lanier Regional Library, 275 Perry St., Lawrenceville 30245. Society: Gwinnett County Historical Society, PO Box 261, Lawrenceville 30245.

73. HABERSHAM COUNTY

Habersham County, formed 1818 from Indian land ceded 1817/8, county seat Clarkesville (30523), fires 1856, 1898, 1923.

GDAH CH microfilms (FHL): annual returns(1819-1957*), Confederate(1897-1911, 1924-37), deed & mortgage(1818-1900*), homestead(1869-1934*), Inferior Court minutes(1819-1964*), inventories & appraisements(1819-1961*), marriage(1824-1964*), Ordinary minutes (1819-1964*), physicians register(1881-1914*), Superior Court minutes(1819-1901), tax(1850), twelve months support(1877-1918*), will(1838-94). Published records in GDAH (etc): Baptist, census(1820RI, 1830R, 1840RP, 1850RAIMS, 1860RAIMS, 1870RAIM, 1880RAIM, 1900R, 1910R, 1920R), county history, DAR, deed, early settlers, Episcopal, genealogical collection, land grant, land lottery(1832), marriage, Methodist, Ordinary minutes, town history, will.

Library: Northeast GA Regional Library, Jefferson at Green Sts., Clarkesville 30523.

74. HALL COUNTY

Hall County, formed 1818 from Indian land ceded 1817/8, county seat Gainesville (30501), fires 1851, 1882, tornado 1936, many records lost.

GDAH CH microfilms (FHL): annual returns(1890-1903), city birth(1865-), city death(1900-), Confederate(1914-38), deed & mortgage(1819-1934*), estate(1819-1937*), homestead(1867-1903*), Inferior Court minutes(1822-73), inventories & appraisements(1819-1903*), lunacy(1900-14*), marriage(1819-1966*), Ordinary minutes(1830-1903), physicians register(1881-1966*), pony homestead(1901-13*), school(1838-47), Superior Court minutes(1834-1901*), tax(1852-3), twelve months support(1850-1929*), will(1819-1966*). Published records in GDAH (etc): Baptist, cemetery, census(1820RI, 1830R, 1840RP, 1850RAIMS, 1860RAIMS, 1870RAIM, 1880RAIM, 1900R, 1910R, 1920R), city history, Confederate, DAR, death, early settlers, estate, genealogy, genealogical collection, jury, land lottery(1832), manuscript, marriage, Methodist, military, Presbyterian, Revolutionary veterans, town history, will.

Library: Hall County Library, 127 Main St., Gainesville 30505. Society: Northeast GA Historical and Genealogical Society, PO Box 907039, Gainesville 30503.

75. HANCOCK COUNTY

Hancock County, formed 1793 from Washington and Greene Counties, county seat Sparta (31807).

GDAH CH microfilms (FHL): annual returns(1797-1903*), Confederate(1890-1939), deed & mortgage(1793-1934*), estate(1793-1900*), free persons of color(1855-62), homestead(1877-94), Inferior Court minutes(1800-71), inventories & appraisements(1794-1880), jury(1833-1918), land lottery(1805/20/5/32), lunacy(1845-85, 1896-1925*), marriage(1808-1962*), Ordinary minutes (1794-1903), pony homestead(1873-93), Superior Court minutes(1794-1900*), tax(1794-6, 1804/12, 1829-70, 1882), voter(1895-1900), will(1794-1909). Published records in GDAH (etc): Baptist, cemetery, census-(1802Su, 1820RI, 1830R, 1840RP, 1850RAIMS, 1860RAIMS, 1870RAIM, 1880RAIM, 1900R, 1910R, 1920R), city history, county history, DAR, deed, early settlers, estate, land lottery(1807/20), manuscript, marriage, Superior Court minutes, tax(1794-5, 1802, 1812-3), will, WPA.

Libraries: Hancock County Library, Sparta 31807; Uncle Remus Regional Library, 1131 East Ave., Madison 30650.

76. HARALSON COUNTY

Haralson County, formed 1856 from Polk and Carroll Counties, county seat Buchanan (30113), fire 1889.

GDAH CH microfilms (FHL): annual returns(1884-1902), Confederate, deed & mortgage(1856-1902*), homestead(1869-1934), Inferior Court minutes(1856-68), inventories & appraisements(1865-1937), liquor/tavernlicense(1856-96), marriage(1865--1909*), Ordinary minutes(1856-1905), pony homestead(1893-1905), Superior Court minutes(1855-1903), tax(1866), twelve months support(1894-1911), voter(1896-7), will(1865-1919). Published records in GDAH (etc): biography, cemetery, census(1860RAIMS, 1870RAIM, 1880RAIM, 1900R, 1910R, 1920R), county history, early settlers, marriage, town history.

Libraries: Haralson County Civic Library, 70 Robertson Ave., Tallapoosa 30176; West GA Regional Library, 710 Rome St., Carrollton 30117. Society: Haralson County Historical Society, Courthouse Square, Buchanan 30113.

77. HARRIS COUNTY

Harris County, formed 1827 from Troup and Muscogee Counties, county seat Hamilton (31811), small fire 1865.

GDAH CH microfilms (FHL): apprentice(1866-7), annual returns(1829-1908), Confederate(1861-5, 1890-

1925), deed & mortgage(1828-1947*), estate(1828-1940*), homestead (1848-1942*), Inferior Court minutes(1828-68), inventories & appraisements(1829-1908), marriage(1828-1923*), Ordinary minutes(1828-1908), physicians register(1881-1952), Superior Court minutes(1828-1909), tax(1831/6, 1841-5), twelve months support(1857-1937), will(1833-1932*). Published records in GDAH (etc): Baptist, census(1830R, 1840RP, 1850RAIMS, 1860RAIMS, 1870RAIM, 1880RAIM, 1900R, 1910R, 1920R), city history, county history, genealogical collection, Jewish, marriage, WPA.

Libraries: Harris County Library, Hamilton 31811; Troup Harris Coweta Regional Library, 500 Broome St., LaGrange 30240.

78. HART COUNTY

Hart County, formed 1853 from Franklin and Elbert Counties, county seat Hartwell (30643), fires 1900, 1967. Superior Court records (deed, physicians register, minutes) in CH, not in GDAH.

GDAH CH microfilms (FHL): annual returns(1857-1903*), Confederate(1861-5, 1921-6, 1933), estate(1854-1945*), homestead(1879-1921*), inventories & appraisements(1857-1916*), marriage(1854-1923*), Ordinary minutes(1854-1945*), tax(1867), twelve months support(1862-1920*), will(1854-1934*). Published records in GDAH (etc): Bible, cemetery, census(1860RAIMS, 1870RAIM, 1880RAIM, 1900R, 1910R, 1920R), county history, DAR, marriage, newspaper, will.

Library: Hart County Library, Benson St., Hartwell 30643.

79. HEARD COUNTY

Heard County, formed 1830 from Troup, Coweta, and Carroll Counties, county seat Franklin (30217), fire 1893, most records lost.

GDAH CH microfilms (FHL): annual returns(1894-1920*), Confederate(1920-1937*), deed & mortgage(1894-1914*), home-tead(1894-1929*), inventories & appraisements(1894-1920*), marriage 1886-1965*), Ordinary minutes(1894-1914*), Superior Court minutes (1894-1914*), tax(1871-2), twelve months support(1894-1925*), will(1894-1965*). Published records in GDAH (etc): Baptist, cemetery, census(1840RP, 1850RAIMS, 1860RAIMS, 1870RAIM, 1880RAIM, 1900R, 1910R, 1920R), church, city history, Confederate, county history, election, jury, justices of the peace, land lottery(1827), petition, town history.

Libraries: Heard County Public, 410 LaGrange St., Franklin 30217; West GA Regional Library, 710 Rome St., Carrollton 30117.

80. HENRY COUNTY

Henry County, formed 1821 from Indian land ceded in 1821, county seat McDonough (30253), fire 1824, some Civil War losses.

GDAH CH microfilms (FHL): annual returns(1836-1949), Confederate(1861-1929), deed & mortgage(1822-1917*),estate(1821-1939*),homestead(1866-94),Inferior Court minutes(1822-91), inventories & appraisements(1821-1954), jury(1888-1914), lunacy(1897-1909), marriage(1821-1945*), Ordinary minutes(1825-91, 1930-44), physicians register(1881-1957), pony homestead(1884-1949), school(1903/813/8), Superior Court minutes(1822-1906), tax(1831/7, 1852-9, 1864-9), twelve months support(1857-93), will(1822-1952). Published records in GDAH (etc): Bible, bonds, cemetery, census(1830R, 1840RP, 1850RAIMS, 1860RAIMS, 1870RAIM, 1880RAIM, 1900R, 1910R, 1920R), Christian church, Confederate, county history, DAR, deed, family history, genealogy, genealogical periodical, land, manuscript, marriage, Methodist, Presbyterian, will.

Libraries: Alexander Public Library, 99 Sims St., McDonough 30253; Flint River Regional Library, 800 Memorial Dr., Griffin 30223.

81. HOUSTON COUNTY

Houston County, formed 1821 from Indian land ceded in 1821, county seat Perry (31069).

GDAH CH microfilms (FHL): apprentice(1866-1930), annual returns(1824-1901*), deed & mortgage(1822-1943*),homestead(1868-1925),Inferior Court minutes(1822-36, 1850-1961*), inventories & appraisements(1834-1919), liquor/tavern license(1834-62), marriage(1833-1919*), Ordinary minutes(1852-1903*), physicians register(1885-1937), school(1841-71), Superior Court minutes(1822-1902*), tax(1829-64, 1869), will(1827-1926*). Published records in GDAH (etc): census(1830R, 1840RP, 1850RAIMS, 1860RAIMS, 1870RAIM, 1880RAIM, 1900R, 1910R, 1920R), county history, DAR, genealogical periodical, Inferior Court minutes, jury, land, land lottery(1832), marriage, Methodist, will.

Library: Houston County Public Library, 1201 N. Washington Ave., Perry 31069. Society: Central GA Genealogical Society, PO Box 2024, Warner Robins 31099.

82. IRWIN COUNTY

Irwin County, formed 1818 from Indian land ceded 1814/8, county seat Ocilla (31774).

GDAH CH microfilms (FHL): annual returns(1822-1923*), Confederate(1890-1924), deed & mortgage(1821-1903*), homestead(1869-1924*),

Inferior Court minutes(1820-78), inventories & appraisements(1822-1923), marriage(1820-1927*), Ordinary minutes(1820-1956*), physicians register (1882-1945*), Superior Court minutes(1820-1902*), tax(1830-2, 1839-58, 1870), twelve months support(1863-96), will(1821-1951*). Published records in GDAH (etc): Baptist, biography, cemetery, census(1820RI, 1830R, 1840RP, 1850RAIMS, 1860RAIMS, 1870RAIM, 1880RAIM, 1900R, 1910R, 1920R), county history, early settlers, jury, land grant, land lottery, marriage, naturalization, Superior Court minutes, tax(1846).

Libraries: Irwin County Library, Beech and First Sts., Ocilla 31774; Coastal Plain Regional Library, Griffin Rural Life Building, Tifton 31794.

---

83. JACKSON COUNTY

Jackson County, formed 1796 from Franklin County, county seat Jefferson (30549). Some original county papers in UGL.

GDAH CH microfilms (FHL): apprentice(1872-1906), annual returns(1800-1903), birth (1875), Confederate(1894-1939), death(1875), deed & mortgage(1796-1906*), homestead(1868-1922*), Inferior Court minutes(1796-1865), inventories & appraisements(1796-1903*), jury(1873-80), Land Court minutes(1796-1877), land lottery(1806/25/32), liquor/tavern license(1851-84), marriage(1805-1911*), pauper(1879-1901), physicians register(1881-1928), pony homestead(1896-1913), school(1852-63), slave importer(1818-30), Superior Court minutes(1796-1904), tax(1797-1811, 1820-66), twelve months support(1875-1908), will(1796-1919). Published records in GDAH (etc): cemetery, census(1802Su, 1820RI, 1830R, 1840RP, 1850RAIMS, 1860RAIMS, 1870RAIM, 1880RAIM, 1900R, 1910R, 1920R), Congregational, county history, court, DAR, genealogical collection, Inferior Court minutes, land lottery (1800/7/25/32), marriage, militia, Ordinary records, Presbyterian, tax(1798, 1803), town history, will.

Libraries: Jefferson Branch Library, Jefferson 30549; Piedmont Regional Library, 301 Midland Ave., Winder 30680.

---

84. JASPER COUNTY

Jasper County, formed 1807 from Baldwin County, county seat Monticello (31064). Organized as Randolph County, name changed in 1812 to Jasper County.

GDAH CH microfilms (FHL): annual returns(1823-1905), Confederate, deed & mortgage(1807-1938*), estate(1809-1941*), homestead(1866-1924), Inferior Court minutes(1820-68), inventories & appraisements(1852-1902*), land lottery(1825), marriage(1808-1900*), Ordinary minutes(1812-32, 1845-1902*), physicians register(1881-1911), pony homestead(1873-1905), state census(1852), Superior Court minutes(1807-1906*), tax(1866/8, 1871-), twelve months support(1875-1912), will. Published records in GDAH (etc): Baptist, Bible, cemetery, census(1820RI, 1830R, 1840RP, 1850RAIMS, 1860RAIMS, 1870RAIM, 1880RAIM, 1900R, 1910R, 1920R), city history, Confederate, county history, DAR, estate, family history, genealogical collection, jury, land lottery(1827), manuscript, marks & brands, marriage, Ordinary minutes, town history, will, WPA.

Libraries: Jasper County Library, Monticello 31064; Uncle Remus Regional Library, 1131 East Ave., Madison 30650.

85. JEFF DAVIS COUNTY

Jeff Davis County, formed 1905 from Appling and Coffee Counties, county seat Hazlehurst (31539). Seek records in CH.

Published records in GDAH (etc): census(1910R, 1920R), WPA.

Libraries: Hazlehurst Public Library, Hazlehurst 31539; Satilla Regional Library, 701 E. Ward St., Douglas 31533.

86. JEFFERSON COUNTY

Jefferson County, formed 1796 from Burke and Warren Counties, county seat Louisville (30434), fire 1861, probate records lost.

GDAH CH microfilms (FHL): annual returns(1815-1922), Confederate(1890-1952), death(1875), deed & mortgage(1797-1808, 1865-1925*), free persons of color(1818-22, 1840-59), homestead(1868-1939), Inferior Court minutes(1796-1868), inventories & appraisements(1801-1923*), land lottery(1825/31), liquor/tavern license(1839-64, 1916-7), marriage(1803-1957*), Ordinary minutes(1801-1921), pony homestead(1868-1939), school(1870-80), Superior Court minutes(1796-1920*), tax(1796-1879), twelve months support(1897-1931), voter(1897, 1902), will(1777-1945*). Published records in GDAH (etc): cemetery, census(1802Su, 1820RI, 1830R, 1840RP, 1850RAIMS, 1860RAIMS, 1870RAIM, 1880RAIM, 1900R, 1910R, 1920R), church, city history, county history, DAR, deed, early settlers, genealogical collection, jury, land, land lottery(1825), marriage, newspaper, petition, Presbyterian, school, Superior Court minutes, tax(1796, 1802, 1812), town history, will, WPA.

Library: Jefferson County Library, 306 W. Broad St., Louisville 30434.

87. JENKINS COUNTY

Jenkins County, formed 1905 from Bulloch, Burke, Emanuel, and Screven Counties, county seat Millen (30442), fire 1919. Seek records in the CH.

Published records in GDAH (etc): Baptist, cemetery, census(1910R, 1920R), county history, family history, Methodist, newspaper, town history.

Libraries: Jenkins County Library, 202 Hendricks, Millen 30442; Screven-Jenkins Regional Library, 302 E. Ogeechee St., Sylvania 30467.

88. JOHNSON COUNTY

JOHNSON COUNTY, formed 1858 from Washington, Emanuel, and Laurens Counties, county seat Wrightsville (31096).

GDAH CH microfilms (FHL): annual returns(1858-1916*), bastardy(1884-1915), Confederate(1861-5, 1890-1929), deed & mortgage(1859-1909*), homestead(1868-1909*), Inferior Court minutes(1859-1941*), inventories & appraisements(1859-1941*), Land Court minutes(1862-1909), marriage(1859-1966*), Ordinary minutes(1859-1904*), physicians register(1881-1946), pony homestead(1897-1960*), Superior Court minutes(1859-1903), tax(1864/6, 1872), twelve months support(1886-1925*), voter(1859-1908*), will(1859-1961*). Published records in GDAH (etc): cemetery, census(1860RAIMS, 1870RAIM, 1880RAIM, 1900R, 1910R, 1920R), county history, marriage, WPA.

Libraries: Fulford Memorial Library, Wrightsville 31096; Oconee Regional Library, 801 Bellevue Ave., Dublin 31021. Society: Johnson County Historical Society, PO Box 86, Wrightsville 31096.

89. JONES COUNTY

Jones County, formed 1807 from Baldwin County, county seat Gray (31032). Also see loose records in UGL.

GDAH CH microfilms (FHL): annual returns(1809-1944), Confederate(1861-2, 1890-1944*), deed & mortgage(1807-1966*), free persons of color(1818-30), homestead(1866-1959*), Inferior Court minutes(1809-74), inventories & appraisements (1809-1903*), land lottery(1820-32*), marriage(1809-1942*), Ordinary minutes (1808-1902*), physicians register(1881-1904, 1912-62), school (1829-61), Superior Court minutes(1808-1903*), tax(1811-79), twelve months support(1865-1924*), will(1809-1951*). Published records in GDAH (etc): Baptist, cemetery, census(1820RI, 1830R, 1840RP, 1850RAIMS, 1860RAIMS, 1870RAIM, 1880RAIM, 1900R, 1910R,

1920R), county history, DAR, deed, estate, family history, land, marriage, Ordinary records, Superior Court minutes, tax(1816), town history, will.

Libraries: Jones County Public Library, 315 W. Clinton St., Gray 31032; Middle GA Regional Library, 1180 Washington Ave., Macon 31201.

90. LAMAR COUNTY

Lamar County, formed 1920 from Monroe and Pike Counties, county seat Barnesville (30204). Seek records in the CH.

Published records in GDAH (etc):
Baptist, cemetery, church, city history, DAR, Methodist, town history.

Libraries: Carnegie Library, Barnesville 30204; Flint River Regional Library, 800 Memorial Dr., Griffin 30223. Society: Barnesville-Lamar County Historical Society, 888 Thomaston St., Barnesville 30204.

91. LANIER COUNTY

Lanier County, formed 1920 from Berrien, Lowndes, and Clinch Counties, county seat Lakeland (31635). Seek records in the CH.

Published records in GDAH (etc): cemetery, county history, DAR, WPA.

Libraries: Lakeland Branch Library, Lakeland 31635; South GA Regional Library, 300 Woodrow Wilson Dr., Valdosta 31601.

92. LAURENS COUNTY

Laurens County, formed 1807 from Wilkinson County, county seat Dublin (31021).

GDAH CH microfilms (FHL): apprentice(1866-1900), annual returns(1811-1901*), Confederate(1890-1938), deed & mortgage(1808-1900*), homestead(1868-1928*), Inferior Court minutes(1808-70), inventories & appraisements(1808-1908*), land lottery(1820), marriage(1809-1935*), Ordinary minutes(1853-1903*), physicians register(1889-1917), state census(1838), Superior Court minutes(1816-1903), tax(1841, 1850-1, 1857-9, 1866, 1871-2), twelve months support(1871-1900*), will(1809-1926*). Published records in GDAH (etc): Baptist, cemetery, census(1820RI, 1830R, 1840RP, 1850RAIMS, 1860RAIMS, 1870RAIM, 1880RAIM, 1900R, 1910R, 1920R), church, city history, county history, court, DAR, Episcopal, estate, family history, land lottery(1819), marriage, Methodist, newspaper, state census, town history, will, WPA.

Library: Laurens County Library, 801 Bellevue Ave., Dublin 31021.
Society: Laurens County Historical Society, Bellevue and Academy Aves., Dublin 31021.

93. LEE COUNTY

Lee County, formed 1825 from Indian lands ceded 1825/6, county seat Leesburg (31763), fires 1856 and 1872, most records lost in 1856. GDAH CH microfilms (FHL): annual returns(1852-1916*), Confederate(1890-1922), deed & mortgage(1826-32, 1858-1915*), homestead(1868-1911*), Inferior Court minutes(1858-78*), inventories & appraisements(1852-1916*), marriage(1867-1905*), Ordinary minutes(1858-1910*), physicians register(1912-39*), Superior Court minutes(1858-1904*), tax(1852), will(1854-1955*). Published records in GDAH (etc): Baptist, Bible, cemetery, census(1830R, 1840RP, 1850RAIMS, 1860RAIMS, 1870RAIM, 1880RAIM, 1900R, 1910R, 1920R), Confederate, DAR, early settlers, land lottery(1827), marriage, will, WPA.

Libraries: Lee County Library, Leesburg 31763; Kinchafoonee Regional Library, 334 N. Main St., Dawson 31742. Society: Lee County Historical Society, PO Box 393, Leesburg 31763.

94. LIBERTY COUNTY

Liberty County, formed 1777 from colonial GA, county seat Hinesville (31313). GA Southern College and Liberty County Historical Society have microfilms not available at GDAH.

GDAH CH microfilms (FHL): apprentice(1866-84), annual returns(1812-7, 1863-4, 1874-1923*), Confederate, deed & mortgage(1777-1958*), free persons of color(1852-64), homestead(1872-1952), Inferior Court minutes(1799-1871), inventories & appraisements(1789-1955*), Land Court minutes(1804-37), marriage(1784-1956*), Ordinary minutes(1826-81, 1890-1940), physicians register(1882-1924), school(1852-75, 1885-1907), Superior Court minutes(1784-1935*), tax(1800-1, 1806-15, 1821, 1827-51, 1861-), twelve months support(1874-1927*), voter(1896-9), will(1780-1942*). Published records in GDAH (etc): bonds, cemetery, census(1756-1815Su, 1790Su, 1802Su, 1820RI, 1830R, 1840RP, 1850RAIMS, 1860RAIMS, 1870RAIM, 1880RAIM, 1900R, 1910R, 1920R), church, Confederate, Congregational, county history, court, DAR, deed, early settlers, estate, Inferior Court minutes, jury, land grant, land lottery(1827), manuscript, marriage, Methodist, militia, Revolution, Superior Court minutes, tax(1801), town history, will, WPA.

Libraries: Liberty County Library, Hinesville 31313; Chatham-Effingham-Liberty Regional Library, 2002 Bull St., Savannah 31499. Society: Liberty County Historical Society, PO Box 797, Hinesville 31313.

95. LINCOLN COUNTY

Lincoln County, formed 1796 from Wilkes County, county seat Lincolnton (30817).

GDAH CH microfilms (FHL): apprentice(1804-31, 1866-1915), annual returns(1806-1968), Confederate(1890-1920), deed & mortgage(1796-1968*), estate(1796-1899*), free persons of color(1819-63), homestead(1867-1930), Inferior Court minutes(1797-1868*), inventories & appraisements(1807-1953), jury(1879-1959), Land Court minutes(1796-1917), liquor/tavern license(1882-5), lunacy(1898-1968*), marriage(1806-1968*), Ordinary minutes(1799-1939, 1948-68*), physicians register(1881-1915), school(1852-70), Superior Court minutes(1796-1966), tax(1801-69), twelve months support(1852-1968*), voter(1896), will(1796-1968). Published records in GDAH (etc): Baptist, bonds, cemetery, census(1802Su, 1820RI, 1830R, 1840RP, 1850RAIMS, 1860RAIMS, 1870RAIM, 1880RAIM, 1900R, 1910R, 1920R), county history, deed, estray, jury, marriage, Superior Court minutes, tax(1818), will, WPA.

Library: Bartram Trail Regional Library, 204 E. Liberty St., Washington 30673.

96. LONG COUNTY

Long county, formed 1920 from Liberty County, county seat Ludowici (31316). Seek records in the CH.

Published records in GDAH (etc): Baptist, cemetery, county history, WPA.

Libraries: Long County Library, Ludowici 31316; Brunswick-Glynn County Regional Library, 208 Gloucester St., Brunswick 31523.

97. LOWNDES COUNTY

Lowndes County, formed in 1825 from Irwin County, county seat Valdosta (31601), fire 1857, Court of Ordinary records burned 1869.

GDAH CH microfilms (FHL): annual returns(1862-1903*), Confederate(1910-28*), inventories & appraisements(1862-1914*), marriage(1870-1934*), Ordinary minutes(1870-1908*), pony homestead(1882-1910*), tax(1830, 1834-40, 1844, 1869-76), twelve months support(1862-1952*), will(1871-1965*). Published records in GDAH (etc): Bible, Catholic, cemetery, census(1830R, 1840RP, 1850RAIMS,

1860RAIMS, 1870RAIM, 1880RAIM, 1900R, 1910R, 1920R), city history, county history, DAR, deed, early settlers, family history, genealogical periodical, Jewish, jury, Methodist, petition, Presbyterian, survey, town history, WPA.

Library: Valdosta-Lowndes County Library, 300 Woodrow Wilson Dr., Valdosta 31601. Society: Lowndes County Historical Society, 305 W. Central Ave., Valdosta 31601.

98. LUMPKIN COUNTY Lumpkin County, formed 1832 from Cherokee County, county seat Dahlonega (30533).

GDAH CH microfilms (FHL): annual returns(1844-1906), birth(1875), death(1875), deed & mortgage(1833-1901*), free persons of color(1848-64), homestead(1866-1912), Inferior Court minutes(1833-59), inventories & appraisements(1844-1906), liquor/tavern license(1833-87), marriage(1833-1908*), Ordinary minutes(1835-1921), pony homestead(1845-1962), school(1847-84), state census(1838), Superior Court minutes(1833-1901), tax(1836, 1866), will(1833-1923*). Published records in GDAH (etc): Baptist, census(1840RP, 1850RAIMS, 1860RAIMS, 1870RAIM, 1880RAIM, 1900R, 1910R, 1920R), Confederate, county history, estate, genealogical periodical, marriage, newspaper, state census(1834/8), town history, will.

Libraries: Lumpkin County Library, Courthouse Hill, Dahlonega 30533; Chestatee Regional Library, 127 N. Main St., Gainesville 30505.

99. MACON COUNTY Macon County, formed 1837 from Houston and Marion Counties, county seat Oglethorpe (31068), fire 1857, most records lost.

GDAH CH microfilms (FHL): annual returns(1857-1901), Confederate(1861-1920), deed & mortgage(1857-1909*), homestead(1866-1932), inventories & appraisements(1872-1913), marriage(1858-1901*), Ordinary minutes(1857-1908), physicians register(1895-1954), Superior Court minutes(1856-1901), tax(1838, 1852), twelve months support(1861-1935), will(1856-1937). Published records in GDAH (etc): cemetery, census(1840RP, 1850RAIMS, 1860RAIMS, 1870RAIM, 1880RAIM, 1900R, 1910R, 1920R), county history, marriage, Methodist, town history.

Libraries: Oglethorpe Public Library, Chatham St., Oglethorpe 31068; Middle GA Regional Library, 1180 Washington Ave., Macon 31201. Society: Andersonville National Historical Site, Highway 49, Andersonville 31711.

100. MADISON COUNTY

Madison County, formed 1811 from Oglethorpe, Clarke, Jackson, Franklin, and Elbert Counties, county seat Danielsville (30633).

GDAH CH microfilms (FHL): amnesty(1865), apprentice(1868-1940*), annual returns(1816-1939*), Confederate(1890-1931), deed & mortgage(1812-1907*), dower(1829-1939), homestead(1827-1917*), Inferior Court minutes(1813-1920*), liquor/tavern license(1881), marriage(1812-1909*), Ordinary minutes(1860-1906*), physicians register(1881-1929), pony homestead(1897-1919*), school(1828-71), Superior Court minutes(1812-1900*), tax(1813-33, 1838-61), twelve months support(1866-1926*), will(1812-1922*). Published records in GDAH (etc): Baptist, cemetery, census(1820RI, 1830R, 1840RP, 1850RAIMS, 1860RAIMS, 1870RAIM, 1880RAIM, 1900R, 1910R, 1920R), Confederate, county history, DAR, deed, early settlers, genealogical periodical, jury, land grant, marriage, Presbyterian, town history, will.

Libraries: Danielsville Branch Library, Danielsville 30633; Athens Regional Library, 120 W. Dougherty St., Athens 30601.

101. MARION COUNTY

Marion County, formed 1827 from Lee and Muscogee Counties, county seat Buena Vista (31803), fire 1845, most records lost.

GDAH CH microfilms (FHL): annual returns(1839-1941*), Confederate(1890-1948), deed & mortgage(1845-1965*), homestead(1866-1950*), Inferior Court minutes(1842-75*), inventories & appraisements (1839-1904*), marriage(1844-1953*), Ordinary minutes (1854-1958), Superior Court minutes(1846-1911*), tax(1848-68, 1877), twelve months support(1864-1904*), voter(1898, 1900/3), will(1846-1940*). Published records in GDAH (etc): cemetery, census(1830R, 1840RP, 1850RAIMS, 1860RAIMS, 1870RAIM, 1880RAIM, 1900R, 1910R, 1920R), county history, early records, marriage, Methodist, will, WPA.

Libraries: Marion County Public Library, Buena Vista 31803; Chattahoochee Valley Regional Library, 1120 Bradley Dr., Columbus 31995.

102. McDUFFIE COUNTY

McDuffie County, formed 1870 from Warren and Columbia Counties, county seat Thomson (30824).

GDAH CH microfilms (FHL): apprentice(1874-1909), annual returns(1871-1915), Confederate(1890-1931), deed & mortgage(1871-1960*), homestead(1871-1909), inventories

& appraisements(1871-1927), jury(1871-96), marriage(1870-1960*), Ordinary minutes(1871-1905), physicians register(1881-1960), Superior Court minutes(1871-1913), tax(1871), twelve months support(1871-1913), voter(1886-94), will(1872-1927). Published records in GDAH (etc): census(1880RAIM, 1900R, 1910R, 1920R), county history, land grant, marriage, newspaper, petition, Quaker, town history, will.

Libraries: Thomson-McDuffie County Library, 149 Main St., Thomson 30824; Bartram Trail Regional Library, 204 E. Liberty St., Washington 30673. Society: Wrightsboro Quaker Community Foundation, 633 Hemlock Dr., Thomson 30824.

---

103. McINTOSH COUNTY

McIntosh County, formed 1793 from Liberty County, county seat Darien (31305), fires 1864, 1872, 1931.

GDAH CH microfilms (FHL): Confederate(1896-1923), death(1875), deed & mortgage(1873-1942*), homestead(1870-1920), inventories & appraisements(1887-1911), jail 1886-1927), jury(1906-42), liquor/tavern license(1882 9), marriage(1869-1957*), Ordinary minutes(1873-1957), physicians register(1860-1901), Superior Court minutes(1873-1922), tax(1825, 1837, 1862), voter(1877-1922), will(1873-1915). Published records in GDAH (etc): cemetery, census(1802Su, 1820RI, 1830R, 1840RP, 1850RAIMS, 1860RAIMS, 1870RAIM, 1880RAIM, 1900R, 1910R, 1920R), county history, deed, early settlers, land, land lottery, Methodist, militia, Scottish Highlanders, town history.

Library: Brunswick Regional Library, 208 Gloucester St., Brunswick 31523. Society: Fort King George Historic Site, Fort King George Dr., Darien 31305.

---

104. MERIWETHER COUNTY

Meriwether County, formed 1827 from Troup County, county seat Greenville (30222), storm 1893, fire 1976.

GDAH CH microfilms (FHL): apprentice(1865-88*), annual returns(1828-1902*), Confederate(1861-3, 1896-1956), deed & mortgage(1827-1963*), estate(1828-1963*), homestead(1866-1910), Inferior Court minutes(1829-90), inventories & appraisements(1828-86*), land lottery(1832 in Duke University Library), marriage(1828-1902*), Ordinary minutes(1877-90), physicians register(1881-1961), power of attorney(1865-88*), school(1898, 1903/13), Superior Court minutes(1828-1905), tax(1863), twelve months support(1866-1905), will(1831-1903). Published records in GDAH (etc): cemetery, census(1830R, 1840RP, 1850RAIMS,

214

1860RAIMS, 1870RAIM, 1880RAIM, 1900R, 1910R, 1920R), church, Confederate, county history, DAR, family history, marriage, Methodist, Presbyterian, town history, WPA.

Library: Troup Harris Coweta Regional Library, 500 Broome St., La Grange 30240.

105. MILLER COUNTY

Miller County, formed 1856 from Baker and Early Counties, county seat Colquitt (31737), fires 1873, 1904, 1974, most records lost in 1873.

GDAH CH microfilms (FHL): annual returns(1871-1913*), birth(1875-6*), death(1875-6*), deed & mortgage(1873-1916*), inventories & appraisements(1880-1913*), marriage(1892-1966*), physicians register(1881-1952*), Superior Court minutes(1904-12*), tax(1871-2), voter (1906-8), will(1871-1965*). Published records in GDAH (etc): census(1860RAIMS, 1870RAIM, 1880RAIM, 1900R, 1910R, 1920R), county history, Methodist, newspaper.

Libraries: Miller County Library, Colquitt 31737; Southwest GA Regional Library, Shotwell and Monroe Sts., Bainbridge 31717.

106. MILTON COUNTY

Milton County, formed 1857 from Cherokee, Cobb, and Forsyth Counties, county absorbed into Fulton County 1932.

GDAH CH microfilms (FHL): annual returns(1866-1931*), Confederate(1911-29), deed & mortgage(1867-1931*), estate(1867-1931*), homestead(1868-1912*), Inferior Court minutes(1858-1904*), inventories & appraisements(1858-1931*), marriage(1865-1932*), Ordinary minutes(1872-1931*), liquor/tavern license(1901-31*), Superior Court minutes(1861-1931*), tax(1866/8), twelve months support(1882-1931*), will(1857-1948*). Published records in GDAH (etc): census(1860RAIMS, 1870RAIM, 1880RAIM, 1900R, 1910R, 1920R), Confederate, DAR, marriage, will.

Libraries: GDAH, Atlanta-Fulton Public Library, One Margaret Mitchell Square, NW, Atlanta 30303; Roswell Memorial Library, 972 Alpharetta St., Roswell 30075. Societies: Roswell Historical Society, PO Box 1309, Roswell 30075; see listings under Fulton County.

107. MITCHELL COUNTY

Mitchell County, formed 1857 from Baker County, county seat Camilla (31730), fire 1869, some records saved.

GDAH CH microfilms (FHL): apprentice(1882-), annual returns (1867-1912*), Confederate(1889-97, 1914-25), deed & mortgage(1856-1907*), homestead(1868-1913*), inventories & appraisements(1896-1948*), marriage(1867-1960*), Ordinary minutes(1858-1907*), Superior Court minutes(1858-1902*), twelve months support(1881-1913*), will(1868-1965*). Published records in GDAH (etc): Baptist, census (1860RAIMS, 1870RAIM, 1880RAIM, 1900R, 1910R, 1920R), county history, jury, marriage, town history.

Library: DeSoto Trail Regional Library, 145 E. Broad St., Camilla 31730.

---

108. MONROE COUNTY

Monroe County, formed 1821 from Indian land ceded 1821, county seat Forsyth (31029).

GDAH CH microfilms (FHL): apprentice(1869-90), annual returns(1823-1905), Confederate, deed & mortgage(1822-1921*), homestead(1868-1956), Inferior Court minutes(1826-49), inventories & appraisements(1851-1954), jury(1892-1912), marriage(1824-1958*), Ordinary minutes(1824-1903), physicians register(1881-1915), pony homestead(1921-32), Superior Court min-utes(1826-1902), tax(1828, 1834, 1841-), twelve months support(1882-1952), will(1824-1958*). Published records in GDAH (etc): cemetery, census(1830R, 1840RP, 1850RAIMS, 1860RAIMS, 1870RAIM, 1880RAIM, 1900R, 1910R, 1920R), county history, DAR, deed, marriage, Methodist, town history, will, WPA.

Libraries: Monroe County Library, W. Main St., Forsyth 31029; Flint River Regional Library, 800 Memorial Dr., Griffin 30223. Society: Monroe County Historical Society, PO Box 401, Forsyth 31629.

---

109. MONTGOMERY COUNTY

Montgomery County, formed 1793 from Washington County, county seat Mt. Vernon (30445).

GDAH CH microfilms (FHL): annual returns(1850-1910), Confederate, deed & mortgage(1790-1916*), homestead(1861-1931), Inferior Court minutes(1809-70), inventories & appraisements(1801-1906), jury(1882-1912),lunacy(1896-1909), marriage(1810-1946*), Ordinary minutes (1809-1903), physicians register (1881-1923), school (1884-9), Superior Court minutes(1807-1904), tax(1797-8, 1805-6, 1811-2, 1828-54, 1859-61, 1867-71), twelve months support(1886-1919), voter(1902, 1909-12), will(1806-1903). Published records in GDAH (etc): cemetery, census(1802Su, 1820RI, 1830R, 1840RP, 1850RAIMS, 1860RAIMS, 1870RAIM, 1880RAIM, 1900R, 1910R,

1920R), Confederate, DAR, deed, early settlers, genealogy, jury, land, land lottery(1805), manuscript, marriage, militia, newspaper, petition, Presbyterian, Superior Court minutes, will.

Libraries: Montgomery County Library, Mt. Vernon 30445; Ohoopee Regional Library, 606 Jackson St., Vidalia 30474.

---

110. MORGAN COUNTY

Morgan County, formed 1807 from Baldwin County, county seat Madison (30650).

GDAH CH microfilms (FHL): apprentice(1866-77), annual returns(1808-1903), Confederate(1890-1930), deed & mortgage(1808-1903*), homestead(1866-1956*), Inferior Court minutes(1808-60), inventories & appraisements(1808-1903), jail(1877-1937), jury(1886-1904), land lottery (1827), liquor/tavern license(1840-6), marriage(1806-1904*), Ordinary minutes(1808-1901), physicians register-(1886), slave importer(1818-24), Superior Court minutes(1808-1903), tax(1808-32, 1838-63, 1869-71), voter(1898, 1905), will(1806-99*). Published records in GDAH (etc): cemetery, census(1820RI, 1830R, 1840RP, 1850RAIMS, 1860 RAIMS, 1870RAIM, 1880RAIM, 1900R, 1910R, 1920R), city history, Confederate, county history, DAR, Episcopal, family history, jury, land lottery(1827/32), marriage, Methodist, Presbyterian, Superior Court, tax, will, WPA.

Library: Uncle Remus Regional Library, 1131 East Ave., Madison 30650.

---

111. MURRAY COUNTY

Murray County, formed 1832 from Cherokee County, county seat Chatsworth (30705).

GDAH CH microfilms (FHL): annual returns(1835-1914*), Confederate(1861-5, 1890-1938), deed & mortgage (1833-1964*), homestead(1874-1932*), Inferior Court minutes(1834-62), inventories & appraisements(1835-1914*), jury(1837/9), marriage(1834-1907*), Ordinary minutes (1853-1905*), physicians register (1877-1955), Superior Court minutes(1833-1907*), tax(1868-9, 1874-8), twelve months support(1882-1918*), will(1840-1922*). Published records in GDAH (etc): cemetery, census(1840RP, 1850 RAIMS, 1860RAIMS, 1870RAIM, 1880RAIM, 1900R, 1910R, 1920R), Confederate, county history, family history, genealogical collection, marriage, Moravian, Presbyterian, state census(1834).

Libraries: Murray County Library, 706 Old Dalton-Ellijay Rd., Chatsworth 30705; Dalton Regional Library, 310 Cappes St., Dalton

30720. Society: Whitfield-Murray Historical and Genealogical Society, 715 Chattanooga Ave., Dalton 30720.

---

112. MUSCOGEE COUNTY

Muscogee County, formed 1825 from Indian land ceded 1826, county seat Columbus (31902), fire 1838, many records destroyed.

GDAH CH microfilms (FHL): annual returns(1839-1903), Confederate(1919-65), deed & mortgage(1837-1905*), homestead(1868-1906*), inventories & appraisements(1839-1909*), marriage(1838-1929*), naturalization(1919), Ordinary minutes(1838-1925*), physicians register(1881-1926*), Superior Court minutes(1838-1907*), tax(1838, 1845/7, 1867/9), twelve months support(1879-87*), will(1838-1964*). Published records in GDAH (etc): Baptist, bonds, cemetery, census (1830R, 1840RP, 1850RAIMS, 1860RAIMS, 1870RAIM, 1880RAIM, 1890R-partial, 1900R, 1910R, 1920R), church, city directory(1859-), Confederate, county history, DAR, death, genealogical periodical, marriage, Methodist, newspaper, Presbyterian, will, WPA.

Library: Bradley Memorial Library, 1120 Bradley Dr. Columbus 31995. Society: Genealogical Society of the Original Muscogee County, 120 Bradley Dr., Columbus 31906; Orangeburg German-Swiss Genealogical Society, PO Box 367, Columbus 31902; Muscogee Genealogical Society, PO Box 761, Columbus 31902.

---

113. NEWTON COUNTY

Newton County, formed 1821 from Jasper, Walton, and Henry Counties, county seat Covington (30209), fire 1883.

GDAH CH microfilms (FHL): annual returns(1822-1902), Confederate(1860-5, 1890-1929), deed & mortgage(1821-1904*), homestead(1850-1954), Inferior Court minutes(1823-76), inventories & appraisements(1822-1915), marriage(1822-1904*), Ordinary minutes(1859-1903), physicians register(1881-1961), pony homestead(1889-1918), state census(1838), tax(1848-51), twelve months support(1856-1961), voter(1895-7), will(1823-1936*). Published records in GDAH (etc): Baptist, Bible, cemetery, census(1830R, 1840RP, 1850RAIMS, 1860RAIMS, 1870RAIM, 1880RAIM, 1900R, 1910R, 1920R), city history, city records, DAR, death, family history, jury, marriage, Methodist, newspaper, town history, will.

Libraries: Newton County-Porter Memorial Library, Covington 30209; DeKalb Library, 3560 Kensington Rd., Decatur 30032.

114. OCONEE COUNTY

Oconee County, formed 1875 from Clarke County, county seat Watkinsville (30677), fire 1887.

GDAH CH microfilms (FHL): annual returns(1875-1915*), Confederate(1862, 1890-1920*), deed & mortgage(1875-1939*), homestead(1875-1912*), inventories & appraisements(1885-1954*), lunacy(1878-97), marriage(1875-1966*), Ordinary minutes(1875-1912*), Superior Court minutes(1875-1913*), twelve months support(1875-1930*), will(1875-1930*). Published records in GDAH (etc): Baptist, cemetery, census(1880RAIM, 1900R, 1910R, 1920R), Christian Church, county history, DAR, Methodist.

Libraries: Oconee County Library, Watkinsville 30677; Athens Regional Library, 120 W. Dougherty St., Athens 30601.

115. OGLETHORPE COUNTY

Oglethorpe County, formed 1793 from Wilkes County, county seat Lexington (30648), fire 1941.

GDAH CH microfilms (FHL): apprentice(1866-1903), annual returns(1798-1903), attorney(1795-1886), birth(1875-8), Confederate(1881-95), deed & mortgage(1794-1901*), homestead(1868-1905), Inferior Court minutes(1794-1869), inventories & appraisements(1793-1911*), jury(1870-93), land lottery(1805/6/20/32), lunacy(1851-88), marriage(1793-1908*), Ordinary minutes(1794-1904), pauper(1851-88), physicians register(1881-1944), pony homestead(1867-1910), school(1829-61), Superior Court minutes(1794-1904), tax(1795-1866, 1871), twelve months support(1856-1903), voter(1886-93), will(1793-1873*). Published records in GDAH (etc): Baptist, cemetery, census(1802Su, 1820RI, 1830R, 1840RP, 1850RAIMS, 1860RAIMS, 1870RAIM, 1880RAIM, 1900R, 1910R, 1920R), county history, DAR, deed, estate, land grant, land lottery(1805/7/32), marriage, militia, Superior Court minutes, tax(1795/6/9), will.

Libraries: Oglethorpe County Library, Lexington 30648; Athens Regional Library, 120 W. Dougherty St., Athens 30601.

116. PAULDING COUNTY

Paulding County, formed 1832 from Cherokee County, county seat Dallas (30132), some Civil War losses.

GDAH CH microfilms (FHL): annual returns(1885-1908*), bastardy(1880-1911*), Confederate(1890-1940*), deed & mortgage(1848-1902*), homestead(1866-1915*), inventories & appraisements(1896-1945*), lunacy(1895-1920*), marriage(1833-

1964*), Ordinary minutes(1866-1932), physicians register(1876-1961*), pony homestead(1876-1911*), Superior Court minutes(1859-1905), tax(1868-9), twelve months support(1895-1919*), voter(1896-1900, 1921), will(1850-1965*). Published records in GDAH (etc): Baptist, cemetery, census(1840RP, 1850RAIMS, 1860RAIMS, 1870RAIM, 1880RAIM, 1900R, 1910R, 1920R), Confederate, county history, early settlers, Methodist, state census(1838), town history.

Libraries: Paulding County Library, Highway 381, Dallas 30132; West GA Regional Library, 710 Rome St., Carrollton 30117.

---

117. PEACH COUNTY

Peach County, formed 1924 from Houston and Macon Counties, county seat Fort Valley (31030). Seek records in CH.

Published records in GDAH (etc): cemetery, city history, county history, DAR, Methodist.

Library: Peach Public Library, 323 Persons St., Fort Valley 31030.

---

118. PICKENS COUNTY

Pickens County, formed 1853 from Cherokee and Gilmer Counties, county seat Jasper (30143), fire 1947.

GDAH CH microfilms (FHL): annual returns(1854-1911*), Confederate(1890-1912*), deed & mortgage(1854-1919*), homestead(1868-81*), Inferior Court minutes(1865-94), inventories & appraisements(1854-1923*), jury(1879-1902*), marriage (1854-1931*), Ordinary minutes(1854-1911*), physicians register(1861-1950*), pony homestead(1895-1928*), Superior Court minutes(1854-1907*), tax(1867), twelve months support(1880-1923*), will(1854-1935*). Published records in GDAH (etc): Baptist, cemetery, census(1860RAIMS, 1870RAIM, 1880RAIM, 1900R, 1910R, 1920R), county history, early settlers, family history, genealogical collection.

Libraries: Pickens County Library, 290 College Ave., Jasper 30143; Sequoyah Regional Library, 400 E. Main St., Canton 30114.

---

119. PIERCE COUNTY

Pierce County, formed 1857 from Ware and Appling Counties, county seat Black-shear (31516), fire 1875, most records lost.

GDAH CH microfilms (FHL): Confederate(1890-1924), deed & mortgage(1871-1914*), estate(1871-1940*), homestead(1892-1940), inventories & appraisements(1875-1911), jury(1880-1902), marriage(1875-1917*), Ordinary minutes(1870-1907), physicians register(1883-1944), pony homestead(1892-1950), school(1892-1902), Superior Court minutes(1872-

1909), tax(1864-71), voter(1896-1916), will(1872-1941). Published records in GDAH (etc): Baptist, cemetery, census(1860RAIMS, 1870RAIM, 1880RAIM, 1900R, 1910R, 1920R), city history, county history, family history, marriage, mortuary, tax(1864/8/9).

Libraries: Blackshear Memorial Library, 600 Main St., Blackshear 31516; Okefenokee Regional Library, 401 Lee Ave., Waycross 31502.

120. PIKE COUNTY

Pike County, formed 1822 from Monroe County, county seat Zebulon (30295).

GDAH CH microfilms (FHL): annual returns(1824-1900), Confederate(1890-1959), deed & mortgage(1823-1906*), homestead(1868-1908), Inferior Court minutes(1825-73), inventories & appraisements(1824-72*), jury(1837-9), marriage(1823-1912*), Ordinary minutes(1856-1901), physicians register(1898-1941), school(1841-66), Superior Court minutes(1823-1903), tax(1825-59, 1864-72), twelve months support(1882-1924), will(1823-1914*). Published records in GDAH (etc): Baptist, census(1830R, 1840RP, 1850RAIMS, 1860RAIMS, 1870RAIM, 1880RAIM, 1900R, 1910R, 1920R), Confederate, county history, DAR, Inferior Court, manuscript, marriage, Masonic, Methodist, tax(1843), will.

Libraries: Pike County Library, Gwyn St., Zebulon 30295; Flint River Regional Library, 800 Memorial Dr., Griffin 30223.

121. POLK COUNTY

Polk County, formed 1851 from Paulding and Floyd Counties, county seat Cedartown (30125).

GDAH CH microfilms (FHL): apprentice(1866-91*), annual returns(1851-1908*), Confederate(1890-1929), deed & mortgage(1852-1907*), homestead(1853-1916*), Inferior Court minutes(1854-60), inventories & appraisements(1866-1950*), lunacy(1895-1912*), marriage(1854-1965*), Ordinary minutes(1865-1910*), physicians register(1881-1963), pony homestead(1895-1912), Superior Court minutes(1852-1901*), tax(1870), twelve months support(1886-1917*), will(1848-1963*). Published records in GDAH (etc): Baptist, cemetery, census(1860RAIMS, 1870RAIM, 1880RAIM, 1900R, 1910R, 1920R), county history, family history, genealogical collection, marriage, Presbyterian, town history.

Libraries: Cedartown Branch Library, Cedartown 30125; Sara Hightower Regional Library, 606 W. First St., Rome 30161.

122. PULASKI COUNTY

Pulaski County, formed 1808 from Laurens County, county seat Hawkinsville (31036).

GDAH CH microfilms (FHL): annual returns(1817-1956), birth(1875*), Confederate, deed & mortgage(1807-1939*), free persons of color(1840-65), homestead(1868-1915), Inferior Court minutes(1809-67), inventories & appraisements(1817-1910), jury(1809-27, 1876-92), land lottery(1832), liquor/tavern license(1882-1906), lunacy(1899-1918), marriage(1810-1956*), Ordinary minutes(1813-1925), physicians register(1881-1954), pony homestead(1915-28), school(1841-50, 1857-68, 1895-7), slave importer(1818-65), Superior Court minutes(1809-1935), tax(1809-11, 1816-29, 1839-70, 1876-8), twelve months support(1863-1913), voter(1886), will(1810-1935). Published records in GDAH (etc): Baptist, census(1820RI, 1830R, 1840RP, 1850RAIMS, 1860RAIMS, 1870RAIM, 1880RAIM, 1900R, 1910R, 1920R), county history, DAR, jury, land, marriage, military, newspaper, tax, town history, will.

Libraries: Roden Memorial Library, Commerce and Dooly Sts., Hawkinsville 31036; Ocmulgee Regional Library, 505 Second Ave., Eastman 31023.

123. PUTNAM COUNTY

Putnam County, formed 1807 from Baldwin County, county seat Eatonton (31024).

GDAH CH microfilms (FHL): apprentice(1869-80), annual returns(1808-1916*), Confederate(1879-1937*), deed & mortgage(1807-1911*), estate(1808-1964*), homestead-(1869-1915*), Inferior Court minutes(1810-46), inventories & appraise-ments(1808-1911*), marriage(1808-1964*), Ordinary minutes(1808-1902), physicians register(1881-1953), school(1825-59), Superior Court minutes(1808-1901*), tax(1812-39, 1844, 1852, 1860-2, 1866), twelve months support(1864-1963), will(1808-1964*). Published records in GDAH (etc): Baptist, cemetery, census(1820RI, 1830R, 1840RP, 1850RAIMS, 1860RAIMS, 1870RAIM, 1880RAIM, 1900R, 1910R, 1920R), Confederate, early records, marriage, Methodist, military, tax(1815), will.

Libraries: Eatonton-Putnam County Library, Eatonton 31024; Uncle Remus Regional Library, 1131 East Ave., Madison 30650. Society: Eatonton-Putnam County Historical Society, PO Box 331, Eatonton 31024.

124. QUITMAN COUNTY

Quitman County, formed 1858 from Randolph and Stewart Counties, county seat Georgetown (31754). Seek records in CH.

GDAH CH microfilms (FHL): marriage(1875-91*), Ordinary minutes(1864-1902). Published records in GDAH (etc): census(1860RAIMS, 1870RAIM, 1880RAIM, 1900R, 1910R, 1920R).

Libraries: Quitman County Library, Georgetown 31754; Chattahoochee Valley Regional Library, 1120 Bradley Dr., Columbus 31995.

125. RABUN COUNTY

Rabun County, formed 1819 from Indian land ceded 1819, county seat Clayton (30525).

GDAH CH microfilms (FHL): annual returns(1855-1910*), Confederate(1891-1910, 1916-9), deed & mortgage(1821-1940*), homestead(1871-1914), Inferior Court minutes(1826-82), inventories & appraisements(1855-96*), liquor/tavern license (1861-75), marriage(1820-1920*), Ordinary minutes(1831-89), school(1857-8), Superior Court minutes(1829-1905), tax(1836, 1861-2, 1869), will(1857-1930*). Published records in GDAH (etc): Baptist, cemetery, census(1830R, 1840RP, 1850RIMS, 1860RAIMS, 1870RAIM, 1880RAIM, 1900R, 1910R, 1920R), Confederate, county history, DAR, early settlers, genealogical periodical, marriage, Methodist, tax(1836).

Libraries: Rabun County Library, Clayton 30525; Northeast GA Regional Library, Jefferson at Green St., Clarkesville 30523.

126. RANDOLPH COUNTY (OLD)

Randolph County (Old), formed 1807 from Baldwin County, county seat Monticello (31064), name changed in 1812 to Jasper County. See Jasper County for records.

127. RANDOLPH COUNTY (NEW)

Randolph County (New), formed 1828 from Lee County, county seat Cuthbert(31740).

GDAH CH microfilms (FHL): annual returns(1861-1912), birth(1875-7), Confederate, deed & mortgage(1837-1903*), homestead(1866-1913), Inferior Court minutes(1845-79*), jury(1841-59), liquor/tavern license(1839-82), marriage(1836-1902*), Ordinary minutes (1852-71*), Superior Court minutes(1841-90), tax(1848-9), twelve months support(1857-8), will(1835-1916). <u>Published</u> <u>records</u> <u>in</u> <u>GDAH</u> (etc): Baptist, birth, cemetery, census(1830R, 1840RP, 1850RIMS, 1860RAIMS, 1870RAIM, 1880RAIM, 1900R, 1910R, 1920R), Confederate, county history, estate, family history, jury, marriage, Methodist, will.

<u>Libraries</u>: Randolph County Library, Cuthbert 31740; Pitts Library, Andrew College, College St., Cuthbert 31740; Kinchafoonee Regional Library, 334 N. Main St., Dawson 31742. <u>Society</u>: Randolph Historical Society, PO Box 456, Cuthbert 31740.

---

128. RICHMOND COUNTY

Richmond County, formed 1777 from colonial GA, county seat Augusta (30903).

<u>GDAH</u> <u>CH</u> <u>microfilms (FHL)</u>: annual returns(1797-8, 1857-81), birth(1823-96), deed & mortgage(1787-1901*), homestead(1867-1921), Inferior Court minutes(1786, 1790-1872), inventories & appraisements(1799-1901), jury(1826-30, 1851-1900), Land Court minutes(1784-7, 1853-70), land lottery(1832), marriage(1785-1900*), Ordinary minutes(1791-1898), slave importer(1818-37), state census(1852), Superior Court minutes(1782-1904), tax(1789, 1795, 1800, 1807-10, 1816-), twelve months support(1799-1901*), will(1777-1957*). <u>Published</u> <u>records</u> <u>in</u> <u>GDAH</u> (etc): Baptist, birth, Catholic, cemetery, census(1756-1815Su, 1790Su, 1802Su, 1820RI, 1830R, 1840RP, 1850RIMS, 1860RAIMS, 1870RAIM, 1880RAIM, 1900R, 1910R, 1920R), city directory(1841-), city history, Confederate, county history, DAR, deed, early records, Episcopal, genealogical periodical, land court, land grant, Lutheran, marriage, Methodist, militia, naturalization, newspaper, petition, Presbyterian, Superior Court minutes, tax, town history, will, WPA.

<u>Libraries</u>: Richmond County Historical Society Library, Reese Library, Augusta College, 2500 Walton Way, Augusta 30910; Augusta Regional Library, 902 Greene St., Augusta 30901. <u>Society</u>: Richmond County Historical Society, Reese Library, Augusta College, 2500 Walton Way, Augusta 30910; Augusta Genealogical Society, PO Box 3743, Augusta 30904.

---

129. ROCKDALE COUNTY

Rockdale County, formed 1870 from Newton and Henry Counties, county seat Conyers (30207).

<u>GDAH</u> <u>CH</u> <u>microfilms (FHL)</u>: annual returns(1876-1906*), Confederate(1890-1952), deed & mortgage(1870-1908*), homestead(1871-1904*), inventories & appraisements(1897-1938*), marriage(1871-1908*), Ordinary minutes(1871-1908*), Superior Court minutes(1871-1905*), tax(1871), twelve months sup-

port(1881-1922*), will(1870-1916*). <u>Published</u> <u>records</u> <u>in</u> <u>GDAH</u> <u>(etc)</u>: cemetery, census(1880RAIM, 1900R, 1910R, 1920R), county history, DAR, newspaper, Presbyterian.

<u>Libraries</u>: Rockdale County Library, 969 Pine St., Conyers 30207; DeKalb Library, 3560 Kensington Rd., Decatur 30032. <u>Society</u>: Rockdale County Historical Society, PO Box 351, Conyers 30207.

130. SCHLEY COUNTY Schley County, formed 1857 from Marion and Sumter Counties, county seat Ellaville (31806).

<u>GDAH</u> <u>CH</u> <u>microfilms</u> <u>(FHL)</u>: annual returns(1858-1907*), Confederate, deed & mortgage(1858-1906*), homestead(1870-97*), Inferior Court minutes(1858-91*), inventories & appraisements(1858-1914*), marriage(1858-1913*), Ordinary minutes (1858-1901*), physicians register(1881-1950*), Superior Court minutes (1858-1911*), tax(1858, 1866, 1870), will(1858-1905*). <u>Published</u> <u>records</u> <u>in</u> <u>GDAH</u> <u>(etc)</u>: census(1860RAIMS, 1870RAIM, 1880RAIM, 1900R, 1910R, 1920R), county history, DAR, deed, marriage, will.

<u>Libraries</u>: Schley County Library, Ellaville 31806; Lake Blackshear Regional Library, 307 E. Lamar St., Americus 31709.

131. SCREVEN COUNTY Screven County, formed 1793 from Burke and Effingham Counties, county seat Sylvania (30467), fires 1860s, 1896.

<u>GDAH</u> <u>CH</u> <u>microfilms</u> <u>(FHL)</u>: annual returns(1821-1915), deed & mortgage(1794-1910*), homestead(1871-1936), Inferior Court minutes(1811-68), inventories & appraisements(1878-1918), jury(1856-60, 1879-1912), marriage(1821-1902*), Ordinary minutes(1811-1904), physicians register(1881-1958), Superior Court minutes(1816-1901), tax(1852, 1864), twelve months support(1896-1933), will(1810-1929). <u>Published</u> <u>records</u> <u>in</u> <u>GDAH</u> <u>(etc)</u>: Baptist, cemetery, census(1802Su, 1820RI, 1830R, 1840RP, 1850RIMS, 1860RAIMS, 1870RAIM, 1880RAIM, 1900R, 1910R, 1920R), county history, DAR, deed, early settlers, estate, Inferior Court minutes, land plat, marriage, militia, Ordinary, petition, will.

<u>Library</u>: Screven-Jenkins Regional Library, 302 E. Ogeechee St., Sylvania 30467.

132. SEMINOLE COUNTY Seminole County, formed 1920 from Decatur and Early Counties, county seat Donalsonville (31745). Seek records in CH.

Published records in GDAH (etc): Baptist, family history.

Libraries: Seminole County Library, Donalsonville 31745; Southwest GA Regional Library, Shotwell and Monroe Sts., Bainbridge 31717.

133. SPALDING COUNTY

Spalding County, formed 1851 from Pike, Fayette, and Henry Counties, county seat Griffin (30223).

GDAH CH microfilms (FHL): annual returns(1851-1905), Confederate(1914-28), deed & mortgage (1852-1901*), homestead(1867-1930*), Inferior Court minutes(1852-64*), inventories & appraisements(1852-1946*), lunacy(1897-1909*), marriage (1852-1966*), Ordinary minutes(1852-1905*), physicians register(1900-49), pony homestead (1897-1915*), school(1852-64), Superior Court minutes (1852-1911*), tax(1852-3, 1861-6, 1871-2, 1876-80), twelve months support(1858-1925*), voter(1895-6), will(1852-1966*). Published records in GDAH (etc): Baptist, cemetery, census(1860RAIMS, 1870RAIM, 1880-RAIM, 1900R, 1910R, 1920R), Church of Christ, city history, Confederate, DAR, family history, jury, marriage, Methodist, tax(1845-6), voter, will.

Library: Flint River Regional Library, 800 Memorial Dr., Griffin 30223.

134. STEPHENS COUNTY

Stephens County, formed 1905 from Franklin and Habersham Counties, county seat Toccoa (30577). Seek records in CH.

Published records in GDAH (etc): Baptist, cemetery, census (1910R, 1920R), county history, DAR, deed, Methodist, town history.

Libraries: Toccoa-Stephens County Library, Toccoa 30577; Northeast GA Regional Library, Jefferson at Green St., Clarkesville 30523.

135. STEWART COUNTY

Stewart County, formed 1830 from Randolph County, county seat Lumpkin (31815), fire 1922.

GDAH CH microfilms (FHL): annual returns(1827-1920), death, deed & mortgage(1828-1907*), homestead(1858-1941*), Inferior Court minutes(1827-73*), inventories & appraisements(1827-1903*), jury(1869-72*), marriage(1825-1961*), Ordinary minutes(1856-1903), physicians register(1881-1958), school(1852-8), Superior Court minutes(1824-1902*), tax(1841, 1853-71), will(1831-1944*). Published records in GDAH (etc): Baptist, census(1840RP, 1850RIMS,

1860RAIMS, 1870RAIM, 1880RAIM, 1900R, 1910R, 1920R), county history, DAR, marriage, town history.

Libraries: Lumpkin Public Library, Lumpkin 31815; Chattahoochee Valley Regional Library, 1120 Bradley Dr., Columbus 31995. Society: Stewart County Historical Commission, PO Box 818, Lumpkin 31815.

136. SUMTER COUNTY

Sumter County, formed 1831 from Lee County, county seat Americus (31709). GDAH CH microfilms (FHL): apprentice(1867-71), annual returns (1850-82), birth(1875-6*), Confederate(1903-52), deed & mortgage (1831-1917*), homestead(1866-1901), Inferior Court minutes(1832-57), inventories & appraisements(1842-1904), jury(1836-43, 1871-3, 1879-1916), liquor/tavern license(1882-91), marriage(1831-1937*), naturalization(1906-18), Ordinary minutes(1829-1902), physicians register (1838-1919), Superior Court minutes(1842-1900), tax(1844, 1852, 1864, 1871), twelve months support(1857-1901), voter(1909-13), will(1838-1926*).

Library: Lake Blackshear Regional Library, 307 E. Lamar St., Americus 31709.

137. TALBOT COUNTY

Talbot County, formed 1827 from Muscogee County, county seat Talbotton (31827), fire 1890. GDAH CH microfilms (FHL): annual returns(1828-1926), Confederate(1895-9), death(1875*), deed & mortgage(1828-1902*), Inferior Court minutes(1828-82), inventories & appraisements(1831-1924),jury(1879-1902),liquor/tavernlicense(1828-33), marriage(1828-1903*), Ordinary minutes(1828-1909), physicians register (1899-1953), Superior Court minutes(1828-1900), tax(1852/6), will(1828-1928). Published records in GDAH (etc): Baptist, Bible, cemetery, census(1830R, 1840RP, 1850RIMS, 1860RAIMS, 1870RAIM, 1880RAIM, 1900R, 1910R, 1920R), church, county history, DAR, deed, Episcopal, family history, marriage, Methodist, petition, will.

Libraries: Talbotton Public Library, Talbotton 31827; Pine Mountain Regional Library, 218 Perry St., Manchester 31816.

138. TALIAFERRO COUNTY

Taliaferro County, formed 1825 from Wilkes, Warren, Hancock, Greene, and Oglethorpe Counties, county seat Crawfordsville (30631). GDAH CH microfilms (FHL): annual returns(1827-1913), birth(1875-6*), Confederate(1890-1920), death(1875-6*), deed & mortgage

(1826-1900*), free persons of color(1796-1864), homestead (1826-1905), Inferior Court minutes(1826-32, 1853-67), inventories & appraisements-(1826-1937), jury(1880-1910), Land Court minutes(1826-58), land lottery (1832), marriage(1826-1973*), Ordinary minutes(1854-1903), physicians register(1881-1911), school(1828-67), state census (1827), Superior Court minutes(1826-1901), tax(1826-70), voter(1892-1903), will(1826-1949). Published records in GDAH (etc): Baptist, Catholic, cemetery, census(1830R, 1840RP, 1850RIMS, 1860RAIMS, 1870RAIM, 1880RAIM, 1900R, 1910R, 1920R), early records, marriage, militia, state census(1837).

Libraries: Taliaferro County Library, Crawfordsville 30631; Bartram Trail Regional Library, 204 E. Liberty St., Washington 30673. Society: Taliaferro County Historical Society, Monument St., Crawfordsville 30631.

139. TATTNALL COUNTY

Tattnall County, formed 1801 from Montgomery County, county seat Reidsville (30453).

GDAH CH microfilms (FHL): annual returns(1857-1913), Confederate(1914-24), deed & mortgage (1802-1938*), homestead(1868-1909), Inferior Court minutes(1805-68), inventories & appraisements(1836-62, 1873-1917), lunacy(1893-1909), marriage(1806-1932), Ordinary minutes(1853-1913), physicians register (1881-1933), pony homestead(1883-1911), school(1852-65, 1928/33/8), twelve months support(1858-1923), will(1854-1939*). Published records in GDAH (etc): Baptist, cemetery, census(1802Su, 1820RI, 1830R, 1840RP, 1850RIMS, 1860RAIMS, 1870RAIM, 1880RAIM, 1900R, 1910R, 1920R), Confederate, county history, DAR, deed, family history, Inferior Court minutes, jury, land grant, land lottery(1805/20), marriage, Methodist, militia, state census(1838), tax(1831), will, WPA.

Libraries: Tattnall County Library, Reidsville 30453; Ohoopee Regional Library, 606 Jackson St., Vidalia 30474. Society: Tattnall County Historical Society, Reidsville 30453.

140. TAYLOR COUNTY

Taylor County, formed 1852 from Talbot, Macon, and Marion Counties, county seat (31006).

GDAH CH microfilms (FHL): annual returns(1858-1911), Confederate(1890-1928), deed & mortgage(1852-1918*), estate, homestead(1887-1931), Inferior Court minutes-(1852-69), inventories & appraisements(1852-1952), marriage(1852-1937*), Ordinary minutes(1866-1913), Superior Court minutes(1852-1903), tax (1852-73), twelve months support(1852-1952), will(1853-1917). Published records in GDAH (etc): Baptist, cemetery, census(1860RAIMS, 1870RAIM, 1880RAIM, 1900R, 1910R, 1920R), Confederate, genealogy, Methodist, town history.

Libraries: Butler Public Library, Butler 31006; Pine Mountain Regional Library, 218 Perry St., Manchester 31816.

---

141. TELFAIR COUNTY

Telfair County, formed 1807 from Wilkinson County, county seat McRae (31055), fire in early 1900s.

GDAH CH microfilms (FHL): annual returns(1879-1937*), Confederate(1861-4, 1867, 1890-1928), deed & mortgage(1806-1904*), homestead(1869-1936*), Inferior Court minutes(1845-54*), inventories & appraisements(1854-1938*), liquor/ tavern license(1869-80), marriage(1810-1902*), Ordinary minutes (1857-1917*), physicians register(1887-1955*), Superior Court minutes(1810-37, 1849-61, 1884-1900), tax(1853-6, 1867, 1870), twelve months support(1898-1961), will(1869-1921*). Published records in GDAH (etc): cemetery, census(1820RI, 1830R, 1840RP, 1850RIMS, 1860RAIMS, 1870RAIM, 1880RAIM, 1900R, 1910R, 1920R), county history, DAR, early settlers, family history, marriage, voter.

Libraries: Telfair County Library, 506 College St., McRae 31055; Ocmulgee Regional Library, 505 Second Ave., Eastman 31023.

---

142. TERRELL COUNTY

Terrell County, formed 1856 from Lee and Randolph Counties, county seat Dawson (31742).

GDAH CH microfilms (FHL): apprentice(1866-1920), annual returns(1855-1910), deed & mortgage (1856-1909*), homestead(1868-1910), Inferior Court minutes(1859-72), inventories & appraisements(1855-1907), marriage(1855-1919), Ordinary minutes(1856-1908), pauper(1886), school(1856/84), state census(1859), Superior Court minutes(1856-1900), tax(1856-71), twelve months support(1855-1921), voter(1895-1909), will(1857-1913). Published records in GDAH (etc): cemetery, census(1860RAIMS, 1870RAIM, 1880RAIM, 1900R, 1910R, 1920R), church, Confederate, county history, DAR, marriage, will.

Library: Kinchafoonee Regional Library, 334 N. Main St., Dawson 31742.

---

143. THOMAS COUNTY

Thomas County, formed 1825 from Decatur and Irwin Counties, county seat Thomasville (31792), storm 1849.

GDAH CH microfilms (FHL): annual returns(1845-1901), Confederate, deed & mortgage(1826-1911*), estate(1826-1957*), free persons of color(1858-64), homestead(1868-1912), Inferior Court minutes(1849-60), inventories & appraisements (1847-1931), liquor/tavern license(1869-1907), marriage(1826-1957*), Ordinary minutes (1826-1902), physicians register(1884-1957), Superior Court minutes(1826-1901), tax(1854, 1870-1), twelve months support(1897-1928), voter(1898), will(1826-1957). Published records in GDAH (etc): Baptist, cemetery, census(1830R, 1840RP, 1850RIMS, 1860RAIMS, 1870RAIM, 1880RAIM, 1900R, 1910R, 1920R), city history, county history, Episcopal, estate, family history, land, manuscript, marriage, Methodist, Presbyterian, WPA.

Libraries: Thomasville Branch Library, 135 N. Broad St., Thomasville 31792; Colquitt-Thomas Regional Library, 204 Fifth St., SE, Moultrie 31768. Society: Thomas County Historical Society, 725 N. Dawson St., Thomasville 31792.

144. TIFT COUNTY

Tift County, formed 1905 from Berrien, Irwin, and Worth Counties, county seat Tifton (31794). Seek records in CH.

Published records in GDAH (etc): cemetery, census(1910R, 1920R), county history, newspaper, physician.

Library: Coastal Plain Regional Library, Griffin Rural Life Building, Tifton 31794.

145. TOOMBS COUNTY

Toombs County, formed 1905 from Emanuel, Montgomery, and Tattnall Counties, county seat Lyons (30436), fire 1919.

Published records in GDAH (etc): Baptist, cemetery, census(1910R, 1920R), county history, DAR, Methodist.

Libraries: Lyons Public Library, Lyons 30436; Ohoopee Regional Library, 606 Jackson St., Vidalia 30474.

146. TOWNS COUNTY

Towns County, formed 1856 from Union and Rabun Counties, county seat Hiawassee (30546).

GDAH CH microfilms (FHL): amnesty(1865), annual returns(1873-1931*), Confederate(1924-41), deed & mortgage(1856-1926*), estate(1857-76*), homestead(1868-1945*), Inferior Court docket(1865-8), inventories & appraisements(1899-1941*), jury(1880-1928), marriage(1856-1908*), Ordinary minutes(1856-1906*), Superior Court minutes(1856-1905*), tax(1869-70), twelve months support(1894-1938*), voter(1898-1900). GDAH CH microfilms (FHL): census(1860RAIMS, 1870RAIM, 1880RAIM, 1900R, 1910R, 1920R), county history, marriage.

Libraries: Helen Community Library, Helen 30545; Northeast GA Regional Library, Jefferson at Green St., Clarkesville 30523.

147. TREUTLEN COUNTY

Treutlen County, formed 1918 from Emanuel and Montgomery Counties, county seat Soperton (30457). Seek records in CH.

Published records in GDAH (etc): Baptist, cemetery, census(1920R).

Libraries: Sparks Memorial Library, Soperton 30457; Oconee Regional Library, 801 Bellevue Ave., Dublin 31021. Society: Treutlen County Historical Society, Treutlen CH, Soperton 30457.

148. TROUP COUNTY

Troup County, formed 1825 from Indian land ceded 1826, county seat LaGrange (30240), fire 1936.

GDAH CH microfilms (FHL): annual returns(1828-1902), deed & mortgage(1827-1927*), estate(1828-1953*), Inferior Court minutes(1828-45*), inventories & appraisements(1828-1902), marriage(1828-1908*), Ordinary minutes(1846-1903), Superior Court minutes(1832-1905), tax(1850-1, 1861-2, 1866-7), will(1832-1929*). Published records in GDAH (etc): Baptist, Bible, cemetery, census(1830R, 1840RP, 1850RIMS, 1860RAIMS, 1870RAIM, 1880RAIM, 1900R, 1910R, 1920R), cemetery, city history, Confederate, county history, DAR, deed, estate, genealogical periodical, Jewish, land lottery(1827), marriage, Methodist, militia(1836), town history, will.

Library: LaGrange Memorial Library, 500 Broome St., LaGrange 30240. Society: Chattahoochee Valley Historical Society, 1213 Fifth Ave., West Point 31833; West Central GA Genealogical Society, PO Box 1051, LaGrange 30241.

149. TURNER COUNTY

Turner County, formed 1905 from Dooly, Irwin, Wilcox, and Worth Counties, county seat Ashburn (31714). Seek records in CH.

Published records in GDAH (etc): census(1910R, 1920R), county history, marriage, Methodist.

Libraries: Evans Memorial Library, 249 College St., Ashburn 31714; Coastal Plain Regional Library, Griffin Rural Life Bldg., Tifton 31794.

---

150. TWIGGS COUNTY

Twiggs County, formed 1809 from Wilkinson County, county seat Jeffersonville (31044), fire in 1901 destroyed practically all records.

GDAH CH microfilms (FHL): miscellaneous(1809-1900), tax(1818/26/30/33/53/63, 1870-80). Published records in GDAH (etc): Baptist, cemetery, census(1830R, 1840RP, 1850RIMS, 1860RAIMS, 1870RAIM, 1880RAIM, 1900R, 1910R, 1920R), county history, DAR, deed, estate, family history, genealogy, genealogical collection, jury, tax(1818/ 26/ 30/ 33/ 53), will.

Libraries: Twiggs County Library, Jeffersonville 31044; Middle GA Regional Library, 1180 Washington Ave., Macon 31201.

---

151. UNION COUNTY

Union County, formed 1832 from Cherokee County, county seat Blairsville (30512), fire 1859, some record losses 1979.

GDAH CH microfilms (FHL): amnesty(1865), annual returns(1877-1920*), Confederate(1863-5, 1914-27), deed & mortgage(1860-1906*), homestead(1877-1937*), Inferior Court minutes(1855-1972), inventories & appraisements(1877-1928*), marriage (1833-1933*), Ordinary minutes(1838-1903), physicians register (1881-1946*), school(1859-64*), Superior Court minutes(1856-1904), tax(1849-51, 1855-9), twelve months support(1877-1933*), voter(1895-1904), will(1877-1942*). Published records in GDAH (etc): Baptist, cemetery, census(1840RP, 1850RIMS, 1860RAIMS, 1870RAIM, 1880RAIM, 1900R, 1910R, 1920R), Confederate, county history, death, early settlers, marriage, Methodist.

Libraries: Union County Library, Blairsville 30512; Mountain Regional Library, College St., Young Harris 30582.

---

152. UPSON COUNTY

Upson County, formed 1824 from Crawford and Pike Counties, county seat Thomaston (30286).

GDAH CH microfilms (FHL): annual returns(1825-1948), Confederate(1890-1933), deed & mortgage(1825-1909*), homestead(1868-1930), Inferior Court minutes(1825-54), inventories & appraisements(1825-1929), lunacy(1892-1920), marriage (1825-1908*), Ordinary minutes(1825-1904), physicians register (1881-

1962), Superior Court minutes(1825-1944), tax(1825-59, 1863-71), twelve months support(1886-1925), will(1825-1915). Published records in GDAH (etc): Baptist, cemetery, census(1830R, 1840RP, 1850RIMS, 1860RAIMS, 1870RAIM, 1880RAIM, 1900R, 1910R, 1920R), church, city history, county history, DAR, genealogical periodical, homestead, Inferior Court minutes, marriage, Masonic, will, WPA.

Libraries: Hightower Memorial Library, Thomaston 30286; Pine Mountain Regional Library, 218 Perry St., Manchester 31816. Society: Upson County Historical Society, PO Box 363, Thomaston 30286.

153. WALKER COUNTY

Walker County, formed 1833 from Murray County, county seat LaFayette (30728), fire 1883, most records lost.

GDAH CH microfilms (FHL): annual returns(1883-1957*), deed & mortgage(1882-1908*), homestead(1883-1909*), inventories & appraisements(1883-1916*), marriage-(1882-1920*), Ordinary minutes(1883-1906*), physicians register(1883-1935), Superior Court minutes(1883-1904*), twelve months support(1883-1906*), voter(1899-1900), will(1883-1956*). Published records in GDAH (etc): Baptist, cemetery, census(1840RP, 1850RIMS, 1860RAIMS, 1870RAIM, 1880RAIM, 1900R, 1910R, 1920R), county history, deed, early settlers, family history, Methodist, newspaper, Presbyterian.

Library: LaFayette-Walker County Library, 305 S. Duke St., LaFayette 30728. Society: Walker County Historical Society, 305 S. Duke St., LaFayette 30728; Delta Genealogical Society, 504 McFarland Ave., Rossville 30741.

154. WALTON COUNTY

Walton County, formed 1818 from Indian land ceded 1818, county seat Monroe (30655).

GDAH CH microfilms (FHL): annual returns(1895-1910), Confederate(1861-5, 1911-30), deed & mortgage (1819-1909*), estate(1819-1965*), homestead(1824-1914), Inferior Court minutes(1819-1910), jury(1823-1920), liquor/tavern license(1868-89), lunacy(1901-18), marriage(1820-1934*), pauper and poverty and poor register(1905-7), physicians register (1947-60), school(1829-1939), Superior Court minutes(1819-1943*), tax(1819/26/31/34, 1849-53, 1859-62, 1828-9), voter(1891-1902, 1909-10), will(1819-1923). Published records in GDAH (etc): Baptist, cemetery, census(1820RI, 1830R, 1840RP, 1850RIMS, 1860RAIMS, 1870RAIM, 1880RAIM, 1900R, 1910R, 1920R), county history, DAR, deed, land, marriage, Methodist.

<u>Libraries</u>: Monroe-Walton County Library, Monroe 30655; Uncle Remus Regional Library, 1131 East Ave., Madison 30650. <u>Society</u>: Historical Society of Walton County, Monroe 30655.

155. WARE COUNTY

Ware County, formed 1824 from Appling County, county seat Waycross (31501), fire 1874, many records lost.

<u>GDAH</u> <u>CH</u> <u>microfilms</u> <u>(FHL)</u>: annual returns(1874-1910), Confederate(1890-1923), deed & mortgage(1874-1916*), homestead(1874-1932), inventories & appraisements (1879-1946), jury(1890-1925), lunacy(1895-1918), marriage(1874-1953*), Ordinary minutes(1874-1911), physicians register(1894-1941), Superior Court minutes(1875-1912), tax(1862, 1867-9), twelve months support(1895-1920), voter(1900), will(1879-1949). <u>Published</u> <u>records</u> <u>in</u> <u>GDAH</u> <u>(etc)</u>: cemetery, census(1830R, 1840RP, 1850RIMS, 1860RAIMS, 1870RAIM, 1880RAIM, 1900R, 1910R, 1920R), county history, deed, early settlers, marriage, tax(1862), town history.

<u>Library</u>: Okefenokee Regional Library, 401 Lee Ave., Waycross 31502.

156. WARREN COUNTY

Warren County, formed 1793 from Wilkes, Columbia, Burke, and Richmond Counties, county seat Warrenton (30828), fire 1909.

<u>GDAH</u> <u>CH</u> <u>microfilms</u> <u>(FHL)</u>: annual returns(1798-1910), Confederate(1890-1932), deed & mortgage(1795-1902*), free persons of color(1844-63), homestead(1857-1913), Inferior Court minutes(1815-68), inventories & appraisements(1794-1857), jury(1870-92), marriage(1794-1902*), Ordinary minutes(1817-1945), school(1856-72), state census(1845), Superior Court minutes(1794-1901), tax(1794/98, 1801/05, 1817-8, 1849-50, 1854-72), twelve months support(1856-1919), voter(1893-9), will(1798-1937). <u>Published</u> <u>records</u> <u>in</u> <u>GDAH</u> <u>(etc)</u>: Baptist, Catholic, cemetery, census(1802Su, 1820RI, 1830R, 1840RP, 1850RIMS, 1860RAIMS, 1870RAIM, 1880RAIM, 1900R, 1910R, 1920R), church, county history, DAR, deed, estate, Inferior Court minutes, land, marriage, militia, state census(1845), Superior Court minutes, tax(1794, 1805/18), will.

<u>Library</u>: Warren County Library, 220 Main St., Warrenton 30828.

157. WASHINGTON COUNTY

Washington County, formed 1784 from Indian land ceded 1783, county seat Sandersville (31082), fires 1855, 1864, most records lost 1855, some lost 1864.

GDAH CH microfilms (FHL): apprentice(1829-76*), annual returns(1843-1912*), Confederate(1861-5, 1896-1920), deed & mortgage (1865-1915*), homestead(1859-1925*), Inferior Court minutes(1843-69), inventories & appraisements(1846-1901*), Land Court minutes(1784-7), marriage(1828-1903*), Ordinary minutes(1858-1906*), physicians register(1881-1917), school(1859-70), Superior Court minutes(1865-1902), tax(1825-30, 1836-8, 1848-51, 1855-6, 1869-70), twelve months support(1861-1906*), will(1852-1903). Published records in GDAH (etc): Baptist, Bible, cemetery, census(1790Su, 1802Su, 1820RI, 1830R, 1840RP, 1850RIMS, 1860RAIMS, 1870RAIM, 1880RAIM, 1900R, 1910R, 1920R), city history, county history, death, estate, land lottery, Land Court, land grant, land lottery(1807), land warrant, marriage, Methodist, militia, surveyor, tax(1825).

Libraries: Wilson Library, Tennille 31089; Oconee Regional Library, 801 Bellevue Ave., Dublin 31021.

158. WAYNE COUNTY

Wayne County, formed 1803 from Indian land ceded 1802, county seat Jesup (31545).

GDAH CH microfilms (FHL): annual returns(1819-78, 1903-15), Confederate(1890-1919), deed & mortgage(1809-1920*), homestead(1835-57, 1875-1909), Inferior Court minutes(1823-68), jury(1880-1906), liquor/tavern license(1856-85), marriage (1809-1926*), Ordinary minutes(1815-1916), pauper(1904-37), physicians register(1883-1956), pony homestead(1905-37), Superior Court minutes (1823-1920), tax(1844/53, 1862-79), voter(1896-1914), will(1819-1927). Published records in GDAH (etc): Baptist, biography, bonds, cemetery, census(1820RI, 1830R, 1840RP, 1850RIMS, 1860RAIMS, 1870RAIM, 1880RAIM, 1900R, 1910R, 1920R), Confederate, county history, DAR, death, early settlers, Episcopal, jury, land, marriage, newspaper, Ordinary.

Libraries: Wayne County Library, Jesup 31545; Brunswick Regional Library, 208 Gloucester St., Brunswick 31523.

159. WEBSTER COUNTY

Webster county, formed 1853 from Stewart County, county seat Preston (31824), fire 1914, was called Kinchafoonee County during 1853-6.

GDAH CH microfilms (FHL): apprentice(1866-9*), annual returns(1863-1914), Confederate(1910, 1931-2), deed & mortgage(1860-1932*), homestead(1856), inventories & appraisements(1863-1914), marriage(1878-83, 1909, 1914-53*), Ordinary minutes(1854-1914*), pony homestead(1893-1914*), Superior Court minutes(1903-13*), tax(1856-64), will(1854-1965*). Published records in GDAH (etc): census(1860RAIMS, 1870RAIM, 1880RAIM, 1900R, 1910R, 1920R), county history.

Libraries: Webster County Library, Preston 31824; Kinchafoonee Regional Library, 334 N. Main St., Dawson 31742.

---

160. WHEELER COUNTY
Wheeler County, formed 1912 from Montgomery County, county seat Alamo (30411), fire 1916. Seek records in CH.

Published records in GDAH (etc): census(1920R), county history, WPA.

Libraries: Wheeler County Library, Alamo 30411; Oconee Regional Library, 801 Bellevue Ave., Dublin 31021.

---

161. WHITE COUNTY
White County, formed 1857 from Habersham County, county seat Cleveland (30528).

GDAH CH microfilms (FHL): annual returns(1859-1902*), Confederate(1861-5), deed & mort-gage(1858-1915*), homestead(1869-1919*), Inferior Court minutes(1857-68), inventories & appraisements(1859-1929*), marriage(1858-1965*), naturalization(1909-14), Ordinary minutes(1858-1911*), pony homestead(1894-1949*), Superior Court minutes(1873-1902*), tax(1858-70), twelve months support(1887-1919*), will(1863-1961*). Published records in GDAH (etc): biography, census(1860RAIMS, 1870RAIM, 1880RAIM, 1900R, 1910R, 1920R), Confederate, county history, DAR, early settlers, genealogical collection, town history.

Libraries: White County Library, Cleveland 30528; Northeast GA Regional Library, Jefferson at Green St., Clarkesville 30523. Society: White County Historical Society, Town Square, Cleveland 30528.

---

162. WHITFIELD COUNTY
Whitfield County, formed 1851 from Murray County, county seat Dalton (3072), fire 1864.

GDAH CH microfilms (FHL): apprentice(1881-1918*), annual returns(1852-1909*), Confederate(1913-37), deed & mortgage(1852-1954*), estate(1852-61), homestead(1880-1922*), Inferior Court minutes(1852-80), inventories & appraisements(1852-1903*), marriage(1852-1906*), Ordinary minutes (1852-1903*), physicians register(1881-1949), pony homestead(1868-81*), Superior Court minutes(1852-1903*), tax(1852-63, 1869-70), twelve months support(1866-1935*), will(1852-1960*). Published records in GDAH (etc): Baptist, cemetery, census(1860RAIMS, 1870RAIM, 1880RAIM, 1900R, 1910R, 1920R), city history, Confederate, county history, genealogical periodical, marriage, newspaper, Presbyterian, town history, will.

Library: Dalton Public Library, 310 Cappes St., Dalton 30720. Society: Whitfield-Murray Historical and Genealogical Society, 715 Chattanooga Ave., Dalton 30720.

---

163. WILCOX COUNTY

Wilcox County, formed 1857 from Irwin, Dooly, and Pulaski Counties, county seat Abbeville (31001).

GDAH CH microfilms (FHL): amnesty(1865), Confederate(1866-7, 1881-2, 1891-3), homestead(1873-82, 1898-1919), Inferior Court minutes(1866-77), inventories & appraisements(1857-1927), jury(1868), liquor/tavern license, marriage(1858-1915), pauper(1866), school(1858-71), twelve months support(1891-1931), voter(1894-8, 1903/8), will(1858-1957). Published records in GDAH (etc): Baptist, cemetery, census(1860RAIMS, 1870RAIM, 1880RAIM, 1900R, 1910R, 1920R), county history, DAR, family history, genealogical collection, land grant, Methodist, newspaper, town history.

Libraries: Wilcox County Library, Abbeville 31001; Ocmulgee Regional Library, 505 Second Ave., Eastman 31023.

---

164. WILKES COUNTY

Wilkes County, formed 1777 from colonial GA, county seat Washington (30673), fires 1780, 1958.

GDAH CH microfilms (FHL): apprentice(1868-1938*), annual returns(1805-1903), Confederate(1861-5), deed & mortgage(1785-1918*), estate(1777-1925*), free persons of color(1819-26), homestead(1868-76), Inferior Court minutes(1790-1882), inventories & appraisements(1794-1925), jury(1826, 1869-78), Land Court minutes(1784-1854), land lottery(1805/7/20/21/27/32), liquor/tavern license(1839-72), lunacy(1888-1908), marriage(1792-1905*), Ordinary minutes(1799-1903), pauper(1800-67), physicians register(1881-1951), pony homestead(1877-1956), school(1829, 1841-5), slave importer(1818-22), Superior Court minutes(1778-1904), tax(1787-94, 1801, 1805-67), twelve months support(1881-1913), will(1786-1921). Published records in GDAH (etc): Baptist, cemetery, census(1756-1815Su, 1790Su, 1802Su, 1820RI, 1830R, 1840RP, 1850RIMS, 1860RAIMS, 1870RAIM, 1880RAIM, 1900R, 1910R, 1920R), church, city history, county history, DAR, early settlers, early records, Episcopal, estate, Land Court, land grant, manuscript, marriage, Methodist, military, militia, newspaper, Presbyterian, Superior Court minutes, tax(1785, 1791-4), will, WPA.

<u>Library</u>: Willis Library, 204 E. Liberty St., Washington 30673.
<u>Society</u>: Washington-Wilkes Historical Foundation, 308 E. Robert Toombs Ave., Washington 30673.

165. WILKINSON COUNTY Wilkinson County, formed 1803 from Indian land ceded 1802/5, county seat Irwinton (31042), fires 1829, 1854, 1864, 1924. Seek original county records in CH, not in GDAH.

<u>Published</u> <u>records</u> <u>in</u> <u>GDAH</u> <u>(etc)</u>: Baptist, cemetery, census(1820RI, 1830R, 1840RP, 1850RIMS, 1860RAIMS, 1870RAIM, 1880RAIM, 1900R, 1910R, 1920R), Confederate, county census(1802), county history, deed, Inferior Court minutes, land, marriage, Methodist, will.

<u>Libraries</u>: Middle GA Regional Library, 1180 Washington Ave., Macon 31201.

166. WORTH COUNTY Worth County, formed 1853 from Dooly and Irwin Counties, county seat Sylvester (31791), fires 1879, 1893.

<u>GDAH</u> <u>CH</u> <u>microfilms</u> <u>(FHL)</u>: annual returns(1879-1912*), Confederate(1890-1927, 1930), deed & mortgage(1892-1912*), homestead(1896-1916), inventories & appraisements(1879-1913*), jury(1879-1904), marriage(1854-1967*), Ordinary minutes(1879-1911*), physicians register(1893-1962), pony homestead (1899-1940*), Superior Court minutes(1879-1910*), tax(1874-87), twelve months support(1897), will(1865-1957*). <u>Published</u> <u>records</u> <u>in</u> <u>GDAH</u> <u>(etc)</u>: cemetery, census(1860RAIMS, 1870RAIM, 1880RAIM, 1900R, 1910R, 1920R), county history, DAR, Methodist, WPA.

<u>Libraries</u>: Sylvester-Worth County Library, Sylvester 31791; DeSoto Trail Regional Library, 145 E. Broad St., Camilla 31730.

LIST OF ABBREVIATIONS

A	=	Agricultural census
CH	=	Court house(s)
FHC	=	Family History Center(s)
FHL	=	Family History Library
G	=	GA State census records
GA	=	Georgia
GDAH	=	GA Department of Archives and History
GHS	=	GA Historical Society (Savannah)
GSU	=	Genealogical Society of UT (Utah)
I	=	Industrial census records
LGL	=	Large genealogical library
LL	=	Local library(-ies)
M	=	Mortality census records
NA	=	National Archives
NAAB	=	National Archives, Atlanta Branch
NAFB	=	National Archives, Field Branch
P	=	Pensioner census, Revolutionary War
R	=	Regular census records
RL	=	Regional library(-ies)
S	=	Slaveowner census records
Su	=	Substitute census records
UGL	=	University of GA Libraries (Athens)
WML	=	Washington Memorial Library (Macon)

Books by George K. Schweitzer

CIVIL WAR GENEALOGY. A 78-paged book of 316 sources for tracing your Civil War ancestor. Chapters include [I]: The Civil War, [II]: The Archives, [III]: National Publications, [IV]: State Publications, [V]: Local Sources, [VI]: Military Unit Histories, [VII]: Civil War Events.

GEORGIA GENEALOGICAL RESEARCH. A 242-paged book containing 1303 sources for tracing your GA ancestor along with detailed instructions. Chapters include [I]: GA Background, [II]: Types of Records, [III]: Record Locations, [IV]: Research Procedure and County Listings (detailed listing of records available for each of the 159 GA counties).

GERMAN GENEALOGICAL RESEARCH. A 252-paged book containing 1924 sources for tracing your German ancestor along with detailed instructions. Chapters include [I]: German Background, [II]: Germans to America, [III]: Bridging the Atlantic, [IV]: Types of German Records, [V]: German Record Repositories, [VI]: The German Language.

HANDBOOK OF GENEALOGICAL SOURCES. A 217-paged book describing all major and many minor sources of genealogical information with precise and detailed instructions for obtaining data from them. 129 sections going from adoptions, archives, atlases---down through gazetteers, group theory, guardianships---to War of 1812, ward maps, wills, and WPA records.

KENTUCKY GENEALOGICAL RESEARCH. A 154-paged book containing 1191 sources for tracing your KY ancestor along with detailed instructions. Chapters include [I]: KY Background, [II]: Types of Records, [III]: Record Locations, [IV]: Research Procedure and County Listings (detailed listing of records available for each of the 120 KY counties).

MARYLAND GENEALOGICAL RESEARCH. A 208-paged book containing 1176 sources for tracing your MD ancestor along with detailed instructions. Chapters include [I]: MD Background, [II]: Types of Records, [III]: Record Locations, [IV]: Research Procedure and County Listings (detailed listing of records available for each of the 23 MD counties and for Baltimore City).

MASSACHUSETTS GENEALOGICAL RESEARCH. A 279-paged book containing 1709 sources for tracing your MA ancestor along with detailed instructions. Chapters include [I]: MA Background, [II]: Types of Records, [III]: Record Locations, [IV]: Research Procedure and County-Town-City Listings (detailed listing of records available for each of the 14 MA counties and the 351 cities-towns).

NEW YORK GENEALOGICAL RESEARCH. A 240-paged book containing 1426 sources for tracing your NY ancestor along with detailed instructions. Chapters include [I]: NY Background, [II]: Types of Records, [III]: Record Locations, [IV]: Research Procedure and NY City Record Listings (detailed listing of records available for the 5 counties of NY City), [V]: Record Listings for Other Counties (detailed listing of records available for each of the other 57 NY counties).

NORTH CAROLINA GENEALOGICAL RESEARCH. A 172-paged book containing 1233 sources for tracing your NC ancestor along with detailed instructions. Chapters include [I]: NC Background, [II]: Types of Records, [III]: Record Locations, [IV]: Research Procedure and County Listings (detailed listing of records available for each of the 100 NC counties).

OHIO GENEALOGICAL RESEARCH. A 212-paged book containing 1241 sources for tracing your OH ancestor along with detailed instructions. Chapters include [I]: OH Background, [II]: Types of Records, [III]: Record Locations, [IV]: Research Procedure and County Listings (detailed listing of records available for each of the 88 OH counties).

PENNSYLVANIA GENEALOGICAL RESEARCH. A 225-paged book containing 1309 sources for tracing your PA ancestor along with detailed instructions. Chapters include [I]: PA Background, [II]: Types of Records, [III]: Record Locations, [IV]: Research Procedure and County Listings (detailed listing of records available for each of the 67 PA counties).

REVOLUTIONARY WAR GENEALOGY. A 110-paged book containing 407 sources for tracing your Revolutionary War ancestor. Chapters include [I]: Revolutionary War History, [II]: The Archives, [III]: National Publications, [IV]: State Publications, [V]: Local Sources, [VI]: Military Unit Histories, [VII]: Sites and Museums.

SOUTH CAROLINA GENEALOGICAL RESEARCH. A 190-paged book containing 1107 sources for tracing your SC ancestor along with detailed instructions. Chapters include [I]: SC Background, [II]: Types of Records, [III]: Record Locations, [IV]: Research Procedure and County Listings (detailed listing of records available for each of the 47 SC counties and districts).

TENNESSEE GENEALOGICAL RESEARCH. A 136-paged book containing 1073 sources for tracing your TN ancestor along with detailed instructions. Chapters include [I]: TN Background, [II]: Types of Records, [III]: Record Locations, [IV]: Research Procedure and County Listings (detailed listing of records available for each of the 96 TN counties).

VIRGINIA GENEALOGICAL RESEARCH. A 187-paged book containing 1273 sources for tracing your VA ancestor along with detailed instructions. Chapters include [I]: VA Background, [II]: Types of Records, [III]: Record Locations, [IV]: Research Procedure and County Listings (detailed listing of records available for each of the 100 VA counties and 41 major cities).

WAR OF 1812 GENEALOGY. A 75-paged book of 289 sources for tracing your War of 1812 ancestor. Chapters include [I]: History of the War, [II]: Service Records, [III]: Post-War Records, [IV]: Publications, [V]: Local Sources, [VI]: Sites and Events, [VII]: Sources for British and Canadian Participants.

All of the above books may be ordered from Dr. Geo. K. Schweitzer, 407 Ascot Court, Knoxville, TN 37923-5807. Send a long SASE for a FREE descriptive leaflet and prices.